All-Pro Performance Training

An Insider's Guide to Preparing for the Football Combine

Loren Landow, CSCS,*D
Chris Jarmon, CSCS

HUMAN KINETICS

Library of Congress Cataloging-in-Publication Data

Names: Landow, Loren, 1973- author. | Jarmon, Chris, 1990- author.
Title: All-pro performance training : an insider's guide to preparing for
  the football combine / Loren Landow, Chris Jarmon.
Description: Champaign : Human Kinetics, Inc., 2021. | Includes
  bibliographical references.
Identifiers: LCCN 2020029052 (print) | LCCN 2020029053 (ebook) | ISBN
  9781492592624 (paperback) | ISBN 9781492592631 (epub) | ISBN
  9781492592648 (pdf)
Subjects: LCSH: Football--Training. | Football players--Rating of--United
  States. | Football players--Recruiting--United States.
Classification: LCC GV953.5 .L36 2021 (print) | LCC GV953.5 (ebook) | DDC
  796.33207/7--dc23
LC record available at https://lccn.loc.gov/2020029052
LC ebook record available at https://lccn.loc.gov/2020029053

ISBN: 978-1-4925-9262-4 (print)

Acquisitions Editor: Michael Mejia; **Senior Developmental Editor:** Cynthia McEntire; **Managing Editor:** Shawn Donnelly; **Copyeditor:** Kevin Campbell; **Permissions Manager:** Martha Gullo; **Graphic Designer:** Dawn Sills; **Cover Designer:** Keri Evans; **Cover Design Specialist:** Susan Rothermel Allen; **Photograph (cover):** Joe Robbins / Getty Images; **Photographs (interior):** Adam Bratten / © Human Kinetics; **Photo Production Specialist:** Amy M. Rose; **Photo Production Manager:** Jason Allen; **Senior Art Manager:** Kelly Hendren; **Illustrations:** © Human Kinetics, unless otherwise noted; **Printer:** Versa Press

We thank Landow Performance in Centennial, Colorado, for assistance in providing the location for the photo shoot for this book.

Human Kinetics books are available at special discounts for bulk purchase. Special editions or book excerpts can also be created to specification. For details, contact the Special Sales Manager at Human Kinetics.

Printed in the United States of America   10 9 8 7 6 5 4 3 2 1

The paper in this book is certified under a sustainable forestry program.

Human Kinetics
1607 N. Market Street
Champaign, IL 61820
USA

United States and International
Website: **US.HumanKinetics.com**
Email: info@hkusa.com
Phone: 1-800-747-4457

Canada
Website: **Canada.HumanKinetics.com**
Email: info@hkcanada.com

E7883

Tell us what you think!
Human Kinetics would love to hear what we can do to improve the customer experience. Use this QR code to take our brief survey.

All-Pro Performance Training

An Insider's Guide to Preparing for the Football Combine

Contents

Foreword by Christian McCaffrey vi

Acknowledgments. vii

Introduction. viii

Key to Diagrams xii

PART I WARM-UP AND INITIAL ASSESSMENTS 1

1 Warm-Up and Movement Prep. 3

2 Physiological Assessments
and Athlete Background. 25

PART II COMBINE TESTS AND DRILLS 39

3 General Athleticism Drills. 41

4 Defensive Position-Specific Drills 55

5 Offensive Position-Specific Drills 65

6 Analyzing Data
and Developing a Training Plan 77

PART III GENERAL MOVEMENT SKILLS TRAINING 87

7 Acceleration 89

8 Agility and Deceleration 115

9 Top-End Speed 143

PART IV STRENGTH AND POWER DEVELOPMENT 155

10 Training for Strength 157

11 Training for Power 181

PART V TRAINING STRUCTURE AND PROGRAMMING 197

12 Structuring Training Cycles 199

13 Nutrition and Recovery. 229

14 Day of Event and Psychological Preparation 237

References. 242
Drill Finder. 246
About the Authors. 251
Earn Continuing Education Credits/Units. 252

Foreword

Great athletes tend to have great coaches. The best athletes and coaches make training about fine-tuning the details of their certain craft. I can honestly say working with Loren had a positive impact on the entire direction of my career. He specified the minor details that turned into major strengths for me.

Training is truly an art, and when done correctly, you should see actual data of growth and, more importantly, understand why. Loren helped me understand how to train, when to do what. He helped me see the bigger picture.

I've always been an extremely hard worker. I still am, but working with Loren made me realize that working smarter is much more difficult than working harder. It takes more time, detail, and effort to figure out *your* exact formula for success. He has shot my career in a positive direction since day one, and I'm extremely thankful to be able to know him as a coach, mentor, and friend. BOOM!

Christian McCaffrey
Carolina Panthers running back
Two-time All-Pro

Acknowledgments

One of our favorite sayings at Landow Performance is: *If you want to go fast, go alone; if you want to go far, go together.* This adage is especially relevant to the process of publishing a book, and we would like to acknowledge the immense help, effort, patience, and guidance we received from others during this project.

First, we would like to offer our deepest gratitude to our magnificent editors at Human Kinetics: Michael Mejia, who first had the idea for this project and got the ball rolling, helping us through some of the book's most difficult early stages and reviews; Cynthia McEntire, who guided us through numerous revisions; and Shawn Donnelly, who navigated us through the final steps. Many thanks to Mark Allemand and Jenny Lokshin from the marketing team, along with the copyeditor and everyone else at Human Kinetics who worked behind the scenes to make this book happen.

We would also like to thank the Landow Performance staff—especially Amber Felchle, our facility manager, who is the vital spark behind Landow Performance's daily business operations and helped coordinate much of the effort from our end. Augustine Agyei, the director of NFL combine preparation and coaches director at Landow Performance, was instrumental in the composition of this book; Augie was extremely accommodating for author interviews, and shared his expertise from the perspective of a coach currently leading an elite-level combine prep program. Augie also did the heavy lifting for this book's novice and elite training programming. Jin Yuan, a sports performance coach at Landow Performance, helped us write eloquent descriptions of elite-level recovery modalities; Jin and Augie were also on site for the book's photo shoot to help ensure quality.

We truly appreciate the excellent work from our book's photographer, Adam Bratten, who is also a sports performance coach at Landow Performance; Adam blended his photographer's precision and coaching expertise together to produce some marvelous photos. We would also like to thank the book's models for being so gracious with their time and effort; Travis Duffle, Marcus Moore, Joe Parker, and Eddie Yarbrough were instrumental in capturing the exact positions we want to display.

A big thanks also goes to Gray Cook at Functional Movement Systems (FMS) for graciously allowing us to show and describe some of the tests involved in the Functional Movement Screen; Kyle Barrow from FMS helped us to ensure that we described these tests accurately.

And finally, we are eternally grateful for all our family members, friends, and colleagues who offered their support throughout the process of writing this book. Words cannot describe how grateful we are for your love and encouragement along the way.

Introduction

Christian McCaffrey wore an unassuming grin as he carried a freshly stitched number 22 jersey into the Carolina Panthers media room for his introductory press conference. Just the previous night in Philadelphia, Panthers linebacker Thomas Davis had taken the podium at the 2017 National Football League (NFL) Draft to announce McCaffrey as Carolina's first-round pick, number eight overall.

Now, facing the media in Charlotte, he fielded his first question to answer as a newly minted NFL player: *What was that split second like, when you heard your name called and your dream came true?*

"A lot of emotions go into it," he replied. "It's such a long process and it's been a long time that I've had this dream, so to see it come true is pretty emotional." To call his journey to the NFL a long process would be an understatement. When McCaffrey took the podium for his first press conference as a pro player, he stood on a foundation built with nearly a lifetime of dedicated training.

When McCaffrey began training for the 2017 NFL combine, he had just finished an outstanding career at Stanford. He finished second in voting for the 2015 Heisman Trophy after his sophomore season, in which he broke Barry Sanders' NCAA single season all-purpose yardage record with a staggering 3,864 yards (Lombardi 2015). Despite struggling through an injury his junior season in 2016, he still managed to lead the Pac-12 in rushing yards (ESPN 2016).

McCaffrey faced public criticism by deciding to sit out Stanford's late December 2016 appearance in the Sun Bowl so he could begin his combine training early. After weeks of intense preparation, he silenced those critics on March 3, 2017, when he ran a blazing 4.48 seconds in the 40-yard dash at the NFL combine. He also displayed his exceptional power with a 37.5-inch vertical jump and posted the second-fastest three-cone drill by a running back at the combine since 2003 with a time of 6.57 seconds (Associated Press 2017).

That brief time window—from the moment he left Stanford Stadium in late November after the Cardinal's last regular-season game, right up until he lined up for his 40-yard dash at the combine—was crucial to McCaffrey's ability to impress NFL scouts and maximize his earning capacity. But more importantly, it was a chance for him to show everyone that he truly belonged at football's highest level.

The Biggest Job Interview of a Player's Life

Football is the ultimate team sport. Each player's role is interdependent with those of his teammates. Football's emphasis on teamwork is often lauded as one of its best qualities, but it also makes it much more challenging to appraise an individual athlete's skills.

Player evaluation is maddeningly difficult, largely due to the variations between football's different levels. In college football, there are wide disparities between Division I FBS, FCS, Division II, Division III, and NAIA. It is difficult for pro scouts to evaluate players while accounting for the level of talent they face during their collegiate careers. Yet players of all college levels still find their way into the professional ranks.

An even wider talent gap exists at the high school level. For sports such as basketball and soccer, excelling at the club level can be vitally important in receiving NCAA scholarship offers. College recruiters in those sports often eschew high school games to scout Amateur Athletic Union (AAU) tournaments and similar club-level events since they often match players of equal skill level.

In football, however, athletes who reach high school age typically choose to play solely for their school. Although AAU clubs exist for football, college scouts tend to be more interested in a player's production at the varsity high school level. This can be problematic because talented players at smaller or less successful high school programs may not be noticed by recruiters.

Because of such challenges, athletic combines are crucial for athletes and scouts alike at all levels. The combine, named for its combined assessment of players' individual medical histories and vitals, general athletic abilities, and position-specific movement skills, helps to create an equal playing field for athletes striving to reach the next level.

The football combine's crown jewel is the 40-yard dash. Sprinting speed is a major indicator of performance, and as such, it is one of the key statistics used to assess football players. At the college prospect level, researchers have found that height, weight, 40-yard dash time, and vertical jump height are all statistically significant across positions in their correlation to a high school recruit's ranking and star value (Ghigiarelli 2011).

Whether a player is looking to catch the eye of college or pro scouts, a stellar combine performance is crucial to maximizing his opportunities. NFL hopefuls often refer to the NFL combine as a job interview, and serious high school athletes take a similar view toward their combine performance. These events are an athlete's chance to show what he is made of and to prove he belongs at the next level.

History of the NFL Combine

For generations, professional football organizations have taken a keen interest in understanding players' medical histories and athletic abilities; however, collecting the data used to be each team's responsibility. In the early 1960s, NFL teams began forming alliances to develop collective scouting organizations, but those scouts' roles were mostly limited to evaluating other pro teams and veteran players (Modrak 1980). NFL Draft selections at the time were largely determined by leafing through publicly available football publications, then dialing up college coaches to ask about players (Knaak 2018).

Throughout the 1970s, this relatively scattered approach to college scouting prevailed in the NFL. Some clubs flew in potential draft picks for individual workouts at their team facilities, an expensive practice that continued until Dallas Cowboys president and general manager Tex Schramm proposed standardized camps for teams to evaluate aspiring NFL players (Crouse 2007).

The first combine workouts were somewhat rudimentary. The 1982 combine held in Dallas by the Quadra scouting organization was essentially an ad hoc smattering of physical assessments. As former longtime scouting and personnel executive Gil Brandt explained, "[I]t was a medical gathering, and we did a few drills. We did the four-square drill, which was a Raider drill, we did the hop-step-and-jump, we did the vertical leap and the 40-yard dash, and that was about it. That was all the combine consisted of" (Knaak 2018).

Meanwhile, also in 1982, National Football Scouting, Inc., held the inaugural National Invitational Camp (NIC) for its 16-member consortium of NFL clubs, and BLESTO (Bears, Lions, Eagles and Steelers Talent Organization) held a combine of its own. By 1985, all 28 NFL clubs had collectively decided to centralize the process and cut costs by agreeing on one league-wide event, the NFL Scouting Combine.

After bouncing around a few different cities, by 1987 the combine settled on its permanent home in Indianapolis, Indiana. The event has grown considerably in the public consciousness since its humble beginnings. Today up to 335 annual invitees face a daunting four-day schedule that includes a plethora of medical evaluations, interviews with teams and media, and tests for general athleticism and position-specific skills.

The NFL Network first began broadcasting the event on TV in 2004, and in the ensuing years it has become a widely consumed and dissected part of the NFL's yearly calendar. Hundreds of thousands of fans tune in to scrutinize each drill and performance metric, attempting to discern tomorrow's star players. As recently as 2015, a single day of NFL combine testing drew a TV audience of 529,000 viewers (Sports TV Ratings 2015).

Other athletes participate in NFL-sanctioned regional or super regional combines, as well as the numerous pro days held by colleges and universities around the nation. Regardless of the stage, these events are critical for aspiring pro players to put themselves on the radar of NFL and Canadian Football League (CFL) teams. Combine testing can be especially important for players from smaller schools who otherwise may be overlooked due to a perceived lack of quality competition.

Meanwhile, an entire industry has sprouted as companies have followed suit in organizing regional and national showcase events for high school players to impress college scouts. Seven-on-seven tournaments often accompany these combines, with major corporations such as Nike and Adidas throwing their weight behind organizing the events.

Purpose of the Book

This book aims to explain how Landow Performance conducts combine training, in hopes that it may help other coaches and athletes by informing their process. The sports performance field is unique in its openness; nearly all practitioners are incredibly generous in sharing their knowledge and ideas. The goal of this text is to provide a comprehensive guide to Landow Performance's general framework for combine training so that coaches and athletes may take away some helpful ideas about how to approach this unique event.

This book addresses the wide variety of factors that must be considered in combine training. As one of the great practitioners, Steven Plisk, often says,

"To be a better specialist, you must become a better generalist." In the context of performance training, this means practitioners must acquaint themselves with general aspects of performance coaching such as biomechanics, biochemistry, anatomy, and programming in order to become effective combine training specialists.

Readers will gain a better understanding of a football combine's unique demands as well as the methods they can use to most efficiently address those demands for individual training scenarios. The book is written to be accessible for football coaches and athletes who may not be fully acquainted with strength and conditioning concepts so that they may know how to master the required tests.

How to Use the Book

Sections are structured to explain the combine preparation process in a logical order. Part I includes how to warm up for each workout, as well as the fundamental assessments that should be completed to better understand an athlete's training needs.

Part II provides detailed coverage of combine tests and positional drills, including not only optimal execution but also how athletes can improve in each assessment. Readers are given methods to collate athlete data and to craft a training plan based on an athlete's proficiency in his key performance indicators (KPIs) and the available training window.

Part III addresses training general movement skills, an area often ignored. Acceleration, agility, and top speed are not simply innate qualities; they are trainable skills that must be constantly rehearsed to improve performance not just in combine tests, but in football generally. The optimal model for each skill is presented along with some favorite drills and coaching methods to optimize movement quality.

Part IV returns the emphasis to the weight room, describing the top exercises Landow Performance athletes use to develop strength and power. Part V then provides eight-week training programs for novice and elite athletes and describes how to maximize results with optimal nutrition, sleep, and psychological preparation.

This book is intended to be a resource for strength and conditioning practitioners, football coaches, and athletes to help them to most effectively prepare for a football combine at any level. Each chapter covers methodology that can be used with virtually any budget or equipment. Prep Like a Pro sidebars throughout the book discuss some of the more elite-level preparation methods so that readers can use or simply better understand the most sophisticated approaches. Coaches and athletes will learn to train at an appropriate level so that they can put their best foot forward on combine day.

Key to Diagrams

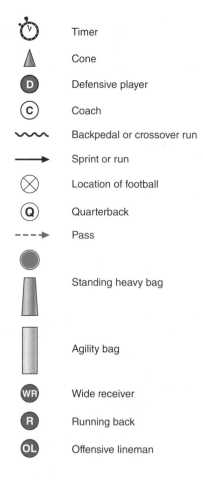

Timer

Cone

Defensive player

Coach

Backpedal or crossover run

Sprint or run

Location of football

Quarterback

Pass

Standing heavy bag

Agility bag

Wide receiver

Running back

Offensive lineman

PART I

Warm-Up and Initial Assessments

CHAPTER 1

Warm-Up
and Movement Prep

During a typical football off-season, players get to enjoy a prolonged developmental training period with potentially tremendous performance gains. Training for a football combine, however, is much different than preparing for a season of play. The length of time players typically have available to train for a combine is much shorter than an average football off-season. With such a brief opportunity to prime themselves and to impress scouts and coaches at the next level, players must take each preparatory step toward their combine or pro day with a calculated purpose. Every detail—no matter how small—matters greatly. Meticulous planning is vital to an athlete's combine training, yet many coaches still neglect a systematic approach to one crucial detail: the warm-up.

Although coaches and athletes might not concur on every training-related subject, nearly everyone recognizes the need to perform some type of warm-up before training or competition. One would be hard-pressed to find a coach who firmly believes, for example, that Chris Johnson from East Carolina University could have simply rolled out of bed on February 24, 2008, and clocked his NFL Scouting Combine 40-yard dash at 4.24 seconds without any kind of warm-up beforehand. Johnson's sprint was a then-unprecedented feat in the combine's modern timing era (since 2006), and it stood as the league's fastest for nearly a decade. It also skyrocketed Johnson's draft stock, from entering the combine as a relatively unheralded second- or third-round draft projection to becoming the 2008 NFL Draft's 24th overall selection in the first round (Katzowitz 2014). But Johnson could never have achieved his earth-shattering 40-yard dash time in the first place without performing a successful warm-up beforehand.

For optimal performance, a warm-up should achieve the necessary physiological responses (such as raising body temperature and increasing circulation) while finding and holding fundamental joint positions and overall posture to improve balance and stability within basic movement skills. Those who do not learn and rehearse these foundational building blocks of athleticism will experience a long-term dip in performance; this effect, known for decades in the motor neuroscience field as the *warm-up decrement,* is thought to stem from the motor system's constant need for "recalibration," even for skills the athlete has rehearsed for a lifetime (Ajemian et al. 2010). There is little debate as to *whether* athletes need to warm up; the question is *how* athletes should warm up to set the stage for optimal performance.

In football, as in many other sports, coaches and athletes treat warm-ups as means to an end: preparing the athlete for his workout or practice. The word itself—*warm-up*—implies something passive and straightforward, like starting a car on a frigid morning and letting the engine run before putting the vehicle in gear. Athletes are often told to focus on "getting the blood flowing" or "breaking a sweat" during their warm-ups. Physiological goals like increases in heart rate and body temperature are essential to the warm-up's purpose, but they tend to be viewed as its only purpose, when in fact it could achieve much more.

Most people's approach to warm-ups is to rehash what they have always done. Many warm-ups that we see today are just half-baked smatterings of movements, thrown together by coaches or athletes based on the drills they have performed throughout their lives. As a result, there are activities that have endured through enough generations to enter the canon of warm-up exercises, even though they provide no tangible benefit besides an elevated heart rate. Some of these activities (e.g., high knees, butt kicks) can even get in the way of learning productive movement skills.

The types of exercises and stretches used during a warm-up can positively or negatively affect the athlete's performance on combine day. For example, college football players' vertical jump heights have been found to improve after a general warm-up with dynamic stretching, whereas those numbers worsen when static stretching is included in the warm-up (Pagaduan et al. 2012). The vertical jump test is a pure display of power and a closely scrutinized combine metric, so an athlete's warm-up choices before the test can be crucial.

It may be tempting to dismiss the warm-up as a throwaway period before the real workout begins, but the exercises performed in the warm-up can offer athletes a chance to learn and rehearse basic skills while still meeting the warm-up's physiological objectives. Effective movement prep in a warm-up also helps to improve the workout's quality. A focused and properly coached warm-up readies the athlete for training by grooving proper athletic positions and movements, thereby enhancing the athlete's ability to learn exercises and drills in the weight room and on the field or turf.

A well-designed warm-up creates neuromuscular movement "problems" for athletes to solve that will make them faster and more mechanically efficient. Like the athletic equivalent of a worksheet in math class, the warm-up is a chance for athletes to improve their ability to solve these movement problems. Coaches can influence players' relative strength, power, and flexibility within a given range of motion, along with overall neuromuscular coordination, speed, agility, balance, stability, and even energy system development—all within this portion of the workout.

The warm-up that Landow Performance coaches use every day was developed over the course of two decades. When performed with the correct intent, it is a truly incredible tool for making athletes more neurologically efficient;

its principles and effects are not specific to combine training or even football. This warm-up applies to athletes across a wide spectrum of sports and levels of competition. It is also a fantastic movement screening tool for coaches. When athletes conduct this warm-up according to the same guidelines every day, a coach can make better decisions based on the daily variations he observes in specific ranges of motion. To ensure athlete consistency, each exercise must be taught slowly and deliberately so that athletes learn its intent. The warm-up's quality, and therefore its benefit, is ultimately only as good as the athlete's level of focus during this valuable time.

This chapter provides a full guide to the warm-up with photos and illustrations—not only the *how* for performing each exercise, but also the *why* behind its intent and structure. Coaches armed with this knowledge will be able to better cue athletes through the warm-up while explaining how each exercise can benefit their long-term development. This will help them to get more buy-in from the athletes, which is critical for long-term performance gains.

This warm-up includes a combination of exercises emphasizing activation, dynamic flexibility and mobility, and movement skills, among other elements. Activation is achieved through muscular isolation, creating movement at specific joint positions to ensure that all of the neuromuscular "lights in the house" are turned on, so to speak, before the real work starts. Dynamic mobility is practiced by maximizing a joint's range of motion in a specific position, then trying to increase that range of motion without losing correct position. The warm-up begins with general skipping and carioca patterns, followed by dynamic stretches and exercises conducted in a series of positions: walking, quadruped, lying, seated, and then standing. An athlete who performs this warm-up lackadaisically before a workout or game will not see its full benefits, nor will he train or perform at his best. But when it is coached and performed in a focused, thorough manner, this warm-up can set the tone physically and psychologically for an excellent workout or performance.

General Movement Prep

The beginning of the warm-up uses different types of skip patterns to raise athletes' heart rates while introducing coordinative tasks that involve the whole body. This helps to kick off the physiological "warming" process described earlier while also beginning to rev up the athlete's nervous system.

SKIPS (CROSS-BODY ARM SWING, WINDMILL ARM SWING)

In a relaxed, rhythmic skip pattern, the athlete simultaneously swings both arms at chest level, alternating between opening them out to the sides and then closing them back in toward each other to cross his body (figure 1.1*a*). He should time this arm swing so that each time his feet leave the ground, his arms are in one of the two end positions: either crossed in front of his chest

Figure 1.1   Skips: *(a)* cross-body arm swing; *(b)* windmill arm swing.

or opened out wide to his sides. He will complete the skip for 25 yards going down and 25 yards coming back.

Next, the athlete repeats the same skip pattern but with a twist, this time swinging both lengthened arms in a circular motion up overhead (figure 1.1*b*) and then back down beside his trunk. He times his arm swing so that each time his feet leave the ground, his arms are in the same position, like a relaxed version of jumping rope. He skips with arms circling forward like a baseball pitcher for 25 yards going down, then turns around and reverses his arm swing like a softball pitcher, skipping back to his starting point.

CARIOCA

The carioca is an exercise for challenging and assessing athletes' coordination and teaching them how to swivel their hips and take crossover steps. There are many different versions of the carioca exercise; for the purposes of this warm-up, athletes take small and quick steps while maximizing their hip swivel. The athlete starts facing sideways to his right. Standing with feet at hip width, he begins taking alternating small steps at a jogging pace (figure 1.2). For the first step he crosses his right foot directly in front of his left foot, then reaches his left foot out to hip width again. The next step starts with his right foot again, which

Figure 1.2   Carioca.

now moves directly behind his left foot; the athlete then moves his left foot out again. He takes these steps in a relaxed and rhythmic pattern, working his hips forward and back as his trailing foot alternates stepping in front of and then behind the leading foot. This variation of the exercise emphasizes hip swiveling in both directions, while the arms stay relaxed at the sides and swing in opposite rhythm of the hips. The athlete does the carioca for one repetition each way—moving out to his left for 25 yards, then facing the same direction and performing the exercise moving back 25 yards to his right.

Ground Series

The ground series begins the process of figuratively turning on all the lights in the house. Through careful setup and movement, athletes can use this series to isolate specific muscles and activate them to do their job correctly.

Quadruped Series

The quadruped series is the point in the warm-up at which coaches can get athletes mentally engaged because of the focus required to maintain body position throughout each exercise. To begin, the athlete must get onto his hands and knees, arranging himself into a stacked position (figure 1.3). This means that each wrist should be placed directly under the elbow and the shoulder with the hands putting pressure into the ground, while the knees are situated directly beneath the hips. Granted, the setup must account for the unique build of each athlete. A group of 10 football players warming up will yield 10 different setups, but coaches should strive to place them into these positions as well as possible.

Figure 1.3   Proper setup for the quadruped series.

Both feet should be actively dorsiflexed, with the toes pulled up toward the shins to create six total points of contact on the ground (hands, knees, and toes). The athlete's intent in this position should be to push his hands into the ground while bracing the abdominal muscles. Simply holding this position should carry a certain level of difficulty due to the required level of muscular engagement.

Many athletes unconsciously put their hips into anterior tilt when entering the quadruped position, creating a visible U-shaped curve in the lower back. Coaches must watch for this tilt carefully because it can begin to jam the facets of the lumbar spine. Some athletes may need to roll their hips down into a slight posterior tilt in order to flatten their backs (think of a dog tucking its tail) to get their hips and lower spine into a more neutral position.

Head position should be similarly neutral. Coaches can identify proper head position by examining the relationship of the ear, shoulder, and hip. If the coach can draw an imaginary straight line neatly through those three landmarks from a side-on view, then the head is properly situated. If the athlete's head is too far back and places the ear out of line with the shoulders and hips, a helpful cue can be to tuck the chin.

Active dorsiflexion of the feet ought to be maintained throughout each quadruped series exercise. This is directed more at overall performance training than at these specific movements. Dorsiflexion is the most difficult position to execute consistently when sprinting, so the quadruped series is an opportunity to hold dorsiflexion and achieve improvements in both muscle memory and local muscular endurance of the anterior tibialis. In this way, an athlete can improve speed even while performing exercises that appear completely unrelated to sprinting ability.

In the quadruped starting position, the athlete's abdominal muscles must be lightly engaged so that his spine remains fixed in its starting posture. Each movement in the quadruped series should be limited to the range an athlete can achieve without violating other positions. For example, an athlete trying to maximally abduct his leg at any cost will bend his elbows, shift his hips, or lose spinal integrity—possibly all at once—to achieve a greater range of motion. Instead, he needs to work exclusively in the range he can control. As he performs each movement carefully and consistently, his range will gradually improve over time.

FIRE HYDRANT

Figure 1.4   Fire hydrant.

The first exercise in the quadruped series is the fire hydrant, aptly named for the classic target of many a dog's micturition. This exercise targets lateral hip activation through abduction, or by bringing a bent leg away from the body's midline in a controlled manner. Without changing the bend in his knee or ankle, the athlete brings one knee off the ground into controlled abduction (figure 1.4). He then lowers the leg to the ground at a similarly smooth pace. As the athlete abducts his leg, his knee should slightly lead his foot, not vice versa. The latter would create excessive hip internal rotation. The exercise should be performed for six repetitions on one side, followed by six repetitions on the other side.

Coaches should watch for elbow bend during the movement and instruct athletes to keep their elbows straight while preventing their hips from shifting out to the opposite side of the abducting limb. Fire hydrants are effective for activating the tensor fasciae latae (TFL) as well as the anterior fibers of the gluteus medius and minimus.

HIP CIRCLE

After completing fire hydrants on both sides, the athlete transitions back to the first leg to perform hip circles. Moving either clockwise or counterclockwise, the athlete circumducts his leg by drawing imaginary circles in the air with his kneecap (figure 1.5). Circles should be as large as possible without opening up to the point where the athlete's hips shift away from his moving leg. Both elbows must be watched carefully throughout the repetitions because athletes will often bend to allow for greater freedom of range in the working hip. The exercise should be completed for six consecutive repetitions on each side.

Figure 1.5 Hip circle.

SCORPION

While maintaining the knee's 90-degree angle of flexion, the athlete focuses on squeezing his glute to drive his heel up to the ceiling or the sky (figure 1.6). He then returns his knee to the ground in a controlled fashion. After performing six repetitions on one leg, he switches to the other leg for six repetitions. The resulting movement resembles a scorpion's stinger, and it can immediately display the degree to which the athlete can extend his hip, as well as the symmetry (or lack thereof) between sides. Coaches should not, however, jump to any conclusions about why an athlete may struggle with hip extension. It is commonly assumed that glute inhibition is the culprit, but the cause may also be anterior tightness in the hip flexors.

Coaches need not worry if they notice a slight external hip rotation while the athlete drives his hip into extension. In fact, this should happen because the structural arrangement of gluteus maximus fibers will cause the femur to externally rotate as the hip extends. The degree of hip extension is much more important in this exercise than the degree of abduction from the midline. Yet this joint extension

Figure 1.6 Scorpion.

should not occur at the expense of lumbar spine integrity. Coaches must be watchful; as they try to maximally drive their heels, athletes will often begin to extend their lumbar spines. When athletes are required to hold their form, the scorpion exercise can help them learn to disassociate their hips and spine while effectively activating the glutes. Athletes who violate lumbar range in a quadruped scorpion often do the same when they are squatting.

An alternate version of the scorpion involves extending the hip and knee together with a dorsiflexed foot so that the heel pushes straight back in line with the head and trunk.

LATERAL LEG REACH

Figure 1.7 Lateral leg reach.

The lateral leg reach is one of the most difficult exercises to perform while holding proper position. The athlete begins with a fully extended leg in line with his head, neck, and trunk. His foot is dorsiflexed and pointing toward the ground. To start the movement, he turns his back leg so that his foot points out to the side. While keeping his knee fully extended and his foot dorsiflexed, he brings his entire leg out in the direction his foot is now pointing (figure 1.7). This exercise does an excellent job of activating the quadriceps, tensor fasciae latae (TFL), and obliques.

Coaches must not allow athletes to cheat a greater range of motion by violating other ranges. A dead giveaway is when the athlete loses tension in his moving thigh or allows his opposite hip to shift out to the side. Coaches must see where the range of motion originates; those who do not will be unable to compare sides and determine asymmetries.

Straight-Leg Series

Typically athletes perform the straight-leg series after the quadruped series due to lever lengths. A straight leg is a longer lever than a bent leg, and thus it makes the torso's job of bracing and holding position more challenging. It makes sense to move from lower to higher difficulty in the warm-up; for optimal performance, preparation must have a ramping-up effect. This is also why the lateral leg reach is last in the quadruped series.

SUPINE STRAIGHT-LEG LIFT

Lying flat on his back in a supine position, the athlete bends one leg so the bottom of his foot is flat on the ground and drawn closer to the hips. With the other leg, he tightens the quadriceps to fully extend his knee and dorsiflexes the foot by pulling his toes up toward the shin. This dorsiflexion puts the posterior lower leg into a stretch, thereby enhancing the length-tension of the overall stretch. From this position, the athlete lifts his leg to create a posterior

Figure 1.8   Supine straight-leg lift.

stretch (figure 1.8) while driving activation in the quadriceps, hip flexors, anterior tibialis, extensor digitorum longus, and extensor hallucis longus. The exercise should be completed for six consecutive repetitions on each side.

The athlete should raise each leg up as far as possible without lifting his hips off the ground, bending his knee, or losing active dorsiflexion in his foot. Upon reaching this maximal stretch, the athlete lowers his leg back to the ground at a controlled tempo. The goal is not to bring the leg higher by any means necessary; instead, it is to lift the limb as high as possible while still influencing the tissue targeted by this stretch. Coaches who see an athlete's knee beginning to bend at the top of this movement should cue him to stop the motion sooner. Also crucial is to teach the athlete to stay engaged in the trunk and to keep the pelvis tight and braced. Otherwise he may augment his range of motion by compensating in the hips or spine.

SIDE-LYING STRAIGHT-LEG ABDUCTION

From a supine position on his back, the athlete rolls to one side and sets his body to create a straight line from ear to ankle. The shoulders, hips, and ankles should be stacked so his top shoulder sits directly over his bottom shoulder, forming an imaginary line pointing straight up. The athlete lays his bottom arm flat on the ground in sequence with his head, trunk, and legs. The athlete can lay his head on his bottom shoulder while placing his top hand close to his chest, settling his palm flat against the ground. Both legs must be perfectly straight, with tight quadriceps and active dorsiflexion, like the moving leg in supine straight-leg lifts. While maintaining perfect body position with an engaged core, the athlete lifts his top leg straight up into roughly 25 to 30 degrees of abduction (figure 1.9). Any further range of abduction in the side-lying position will cause the athlete to bend his spine laterally; the coach must ensure that the desired tissue is activated without violating other ranges. The athlete should

Figure 1.9   Side-lying straight-leg abduction.

complete six repetitions on one side, then perform the next exercise (side-lying straight-leg adduction) on the same side before switching onto his other side and performing both exercises for six repetitions in the same sequence.

SIDE-LYING STRAIGHT-LEG ADDUCTION

After completing the desired number of side-lying straight-leg abductions, the athlete remains on the same side and performs leg lifts with his bottom leg. The only adjustment in position necessary is moving the top leg across his body so that his top foot rests on the ground near his hips. Shoulders and hips remain stacked, while the bottom arm, shoulder, hip, knee, and ankle continue to form a straight line.

For this exercise, the athlete's focus should be on lifting the bottom leg off the ground into adduction (figure 1.10), activating the adductor magnus and gracilis. Coaches should emphasize not how high the athlete lifts his leg, but how aligned he can keep his body throughout the repetitions. If the athlete's bottom leg begins to drift out of line with the rest of his body, the cue should be to squeeze the quadriceps and glutes to maintain correct posture. The athlete should complete six repetitions of his top leg abduction and bottom leg adduction on one side, then roll over and perform the same sequence on the other side.

Figure 1.10   Side-lying straight-leg adduction.

PRONE STRAIGHT-LEG ABDUCTION

Rolling onto his abdomen, the athlete brings both legs together and bends his right arm with his palm flat against the ground so that he may rest his forehead on his right hand. His left arm stays out to the side for balance as he abducts a fully straightened right leg and dorsiflexed foot roughly 30 degrees out to his right (figure 1.11), then brings it back to neutral position. When he completes six repetitions on the right side, he switches his arms and performs the same exercise for six repetitions with his left leg. Much like the side-lying straight-leg abduction, coaches must watch the spine for any side bend.

Figure 1.11   Prone straight-leg abduction.

Rockers and Wipers

To round out the ground series, athletes complete two exercises that start from a seated position. The quadruped series and straight-leg series are intended to isolate and activate muscles from relatively static body positions. Back rockers and windshield wipers, however, are more dynamic and help transition athletes into the rest of the warm-up.

BACK ROCKER

For those conducting a sit-and-reach flexibility test at a combine, it may be hard to determine whether a poor score is due to the hamstrings, the erector spinae, or simply an unfavorable leg-to-torso length ratio. The back rocker exercise drives mobility improvements in the first two categories. It also serves as an excellent cool-down exercise following an intense movement training session.

Beginning in a seated position with both legs straight out in front of his torso, the athlete rolls onto his back, anchoring his body weight onto the shoulder blades while bringing straight legs back over the rest of his body and remaining engaged in the midsection (figure 1.12*a*). The goal should be for the athlete to move back as far as he can while keeping his legs perfectly straight. While rocking backward, the legs should remain as straight as possible with tightened quadriceps and active dorsiflexion of the feet. This creates excellent leverage for a stretch on the thoracolumbar fascia and the erector spinae.

Figure 1.12   Back rockers: *(a)* rock backward; *(b)* rock forward into straddle position; *(c)* rock forward into figure-four position.

Next, the athlete rolls forward, reaching up high with both hands and hinging forward at the hips as he lands in a seated position. He rotates through three different seated variations, rolling back between variations. First, he rolls forward into a straddled seated position, forming a V-shape with straight legs (figure 1.12*b*). After rolling back again, he makes a figure-four position (figure 1.12*c*): left leg straight, with the right leg bent at the knee and hip so his right foot meets his left thigh (forming the shape of a 4). A third roll back onto the shoulder blades is followed by the opposite figure-four position, this time with his right leg straight and his left leg bent. The athlete makes three full cycles through this three-part sequence with a constant and controlled tempo, rolling back after each seated position. This is a total of nine repetitions rolling back and forward: three straddle or V-sits, three left-side figure-four sits, and three right-side figure-four sits.

Two critical safety points regarding back rockers must be addressed. First, the shoulder blades or scapulae, not the neck, should be the aiming point during the roll back. Second, athletes must not remain in the rolled-back position of the back rocker for too long. Although athletes often like the stretch this provides, remaining there in a static position can create prolonged intense pressure on the lumbar spinal discs. Maintaining trunk engagement throughout the movement to hold intervertebral pressure will greatly mitigate any possible danger of spinal injury. Coaches must be aware of each athlete's injury history and consider whether this exercise could pose a risk for the athlete. The back rocker is a dynamic stretch, not a static one. Athletes should cycle through repetitions at a controlled pace without prolonging the rolled-back position. When performed properly, back rockers allow athletes to achieve a quality stretch in muscular groupings at the upper back, pelvis, and hamstrings.

WINDSHIELD WIPERS

Windshield wipers combine hip internal and external rotation with a dynamic reaching stretch in the piriformis, glutes, latissimus dorsi, and erector spinae. Returning to a seated position after completing back rockers, the athlete orients both legs at a 90-degree angle on the ground with his knees pointing toward the right side. He positions his right leg so the lateral (outer) side of his right foot is on the ground and his heel is close to his left knee. His left leg mirrors his right leg, so the thighs and lower legs are parallel to each other. Both feet are actively dorsiflexed, with the heels remaining in a fixed position throughout the stretch. The athlete may place his hands on the ground behind him for support and balance (figure 1.13a). Mimicking a windshield wiper's motion, he keeps his hips and heels on the ground while bringing his knees up and across, pivoting from the heels. When the athlete's legs reach the ground, they are now a mirror image of their starting position. His hip and knee angles remain the same, so his knees point out to the left with his left heel close to his right knee (figure 1.13b). The athlete then brings his knees all the way back over to the right side, then to the left again to complete three wiper movements.

After completing the third motion, the athlete extends his hands far out to the left along the ground in perfect line with the direction in which his left femur is pointing. He leans his trunk as he reaches, creating an excellent hip stretch. After a brief pause in this stretch, he returns to his seated position with his legs remaining in the same spot. This completes a single repetition. Now he completes three more wiper motions—to the right, then left, then right again—now reaching out in line with his right femur (figure 1.13c). The heels and hips remain in their starting position throughout all repetitions. The athlete thinks only about moving his knees and then his upper body. He completes three repetitions of reaches on each side, for six total repetitions.

Figure 1.13   Windshield wiper: *(a)* wiper motion right; *(b)* wiper motion left; *(c)* reaching to the right.

Walking Series

Upon completing the ground series exercises, the athlete begins a series of walking dynamic mobility exercises. Joint position dictates muscle function—meaning that the exact way an athlete moves during an exercise will determine which muscles are used. Even a slight deviation from the exercise's acceptable margin of error may cause the athlete's nervous system to call upon different muscles than intended. And because athletes will adapt, each exercise requires the athlete to move in a very detailed way to isolate and activate the intended muscles. The walking series addresses posture, balance, strength, and stability while expanding selected ranges of motion. To make these improvements, however, athletes must concentrate on using only the individual exercise's targeted joint range.

Focusing on holding posture during this warm-up can be more difficult than expected because the goal of these exercises often seems counterintuitive. Most athletes try to do their exercises as well as possible, which to many means getting as far as possible in the movement. Competitive athletes training in a group are especially apt to chase range of motion at all costs. Doing this without emphasizing postural control will inevitably cause athletes to violate other ranges of motion, however, negating a coach's ability to use the warm-up as a movement screen for potential athlete deficiencies or asymmetries.

Movement through ranges of motion an athlete cannot control will not achieve much. If the coaching cue for a straight-leg march is simply, "kick your foot above your head," the ever-competitive athlete will surely violate any number of joint ranges to kick as high as possible. Coaches will then be unable to detect movement restrictions, asymmetries, and potential future injuries because they cannot determine the true range of motion and condition of the targeted joints and muscles. Not only must parameters for each drill in the warm-up be set and clearly explained, but also they must be constantly reinforced through attentive coaching.

The athlete will begin each exercise in the straight-leg series (except for the inchworm) with the same setup posture: standing tall with his feet hip width apart and toes pointed straight ahead, his shoulders back, and his eyes straight ahead (figure 1.14). Each exercise is typically conducted at a controlled pace for 10 yards unless otherwise specified. Coaches should make a top priority of perfect posture throughout each movement. Single-leg balance requires serious focus, so this sequence of dynamic stretching helps athletes to become attuned to their bodies as they prepare for their training session. Initially they should conduct the walking series slowly and deliberately, increasing speed as their competency, balance, and ability to properly stack joints improve, but never to an extent that feels rushed.

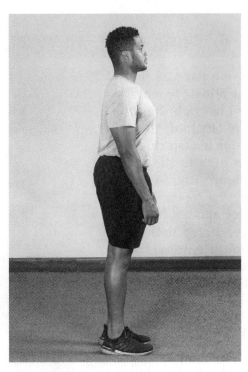

Figure 1.14 Setup posture for the walking series.

WALKING KNEE HUG

From the tall, standing setup posture, the athlete dorsiflexes his left foot as he lifts his left knee toward his torso, allowing his lifting knee to bend as he grasps his shin with both hands just below his raised knee (figure 1.15). He pulls his shin further up and in toward him, hugging his knee tight to his chest as his hip and knee ranges of motion allow. His down leg is fully extended, with the foot flat on the ground, actively pushing the ground away to get as tall as possible. His shoulders remain back with his eyes fixed straight ahead; there should be no collapsing of his chest, back, or neck to allow for further range. After a brief hold in the top position, the athlete returns his leg to the ground in a controlled manner, then performs the same movement on his right side. He will continue alternating sides, gaining some ground with each step as he performs this exercise for 10 yards.

Figure 1.15 Walking knee hug.

WALKING QUAD STRETCH

Continuing at the same pace as the walking knee hug, the athlete reaches behind his body with his right hand to grip the top of his left foot, then stands tall while pulling his left thigh back and reaches up high in the air with his left hand (figure 1.16). After a controlled lowering, he repeats the same with his right leg and left hand, gaining ground with each step. In their cueing, coaches should emphasize bringing the thigh back; if an athlete's knee points straight at the ground, he will feel a considerable quadriceps stretch, whereas the intent to drive his knee backward will put his hip flexors and adductors into an additional stretch. The walking quad stretch will quickly expose an athlete's limitations in movement, making the exercise helpful for coaches to watch closely. Complete the exercise for 10 yards.

Figure 1.16 Walking quad stretch.

LEG CRADLE

This dynamic stretch bears a slight resemblance to the walking knee hug, with some key differences. The athlete externally rotates his left leg to a 45-degree angle as he lifts it, cradling his left hand under the knee while his right hand grips his left shin just above the ankle (figure 1.17). He uses both hands to bring the leg further up toward his chest, maintaining the lower leg's 45-degree angle and not trying to externally rotate his thigh any further. The athlete should not feel any twisting pressure on his knee. A careful lowering is followed by the same movement on the right side, then continuing to alternate sides for 10 yards.

Figure 1.17   Leg cradle.

WALKING TOE TOUCH

In this dynamic stretch, the athlete maintains a normal hip-width relationship between his feet as he alternates reaching for his toes on one leg and then the other, hinging at his hips. He first steps his left foot forward so that his left heel is in line with his right big toe. He keeps his left heel on the ground and flexes his ankle to pull his toes up toward his shin. He locks out his left knee, while his right leg behind him remains slightly bent. The athlete then pushes his hips back, hinging directly at his hips to reach his arms down toward his left big toe. All the while, he must maintain excellent upper-body posture with his shoulders back, his back perfectly flat, and his chin in a neutral position (figure 1.18). As the athlete hinges, he reaches both hands down toward his front foot.

Figure 1.18   Walking toe touch.

The athlete should not necessarily be directed to get his hands all the way to his front foot; keeping good posture is much more important than whether he touches his toes. The emphasis should be on holding spinal integrity while hinging at the hips so that the coach can observe the athlete's true hamstring range of motion. The athlete should merely reach toward his feet; at the end of his hamstring range, he finishes the repetition by hinging back upward as he steps his right foot through and reaches both arms overhead. He takes a short step between repetitions to transition into an opposite-side stretch, now with his right leg in front and his left leg behind.

INCHWORM

The inchworm targets some of the same ranges as the walking toe touch, but with more involvement from other posterior chain muscles such as the glutes and spinal erectors. It also helps begin to warm up the athlete's upper body. Beginning in a push-up position with arms extended and body in a straight line from ear to ankle, the athlete inches forward on the balls of his feet toward his hands, maintaining straight legs and a flat back to hinge at the hips (figure 1.19). Emphasizing dorsiflexion as the feet move forward will improve the length-tension of the lower leg tissues. When he reaches the point at which he cannot move further

Figure 1.19　Inchworm.

without bending his knees, the athlete walks his hands forward to return to a push-up position. He then drops his hips and brings his head back to look up, keeping his hips and knees off the ground. Landow Performance athletes typically complete this exercise for five full repetitions, although coaches may prescribe it for five yards of distance instead.

Athletes who have potential lumbar extension dysfunction should avoid dropping their hips and instead simply return their hips to neutral before beginning the next inchworm. Athletes typically find this exercise the least enjoyable, and they often rush through repetitions by taking the biggest steps possible. To accurately assess an athlete's limitations, coaches should insist they take the smallest steps possible during each inchworm repetition.

STRAIGHT-LEG MARCH

Often referred to colloquially as "tin soldiers" or "Russian walks," the straight-leg march is a warm-up exercise commonly used across the globe. Despite its universality, this dynamic stretch often is performed in a manner that diminishes its potential benefits.

The athlete brings his left leg up in a forceful yet controlled manner with a fully extended knee and dorsiflexed foot, while maintaining ideal upper-body posture. He simultaneously lifts his right hand to shoulder height to mimic the contralateral movement aspect of walking, skipping, or running (figure 1.20). The arm should not actively reach forward, however, because that would encourage breaking posture in the thoracic spine. After lowering the left leg and right arm, he performs the movement with his right leg and left arm, alternating back and forth as he moves forward for the prescribed distance.

For the purposes of this warm-up, athletes are cued to concentrate only on kicking each leg as high as possible without rounding the spine to achieve a higher leg position. They could certainly kick higher, but doing so would violate other ranges, thereby limiting the extent to which they can activate and improve the desired joint range. Maintaining optimal posture also prevents athletes from concealing limitations that a coach can easily spot when the drill is done correctly.

Figure 1.20   Straight-leg march.

STRAIGHT-LEG SKIP

The athlete performs the straight-leg march with a double-skip rhythm, similar to that of an A-skip (see chapter 7). Just as in the straight-leg march, his abdominals must remain engaged to preserve upper-body posture. His arms move in a relaxed manner, swinging opposite to the kicking leg (figure 1.21). The straight-leg skip also requires applying more force into the ground through the ball of the foot. From a side view, coaches should see their athletes remaining rigid in the midsection throughout the skip, rather than collapsing at the chest or the lumbar spine. This will enable coaches to notice asymmetries (e.g., an athlete with tighter right-side hamstrings).

Figure 1.21   Straight-leg skip.

ELBOW TO INSTEP

Figure 1.22   Elbow to instep.

Lunging forward with his left leg, the athlete lowers his torso toward the ground, bringing his left elbow toward his left ankle while keeping the left foot flat on the ground (figure 1.22). He braces his right hand flat on the ground on his right side for balance. The athlete steps up to a standing position, bringing the legs together and restoring his hips to a neutral position before lunging forward with his right leg. As he moves through the drill, he alternates sides for 10 yards.

Practitioners often debate how far the lunging leg's knee should travel out over the toes. Some argue that the knee must remain at a perfect 90-degree angle, and it should never violate that angle by moving past the toes. However, consider that football players violate that angle constantly in their sport, so they must learn to properly control tibial motion over the foot. If athletes do not condition that range during the warm-up, they risk losing it. Therefore, the rule for elbow to instep is to let the knee track neutrally over the toes as far as the athlete can manage without his heel coming off the ground. There are always exceptions for athletes with less range due to injury or age. It is the practitioner's responsibility to cue this exercise appropriately for each athlete.

Standing Series

After completing the walking series, the athlete performs more dynamic exercises, but this time from a standing position.

ANKLE ROCKER

The first standing exercise, the ankle rocker, helps to activate the ankle plantar flexor and dorsiflexor muscles. Standing tall, with his feet at hip width and pointing straight ahead, the athlete raises up onto his toes (figure 1.23a), then after a controlled lowering, pulls his toes up as far as possible (figure 1.23b). A return to the ground after dorsiflexion completes one full repetition, and the athlete completes 10 repetitions. During the dorsiflexion portion of this exercise, coaches must ensure that athletes' hips do not drift back excessively to help them lift their toes higher. Active range of motion in plantar flexion and dorsiflexion is the goal.

Figure 1.23   Ankle rocker: *(a)* up on toes; *(b)* lift toes.

BODYWEIGHT SQUAT

The bodyweight squat allows the athlete to continue working on dorsiflexion, this time stressing a passive range of motion. Knee and hip mobility can also be assessed and improved. Sitting back into a squat position, the athlete counterbalances with his arms out in front of his torso (figure 1.24).

Width of stance and depth of squat are purposely not prescribed in this description because athletes differ in limb length ratios, ranges of motion, and injury history.

Figure 1.24   Bodyweight squat.

However, the athlete's shins should begin angling forward into ankle dorsiflexion as the athlete lowers into his squat; ideally he will lower his squat and dorsiflex at an angle where his knees travel forward neutrally over the toes, so that his bottom squat position ends with the athlete's knees just past his toes—but not to a point that creates pain or any dysfunction elsewhere in the movement. Coaches and athletes should try to find an approach that suits each athlete, aiming for a pain-free range where an athlete can get his thighs parallel with the ground, or as close to this depth as is appropriate.

TOE GRAB

Figure 1.25   Toe grab.

Widening his feet just outside his squat stance, the athlete hinges forward, bending his knees as much as necessary to reach his toes. Grasping both toes, the athlete then squats toward the ground while keeping his elbows inside his knees (figure 1.25) and raises his chest and head.

After lowering his hips to maximum depth with both heels remaining on the ground, he then drops his chest and head again to lift his hips back up while keeping his hands in position. Moving down into the bottom squat and back up into the top position comprises one full repetition; complete 10 repetitions.

Conclusion

Athletes should finish their warm-up with a few transit mobility series, customized for the workout to come. This final portion of the warm-up typically includes exercises like A-skips (described in chapter 7) or more carioca drills prior to a multidirectional movement training session. The goal is to finish with more dynamic and specific movements that will develop skills and contribute to the session ahead. The number of repetitions for these exercises in the warm-up is low, usually two to three repetitions. Upon completing their warm-up, athletes take a three-minute rest before continuing their movement or weight room session.

For combine athletes, this warm-up should be performed the same way whether it precedes a workout or competition. Although some athletes can benefit from a special competition warm-up, most are creatures of habit (like most humans) who can benefit greatly from the consistency derived from a routine warm-up, an effect that is often affectionately called the "warm fuzzies." Combines and pro days are unfamiliar and stressful, and many athletes can benefit psychologically from the comfort and familiarity of a ritual warm-up.

Ultimately, the devil is in the details. Any practitioner could regurgitate these exercises to athletes without fully understanding them, but the way the warm-up is conducted and coached will determine its effectiveness. All practitioners should practice this warm-up themselves regularly, working through each exercise with the conscious intent to contract or stretch the proper muscles. Coaches who know how this warm-up should feel, who have a strong understanding of human biomechanics, and who closely watch an athlete's every movement can make this warm-up a remarkably effective tool.

CHAPTER 2

Physiological Assessments and Athlete Background

Most strength and conditioning coaches exhibit a tremendous passion for training. Their ardor for hard work and physical preparation motivates them to give their utmost to foster athlete development, and they seek to learn more from the vast wealth of published knowledge to keep improving as coaches. This enthusiasm for the nuts and bolts of training, however, can lead coaches to get ahead of themselves. Some will flip through the assessment chapters in their strength and conditioning books to get to the more "exciting" parts about training. But a coach who knows nothing about the person in front of him will produce suboptimal—or possibly even disastrous—training results for his athlete.

To effectively prepare football players for a combine or pro day, coaches must know as much as possible about each athlete's starting point. This information should not be limited to measuring jumps and clocking sprints and agility drills. Those data points are helpful, but they are only a small part of the larger picture illuminating where the athlete stands at the beginning of his combine preparation.

This chapter will guide coaches through the necessary initial evaluation steps. It may be tempting to launch headfirst into workouts without first conducting a detailed intake process, but this is inadvisable. The athlete's training will likely be less effective without the most complete picture possible of his starting position. Physiological assessments and an athletic history interview will produce a comprehensive snapshot, informing each coach's decisions leading up to combine day.

Physiological Assessments

A practitioner can begin the intake process by gathering some objective data about the athlete's body. This includes measuring basic athlete vitals and assessing various joint movement ranges.

Athlete Vitals

A player's height, weight, and body fat percentage are important to consider before beginning combine training since his nutritional intake may need to be adjusted for weight gain or loss. The goal should be to bring his weight and body composition as close as possible to his football position's archetype at the next competitive level (accounting for variations in height and bone density). Football scouts and coaches typically view these vitals as benchmarks during their evaluations, so strength and conditioning practitioners must know where their athletes stand relative to team expectations.

When a football player joins the Landow Performance combine training program, coaches and personnel record height, weight, and body fat percentage on the first day. Though coaches could simply use the height and weight provided by the school's roster or media guide, it is best to measure these vitals in person. Player weight often varies in the course of a season, and sometimes rosters will list players as taller or heavier than their actual numbers.

Body fat percentage can be assessed using a number of methods that vary in cost and accuracy. At the NFL combine training level, where cost is less of a concern and accuracy is more consequential, advanced devices such as the Bod Pod are prevalent. Dual-energy X-ray absorptiometry (DEXA) scans are also popular for evaluating both body fat and bone density. For coaches without access to these methods, calipers can be acquired for minimal cost and can provide a useful ballpark number for determining what nutritional approach players should take during their preparation. Specific nutritional guidelines are covered in chapter 13.

Before participating in the Landow Performance combine training program, athletes must undergo a doctor's physical examination to identify potential medical issues that a coach cannot detect.

Range of Motion Assessment

Nearly all sprint-based sports cause athletes to frequently place their limbs in compromising joint positions. A joint with poor range of motion can be at higher risk of injury when it is forced to move too far. Limited range of motion in one joint can also produce undesired movement in other joints, creating injury risks there as well. When the neuromuscular system is called on to move a joint, that movement's limit is termed *active range of motion*. An athlete with active range limitations will compensate by automatically manipulating surrounding joints. *Passive range of motion*, or a joint's full movement range independent of the neuromuscular system, can be problematic when it is either too narrow or too wide. If passive range is limited, active range will not surpass it; the neuromuscular system cannot move the joint past its structural ability to move.

A wide gap between passive and active range of motion in a joint represents an unstable zone known as the *range of motion deficit*. When a joint is within its range of motion deficit, the inability to control the joint in this position poses an injury risk. Various tests may be used during the intake process to determine the athlete's flexibility and his range of motion deficit (figure 2.1). Awareness of this deficit helps a coach to decide where joint mobility and stability must improve.

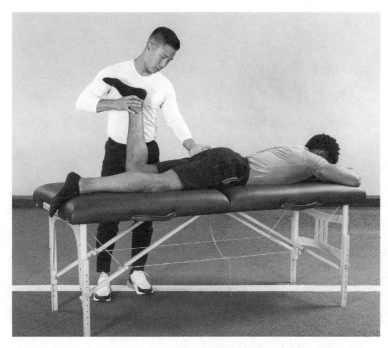

Figure 2.1   Athlete passive/active joint assessment conducted on table.

As part of the initial football combine athlete intake process at Landow Performance, coaches conduct the Functional Movement Screen (FMS) series of tests developed by Gray Cook and Lee Burton. These tests—described and illustrated on the following pages—can give coaches an initial idea of an athlete's fundamental quality of movement by looking at mobility and stability during basic movement patterns, potentially helping to reveal compensation patterns and structural limitations. The practitioner scores each test on a scale of 0 to 3. Any test that causes pain is scored as a 0. In the absence of pain, an athlete will receive a score of 1 if he cannot complete the test or achieve the desired position. He scores a 2 if he uses compensatory patterns during the test. Successfully completing the test without compensation earns him a 3 (Cook et al. 2014a, 2014b).

DEEP SQUAT

While standing, the athlete places the inside edges of the feet in vertical alignment with the creases of the armpits to establish a reliable shoulder-width stance. The athlete rests a dowel or PVC rod on top of his head to adjust the hand position, placing the elbows at a 90-degree angle. From that position, he presses the PVC rod overhead (figure 2.2a). He then descends slowly into the deepest possible squat position with the heels on the floor, head and chest facing forward and the rod maximally pressed overhead. The knees should align over the feet with no valgus collapse (figure 2.2b). He holds the bottom position for a full second before rising back to his starting position, completing 1 to 3 full repetitions.

Figure 2.2   Deep squat: *(a)* starting position; *(b)* squat.

This test allows practitioners to assess the athlete's range in ankle dorsiflexion and knee and hip flexion as well as overhead shoulder mobility and trunk integrity throughout the movement. It is important for the athlete to demonstrate lower-body mobility without robbing movement from the torso and upper extremities. Ankle dorsiflexion is a key range to note for the purposes of combine training because it is critical to several general athleticism tests in the combine.

HURDLE STEP

The athlete stands directly in front of a test kit with feet together and his toes up against its base. The practitioner adjusts the hurdle's height to somewhere between the athlete's mid-shin and his tibial tuberosity, or the bony bump on the knee located at the top of the tibia. Holding a dowel or PVC rod with both hands behind the neck at shoulder level (figure 2.3*a*), like a high bar position in a barbell squat, the athlete tries to step one leg slowly over the hurdle while staying as tall as possible in the rest of his body (figure 2.3*b*). After touching his heel on the other side of the hurdle, he reverses his stepping leg's direction to bring it back over the hurdle toward him and return it to the starting position. He completes the movement for 1 to 3 repetitions with each leg, with each side scored individually.

The hurdle step pattern is fundamental to our ability to walk and basic to our locomotive mechanics. It is a display of our ability to control our center of mass with a changing base of support. This transfer from double leg to single leg is required in many sport performance skills.

Along with the warm-up's walking series (chapter 1), this test reveals single-leg balance and hip stability as well as hip and knee flexion range. Compensations observed in this test will also likely be noticeable in the walking series.

Figure 2.3   Hurdle step: *(a)* starting position; *(b)* first step over the hurdle.

IN-LINE LUNGE

For this assessment, the practitioner first measures the athlete's tibia length on one leg from the floor to his tibial tuberosity. Noting this measurement, she asks the athlete to place the back end of his heel at the edge of a flat measured surface with his foot pointing straight ahead; a board or floor with a measuring tape will suffice. Next, starting from the athlete's big toe, the practitioner measures out the previously recorded tibial length along the board and makes a mark.

The athlete holds a PVC rod or dowel in a vertical position along his spine. His hand on the same side as the measured leg grasps the rod behind his neck, while his opposite hand grasps the rod at his lower back. Keeping his measured leg in place, he steps forward with his opposite foot and aligns the back of that heel with the practitioner's mark (figure 2.4*a*). Next, keeping both feet positioned, he slowly lowers his back knee toward the ground, allowing his heel to come off the ground, and attempts to touch his back knee to the surface behind his forward heel (figure 2.4*b*). He then raises back out from that position in a controlled manner. He completes 1 to 3 repetitions on this side. Next, the practitioner measures the athlete's other tibia and the athlete attempts the same movement on that side for 1 to 3 repetitions.

The in-line lunge test can be helpful in spotting potential stability and range of motion issues in the ankle, knee, and hip as well as overall balance. It mimics the joint angles required to find an optimal starting position for the 40-yard dash, and therefore it may identify areas that require more mobility work during training.

The lunge reflects an athlete's ability to lower his center of mass in a stride or asymmetrical foot position, which is most commonly used during deceleration and direction change. This pattern requires the athlete to lower his center of mass as in the squat pattern, but in a more dynamic way. The lunge is

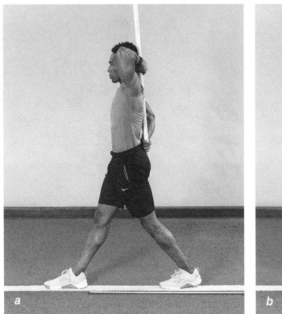

Figure 2.4   In-line lunge: *(a)* starting position; *(b)* lunge.

a natural extension of developmental patterns and the developmental posture called the half kneel position.

SHOULDER MOBILITY

To assess various shoulder, scapular, and thoracic ranges, the practitioner first measures the athlete's hand lengths—in this case, the distance from his distal wrist crease to the tip of his ring finger. For the test, the athlete makes

two fists with his thumbs inside his other fingers. In a standing position, the athlete lifts one arm overhead while keeping the other down close to his side. He bends both elbows and smoothly reaches behind his back with both arms, attempting to make both fists meet behind his upper back (figure 2.5).

When the athlete reaches the end point of his range of motion, the coach measures the distance between the closest bones of the athlete's two fists. The test is scored a 3 if the fists are within one hand length of each other, a 2 if they are one and a half hand lengths away, and a 1 for any further distance. This test can be performed for up to 3 repetitions on each side, with the top arm scored on the assessment.

Figure 2.5   Shoulder mobility.

The ability to carry, push, pull, reach overhead, and even walk is influenced by the upper-body reciprocal pattern and upper-limb mobility and control. In sports, the upper-body reciprocal pattern is fundamental to a wide array of throwing, striking, and swinging movements. The opposing actions of the arms in the tennis serve, javelin throw, or baseball pitch allow for accurate and powerful movements.

ACTIVE STRAIGHT-LEG RAISE

This test closely mimics the supine straight-leg lift exercise described in chapter 1, in which the athlete begins on his back with one leg bent and the other leg straight. For the FMS assessment, the coach places the end of a dowel or PVC rod on the ground directly next to the tested straight leg at the midpoint of that knee's patella and the same-side anterior superior iliac spine (ASIS; figure 2.6a). With one leg remaining straight and the back of the opposite leg maintaining contact with the ground, the athlete raises his leg as high as possible (figure 2.6b).

Once the athlete's test-side leg reaches its end range, if his test-side ankle bone (malleolus) has moved past the previously measured midpoint of his thigh (indicated by the dowel's position), the test is scored a 3 for his moving leg. If his malleolus does not reach the target, the dowel is moved out to match that malleolus position. An end range between the athlete's knee and his thigh's midpoint is scored a 2, whereas any point below the knee without pain receives a score of 1. The athlete may perform 1 to 3 repetitions on each leg.

The active straight-leg raise gives coaches a quantitative assessment of lumbopelvic control, extension of the down leg, and flexion of the raising leg. This pattern is also expressed in the hip hinge. The control of center of mass and weight shifting through the hips while protecting the spine is a critical component of many daily, work, and sport movements—for example, when deadlifting a heavy object or sitting back into the hip on one side to stop

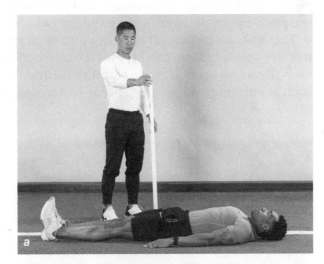

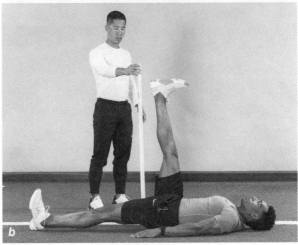

Figure 2.6 Active straight-leg raise: *(a)* starting position; *(b)* leg raise.

and change direction on the field. One can imagine how limitations in this pattern can affect acceleration, deceleration, and ability to change direction. This can affect a multitude of sport and recreational activities. Dysfunction in the pattern could produce a cascade of undesirable movements, postures, and positions. With this information, a coach who diligently watches his athlete's warm-up can note daily range and asymmetry variances.

TRUNK STABILITY PUSH-UP

Beginning in a prone (facedown) lying position with both feet together, the athlete places his hands on the ground at shoulder width, aligning both thumbs with the top of his forehead so that his arms make the shape of a field goal post (figure 2.7a). Both legs are fully straightened, and both feet are dorsiflexed so that his toes are on the ground. Maintaining a flat back and a neutral chin position, the athlete tries to complete a push-up from this position (figure 2.7b). If he cannot, he moves his thumbs to chin level for another attempt, and then to shoulder level if he fails his second attempt.

If the athlete can complete this push-up in the first position without any bending in his spine, he receives a 3 on the test. If he completes a similarly perfect push-up with thumbs at chin level, the test is a 2. If he cannot perform the push-up properly with the hands at chin level, the test is scored a 1.

This test can be helpful entering into combine training because it indicates reactive sagittal plane stability and the connection between the upper and lower body. Reactive sagittal plane stability is fundamental to many sport activities such as running and jumping because it resists extension and transfers forces from the lower body to the upper body. This strong connection between the upper and lower body also allows athletes to perform high-level skills that resist extension.

Upper-body strength is a component of this test and a possible predictor of performance on the combine bench press test. Even more importantly, it reveals sagittal trunk stability. An athlete who can hold trunk integrity at a steeper angle during the initial phase of the 40-yard dash will be able to better accelerate out of his starting position.

Figure 2.7 Trunk stability push-up: (a) starting position; (b) push-up.

ROTARY STABILITY

Assuming the quadruped series starting position as described in chapter 1, the athlete raises his arm forward and extends his leg back on the same side enough to get both limbs roughly 6 to 8 inches off the ground (figure 2.8*a*). For those familiar with the bird dog exercise, the first portion of this test has a similar setup and execution, but it is performed ipsilaterally (by same-side limbs) instead of contralaterally (by opposite-side limbs).

Next, the athlete reverses the direction of his limbs and tries to pull his same-side elbow and knee together beneath his trunk (figure 2.8*b*). Successful completion of both the reaching and pulling movements, with up to 3 attempts per side, is scored as a 3 on that side. If he cannot perform it successfully, the athlete may then attempt the contralateral version of the movement (or the bird dog) up to 3 times per side. A successful contralateral movement earns a score of 2, and failure at this second version receives a 1.

This test further informs the core integrity assessment from the trunk stability push-up, now adding a rotational stability aspect. It can be beneficial in predicting the athlete's ability to hold an aggressive lean during the acceleration phase of the 40-yard dash.

Active and passive range of motion testing can provide useful information entering a combine training phase. However, coaches should not be concerned only with active versus passive flexion, extension, or rotation. The crucial aspect of active range of motion is *where* an athlete creates his range. For example, athletes can often create a passable level of active dorsiflexion with much of their range coming from the toes and almost none from the ankle joint. This is where the warm-up comes in handy; instructing the athlete to isolate his

Figure 2.8   Rotary stability: *(a)* arm and leg extended; *(b)* elbow to knee under trunk.

PREP LIKE A PRO: JOINT-BY-JOINT ASSESSMENTS

NFL Scouting Combine medical personnel look at players' joint ranges of motion with a joint-by-joint passive range of motion examination. During intake for the Landow Performance combine prep program, a team of physical therapists and athletic trainers evaluate the athletes in a very similar way. In both cases, these medical personnel are not interested purely in determining how far an athlete's joint can move within a specific range. They want to feel how the range ends. Maybe they notice laxity at the joint's end point, or perhaps an abrupt halt to movement caused by structural issues, or asymmetries between sides. These examinations can reveal potential injury concerns, so practitioners involved in the athlete's preparation should be aware of his passive ranges.

warm-up exercise movements to the desired joint ranges will make any deficiencies and asymmetries readily apparent to a disciplined coach's eye.

Dorsiflexion, for example, is a crucial detail coaches can observe during an active warm-up. Even during a walking knee hug, for example, practitioners can glean insight from paying attention to what happens in the forefoot of the athlete's shoe. Coaches often tell athletes to "pull your toes up," a common cue for teaching dorsiflexion. However, some athletes actually *are* bringing their toes up by extending at the phalanges. Extending the phalanges causes the midfoot to plantar flex rather than extend like it should. In their response to this cue, these athletes structurally prevent themselves from achieving the desired outcome. Even when the coach thinks dorsiflexion is improving, there may be no real progress occurring. Coaches must pay attention to what happens at the midfoot and at the rear foot to make sure athletes are getting to dorsiflexion because the ability to dorsiflex is crucial in both sprinting and change of direction. To take a closer look, the coach could observe his athlete conducting a dynamic warm-up, watching whether the athlete actually gets motion through his talocrural joint (ankle joint).

Athlete Background

Athlete vitals and joint testing results are helpful, but they only offer a small slice of the overall picture. Background interviews should also be part of the intake process. With these interviews, coaches seek to understand the types of coaching and training an athlete has received and to learn about past injuries and existing medical conditions. Each Landow Performance combine prep athlete's intake process begins with a call or video chat before he even sets foot in the training facility. One of the first subjects addressed is the athlete's training background, since this will affect how coaches approach his preparation.

Training Age and Long-Term Athletic Development

Generally, *age* refers to chronological age—the number of years a person has been alive. But other types of age more pertinent to athletic development exist. Among those discussed in the literature are developmental age (including physical, cognitive, and emotional maturity), skeletal age, an athlete's relative age compared to that of his competitors, and *training age*—which is subdivided into general and sport-specific training age (Balyi and Way 2005).

Coaches may take all these types of age into account, but one of the most important is the training age. Istvan Balyi, one of the preeminent experts on the subject, defines general training age as the number of years an athlete has spent in training; sport-specific training age refers to the athlete's history after specialization in a single sport (Balyi and Way 2005). Balyi developed a four-stage *long-term athletic development* (LTAD; figure 2.9) model for early specialization sports (e.g., gymnastics, figure skating, and diving) and a six-stage model for late specialization sports (including all team sports) that describe the ideal training objectives for athletes of particular age ranges.

One of Balyi's most critical developmental phases, the *learning to train* stage, takes place roughly between the ages of 9 and 12 for boys. He describes this period as the "window of accelerated adaptation to motor coordination" and insists, "If fundamental motor skill training is not developed [during this stage] … a significant window of opportunity has been lost, compromising the ability of the young player/athlete to reach his/her full potential" (Balyi and Hamilton 2004).

Most collegiate and professional football players have a relatively low general training age because they specialized early in their sport and missed out on Balyi's window of accelerated adaptation. The American trend toward early specialization often produces football players who lack the foundation of a long-term athletic development program that aims to develop a robust general training age before moving into sport-specific training.

Other sport performance experts have stressed the need for a foundation of general athletic skills. In its official position statement on long-term athletic development, the National Strength and Conditioning Association (NSCA) contends that "…developing a proficient physical 'vocabulary' of fundamental motor skills during early childhood should serve as the foundations on which more advanced and complex specific motor skills can be later developed" (Lloyd et al. 2016). Similarly, Sergey Matveyev emphasizes that "…for a maximum development of certain physical abilities the general level of the organism's functional abilities has to be increased. No matter how narrow is the subject of the sports specialization, the progress in it is conditioned … by the many-sided physical development of an athlete" (Matveyev 1977). The NSCA's position paper and Matveyev's *Fundamentals of Sports Training* both essentially describe the same concept, but they were published 39 years apart, which illustrates the timeless significance of general physical preparation.

Football combines exist mainly to measure football players' general athleticism, so it makes sense to view combine training as a chance to make up for some of the long-term athletic development these players missed out on during their athletic careers. The condensed training cycle leading into these events does not allow for a highly specialized programming approach anyway, so it's logical to aim to improve only these general qualities.

The initial interview includes questions to gauge the player's training age: how he feels about his weight room performance, as well as how many strength and conditioning coaches he's had in his career. The second question—the number of previous strength coaches—provides valuable insight into training age. If the athlete has had multiple strength coaches, there is a great chance he has learned from multiple training philosophies. Asking about injury history is also vital in helping a coach determine which exercises should be omitted from the athlete's training. Coaches should also ask athletes about their motivations to reach the next level of football. To what extent are they motivated

Long-Term Development in Sport and Physical Activity

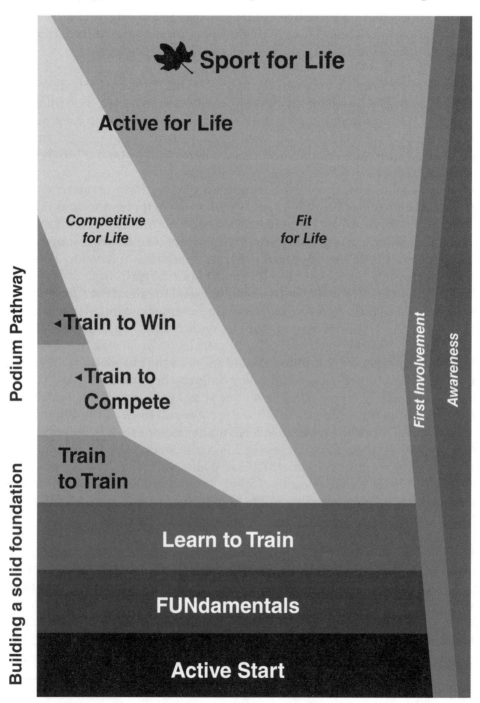

Figure 2.9 Stages of long-term athletic development.
Used with permission of Sport for Life Society.

by internal rewards, like the satisfaction of maximizing their development, versus external rewards such as recognition or money?

In addition to intake interviews, coaches can use the warm-up and the first few training sessions to visually assess an athlete's competence, including weight room workouts and movement sessions on the turf or grass. Athletes who lack exposure to one aspect or the other will often shy away from their weaknesses and gravitate toward their strengths.

Evaluation of Injury and Medical History

Throwing an athlete into workouts without a full picture of his training background likely will create suboptimal training adaptations and may even injure the athlete. Doing the same without a strong knowledge of his medical history and prior injuries could have downright catastrophic outcomes, which could ultimately prevent the athlete from testing at his combine or pro day.

There is a reason the warm-up was covered in chapter 1 before this chapter on athlete intake assessments. Although it certainly sets the tone for a workout and teaches athletes new skills, the warm-up also is an incredibly helpful assessment tool. For example, an athlete who performs walking toe touches with correct intent and form may display a major discrepancy in range of motion between sides. A coach who spots this abnormality now has a key piece of data to inform the questions she asks the athlete. Perhaps back in high school, the athlete dealt with hamstring problems that he forgot to mention because they never resurfaced during his college career. Maybe he slightly tweaked a hamstring the other day during a top-end speed session but neglected to mention it because he assumed he could "tough it out." The root issue also could be that the athlete simply has always had tighter hamstrings on his right side. Any of these variables could lead a coach to alter the session's structure by changing volume or exercise selection.

Regardless of the reason for the range imbalance, dedicated coaching and careful observation of the warm-up allows coaches to spot potential issues they likely would never have known about otherwise, which can inform training decisions. Situations like this are common, especially in a sport with high injury rates such as football. In combining the warm-up with FMS joint assessments, athlete vitals, and medical exams, coaches can better understand their athletes' current situations.

Conclusion

The athlete intake process may not be the most thrilling part of combine preparation, but it is vital to success on testing day. At Landow Performance, these initial assessments are followed by general athleticism tests (chapter 3), conducted for the first time with minimal instruction to create a performance baseline for comparison; these tests also can give coaches an early indication of where individual athletes most need to improve. The next three chapters will explain these general athleticism tests, as well as the position-specific drills encountered at most combines and pro days. Chapter 6 describes how to use intake results from this chapter, along with more advanced data, to design an individual athlete's training plan.

PART II

Combine Tests and Drills

CHAPTER 3

General Athleticism Drills

This chapter provides a detailed guide for the most common general athletic assessments used at football combines. Players who wish to reach the next level of competitive play must succeed in these drills. Coaches and scouts often cross a player's name off their lists if he does not meet or exceed the benchmark level of performance in the tests that are most pertinent to his position. These evaluators know what numbers each athlete should achieve in order to play successfully at their level. For example, scouts know that a prospective NFL defensive back generally will run the 10-yard split of the 40-yard dash in 1.58 seconds or faster. This player might be extremely skilled in his coverage techniques and his tackling ability, but if he cannot run 10 yards in 1.58 seconds, he will likely be unable to keep up at the professional level. His performance in position-specific drills becomes less relevant if his numbers already suggest that he lacks the physical tools to succeed at the next level.

During the NFL Draft process, media analysts often refer to the NFL combine's general athleticism testing as a player's opportunity to "check the boxes" for teams. After poring over current and historical combine testing data, teams can decide on their ideal metrics for different positions, and then take a closer look at the players who check enough boxes off their figurative wish lists.

The following general athleticism tests and drills are nearly universal at combines of all levels, and a football player who trains to improve his performance in these tests is also training to become a better athlete.

VERTICAL JUMP

Purpose

Evaluate lower-body explosive power in a vertical plane.

Execution

In a tall, relaxed standing position with feet hip-width apart, the athlete takes a couple of deep breaths and begins to lightly swing both arms forward and back. After a few seconds, he slowly brings his arms above his head with elbows bent, still relaxed in his entire body, and, when ready, rapidly drops his hips while simultaneously throwing his arms down (figure 3.1*a*). When he hits his predetermined countermovement position, he recoils out, throwing his arms up vertically toward his target while extending and looking up at that target (figure 3.1*b*).

For those without access to a Vertec, the tool that is commonly used for this test, jump mats are popular for calculating athletes' jump heights based on time spent in the air. New mobile applications and low-cost measuring devices also continue to emerge. Athletes can even jump holding a piece of chalk and mark a wall next to them at the top of their jump in order to measure their jump height.

Common Errors

Many athletes go into the vertical jump test without having worked with a Vertec. As a result, they don't know where they should stand or how to properly reach their hands at the apex of their jump. Even though the vertical jump is

Figure 3.1   Vertical jump: *(a)* countermovement; *(b)* jump.

directed straight upward, it still produces a slight forward arc. So if an athlete jumps from directly under the Vertec, he will reach the top of his jump a few inches past the Vertec. Athletes often blindly reach for the Vertec pegs while looking down or straight ahead as they jump, instead of aiming and looking toward their target. Many display asynchronous arm and lower-body movements during either the loading or the takeoff portion of the jump and often during both. One of the most common errors occurs when an athlete's bottom countermovement position is either too high or too low relative to his optimal depth—which can be determined in part using testing in this chapter and in chapter 6.

Methods to Improve

Athletes should rehearse the vertical jump's rhythm and timing through the countermovement and takeoff phases. Arm and hip action in both phases must be perfectly synchronized to create maximal jump height. When an athlete swings his arms effectively, he places more force into his countermovement, thereby creating a greater stretch-shortening cycle (SSC) response. Then, as he reverses direction and begins his takeoff phase, proper arm swing timing generates greater momentum into the jump as his lower body propels him off the ground.

Each athlete should practice lowering his hips to the ideal lowest point of his countermovement. This point is by no means universal among athletes. Each athlete and his coach must work together to determine the athlete's sweet spot, which is dictated by his elasticity—that is, his effectiveness in using his stretch-shortening cycle. This is where the eccentric utilization ratio (EUR) and reactive strength index (RSI), both explained in chapter 6, become extremely helpful for testing improvements. These values determine how far an athlete should pull himself down before reversing direction and moving up. A more elastic athlete benefits from a shallow and quick countermovement because it allows him to rely more heavily on his stretch-shortening cycle. Meanwhile, a more strength-based athlete will test higher if he uses a deeper countermovement since he has more time to produce force for the jump.

PREP LIKE A PRO: VERTICAL JUMP

An athlete's placement relative to the Vertec device can affect how he tests in the vertical jump. As he takes off in his jump, his hip extension will cause a slight movement forward in the air. Athletes who stand directly underneath the Vertec to begin their countermovement, as many are coached, will have actually passed the Vertec as they reach their jump's apex. Landow Performance coaches teach combine prep athletes to move their starting position about 6 inches back from underneath the Vertec. This way, after extending their hips in takeoff, they will migrate to the middle of the Vertec by the apex of their jump, thus maximizing their contact point with the Vertec pegs.

STANDING BROAD JUMP

Purpose

Evaluate lower-body explosive power in a horizontal plane.

Execution

For his starting position, the athlete stands tall with his feet hip-width apart and his toes pointed straight ahead. Just as in the vertical jump, he begins a relaxed, rhythmic, shallow arm swing, then brings both arms overhead with bent elbows (figure 3.2*a*). When ready, he throws his hips and arms simultaneously down and back into his countermovement position. The countermovement position for the standing broad jump is different than that of the vertical jump; instead of launching straight up, he projects up and out. This requires a different loading of the hips. The countermovement will look more like a cross between a Romanian deadlift (RDL) and a squat, with the shins angling forward as the hips move back (figure 3.2*b*).

The athlete reverses his countermovement to project out and up, fully extending his hips, knees, and ankles, with a synchronized arm swing in the direction of his takeoff (figure 3.2*c*). Once his hips and knees have fully extended and launched his body, the athlete pulls his feet back underneath him to land; he should try to pull his feet up and in front of his body as he returns to the ground, like a long jumper, to create a slightly longer hang time. This

Figure 3.2   Standing broad jump: *(a)* starting position; *(b)* countermovement.

added time spent in the air allows him to glide further forward and cover more distance. After carrying his jumping arc as far as possible, he lands with both feet flat on the ground, sticking the jump with his knees and hips bent (figure 3.2*d*). Falling over backward or moving the feet upon landing will immediately disqualify his attempt.

Common Errors

A jump stance with feet wider apart than hip width will diminish the athlete's ability to produce maximal force. Another common mistake is taking a "flat" jump, trying to move as far horizontally as possible. In other words, the athlete projects at a shallow angle and barely hovers over the ground while moving forward. Many athletes are also unaware of what they should do with their legs in the air, so their legs remain relatively straight during flight, which will negatively affect their jump distance. Instead, they should bring their feet up and underneath them as described earlier.

Methods to Improve

Athletes who jump too low to the ground must project at a greater arc. If an athlete's feet barely leave the ground as he jumps forward, he must jump more vertically. Coaches first should cue athletes to project at a 45-degree angle, then make small tweaks as needed. Refer to the Prep Like a Pro sidebar for this exercise to find more information on adjusting takeoff angle.

Figure 3.2 Standing broad jump: *(c)* jump; *(d)* landing.

PREP LIKE A PRO: STANDING BROAD JUMP

At the elite level, coaches use video analysis to optimize each athlete's launch angle. Many free or inexpensive camera applications allow a smartphone or tablet to become an analytical tool. With these apps, a coach can cue individual athletes to project up and out at 45 degrees, then film the jump from a side-on view. In reviewing the recording, the coach can break down each phase of the athlete's jump and show the athlete where his body is compared to optimal positions. Video analysis helps coaches to adjust an athlete's takeoff angle to maximize jump distance. When examining frozen video stills of the athlete's takeoff point from a side-on view, the coach should see the athlete's ankle, knee, hip, and shoulder align at the desired angle.

40-YARD DASH

Purpose

The 40-yard dash (figure 3.3) is regarded as the crown jewel of combine testing, and for good reason. The test contains several valuable metrics that football teams rely on to gauge a prospect's general athleticism.

The split recorded at 10 yards—indicative of lower-body explosiveness and pure acceleration—is critical across all position groups. The 20-yard split reveals how long an athlete can continue to accelerate, and at what point he begins to transition into top-end speed mechanics. The back end of the 40-yard dash indicates the athlete's ability to maintain his speed.

Execution

The athlete approaches the starting line with both feet together and pointing straight ahead. From this position, he steps back with one foot so that his feet are in a heel-to-toe relationship, then brings his other foot back to meet it so he is standing a full shoe's length behind the starting line. The athlete again moves one foot back, creating the same heel-to-toe relationship with his front

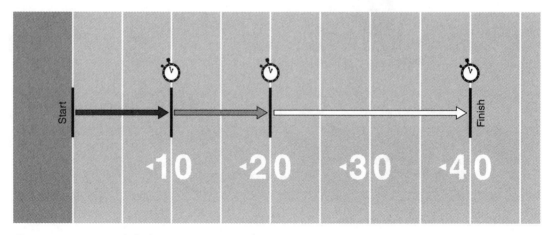

Figure 3.3 40-yard dash course.

foot. Next, he moves his back foot out to the side so that he is standing with his feet hip-width apart, with his front foot's heel and back foot's toes still aligned. He wiggles his back foot on the ground back about 3 to 4 inches and drops to a kneeling position with the toes of both feet remaining in place.

Now in a kneeling position with one leg back and one forward, the athlete places the arm opposite his front leg—referred to here as the *lead arm*—rotating his hand so that his biceps points toward the finish line. His lead hand should take the full starting line by placing the inside of his thumb and index finger as far forward as possible, right along the very edge of the line. The athlete then raises his hips, maintaining only three points of contact with the ground: front foot, rear foot, and lead hand. His weight shifts forward, but he maintains some weight on his rear leg, a distribution of 75 percent weight forward and 25 percent on his back leg.

Shifting his body weight forward allows the athlete's shin to move forward over his toes, a term referred to hereafter as *shin angle*. This forward lean should result in the hips being in a higher position than his shoulders in the starting stance. The forward body weight is evenly distributed between the athlete's front leg and lead hand so that if he were to pick up his lead hand from the ground, he would fall. His other arm, referred to here as the *up arm*, reaches back to hip height with a slight elbow bend. (See figure 7.8 on page 108 for a photo of this position.)

The 40-yard dash start is an orchestration of several movements occurring at once. The athlete simultaneously pushes off both feet, punching his back leg forward as the front leg drives back into the ground, fully extending. This push creates an aggressive split of the legs, which he mirrors by concurrently splitting his arms the opposite way. He swings his up arm forward into a "block" position, elevating his forearm and bending at his elbow so that his forearm crosses in front of his head. The block position shortens the athlete's arm, allowing him to quickly move it from a somewhat awkward starting position to synchronize with extension of that same-side leg. From there, the athlete focuses on driving his arms back, swinging at the shoulders and aiming his hands for just outside hip level. As he picks up speed and his stride quickens, the athlete's elbow will bend slightly more so that his arm swing speed can match the turnover rate of his legs.

Common Errors

An athlete's vertical and broad jump numbers are generally predictive of performance in the 10-yard split, but sometimes these results differ. When athletes run a slower 10-yard split than their jump numbers forecast, the disparity typically is due to a mechanical breakdown in the setup of the sprint. Restrictions in lower-extremity ranges of motion can prevent an athlete from setting up at the right angles to execute his start; improper limb positioning coming out of the start may also negatively affect his sprint times.

Many athletes crowd too close to the line when taking the starting position. Although it is helpful to place the hand as far forward on the starting line as possible, the rest of the body need not follow suit. A cramped starting position forces the athlete's front shin angle to remain vertical. The thigh will move to wherever an athlete's shin angle points. If he pushes into the ground with a vertical shin angle, his thigh will follow, and he will pop straight up out of his stance. Too much or too little forward lean causes an unbalanced start, which disrupts acceleration mechanics.

At combine and pro day events, the back hand often is seen positioned high above the hip in the starting stance because that is where countless athletes are taught to place it. For coaches or scouts standing 10 to 40 yards away, that hand movement will be the first movement they see to start their stopwatches. The same goes for lifting up one's front hand from the ground before the rest of the body begins moving; every movement in the start should happen all at once.

Coaches commonly cue athletes to "stay low" as they accelerate. Although acceleration position is indeed based on a leaning torso angle, the torso should come up naturally. Attempting to hold body lean for too long generally results in a slumped chest and head, which diminishes speed. Coaches should never tell athletes when they should or should not be in an upright position. Ankle range of mobility, trunk stability, and lower-body explosiveness (estimated using vertical jump height) are all indicators of the body angle an athlete can find and maintain as he accelerates.

Cyclical leg motion in the acceleration phase is another common error in the 40-yard dash. As discussed in chapters 7 and 9, the technical model for acceleration mechanics differs from that of top-end speed; the former requires a piston-like movement of the legs, whereas the latter is a cyclical motion. Athletes who accelerate cyclically will not be able to produce optimal force into the ground, and this will produce slower 10-, 20-, and 40-yard dash times.

During the second half of the 40-yard dash, athletes often begin to display sloppy recovery mechanics, delaying their back-side recovery, which then results in a lower thigh position upon front-side recovery. This places great strain on the hip flexors and adductors, which could eventually cause injuries. Sometimes athletes lack dorsiflexion in the foot as they recover. Similarly, sub-optimal strike patterns—casting the foot out to strike in front of their hips, or striking on the fourth and fifth metatarsal rather than the ball of the foot—will not only slow athletes' times but also put them at risk for hamstring injuries.

One fundamental error seen in the 40-yard dash may seem to be the most obvious and the easiest to fix, but it must be stated because of how prevalent it is: athletes who do not finish the test. Sadly, many players clock a slower time than they are capable of running because they begin to slow down before reaching the finish line. At Landow Performance, this is known as "running 38" instead of the full 40 yards.

Methods to Improve

Simply positioning the back arm correctly in an athlete's starting stance can shave substantial time off his measured 40-yard dash time. Landow Performance coaches teach combine athletes to keep their back hand hidden right at their hip so that it does not serve as a flag for scouts to start their watches.

Improving total body strength and lower body explosiveness in the weight room will certainly produce a faster 40-yard dash time. Yet many coaches and athletes overlook the dedicated practice of movement mechanics because they don't know how to go about it properly. Practitioners who study, practice, and coach the preeminent technical models for acceleration and top-end speed will help their athletes make significant improvements not only in this test but also on the football field.

PREP LIKE A PRO: 40-YARD DASH

Moving back from the line an adequate distance can significantly aid the athlete's mechanical ability to accelerate. Many athletes crowd the line with their stance in a seemingly logical attempt to start as close as possible to the finish line. However, for the 40-yard dash, consider "trading inches for angles." This means to sacrifice a small bit of distance to the finish line so the athlete can have a greater forward shin angle on his lead leg, thereby creating a better position from which to accelerate. He should not try to create more of an angle than he can hold in acceleration, however, or he will begin to stumble forward out of his start. If the athlete can execute an excellent first three acceleration steps, he stands a chance to run a great 40-yard dash.

PRO AGILITY (5-10-5)

Purpose
Evaluate quickness and lateral change of direction.

Execution
Facing the three cones, the athlete approaches the middle cone and takes an athletic stance with his feet shoulder-width apart, then gets down in a three-point stance at the starting line, barely touching the line with the same-side lead hand as his starting direction. His weight remains back and loaded in his hips, with outside pressure on his lead foot and inside pressure on his trail foot.

Much like the 40-yard dash start, orchestration is crucial—everything should happen at once. The athlete stays low coming out of his stance, taking crossover steps to reach the first line (figure 3.4). (For more information on this skill, refer to chapter 8.) For the first change in direction, the athlete keeps his weight shifted inside, simultaneously planting his feet and touching the line with his outside hand only. Next, he makes a crossover transition into acceleration.

After making it past 8 of the 10 yards, the athlete begins preparing for his second change of direction. This change resembles a suicide drill in basketball; the athlete drops his hips, pivots his inside foot, touches the second line, and transitions back into acceleration to finish through the original starting line.

Common Errors
When changing direction in this drill, athletes often try to propel off the outside foot. Rather than helping them explode back in the other direction, this tactic merely forces them to fight against inertia and often causes them to slip. Another typical strategy that results in a slower change of direction is when coaches teach athletes to "reach for the line." Though this may seem to shorten the distance of the drill, it merely throws the athlete off balance.

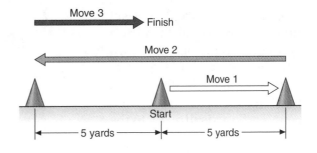

Figure 3.4   Pro agility (5-10-5).

Some coaches tell athletes to get up and extend immediately out of the stance to start generating speed for the first 5 yards. Instead, athletes should stay low since they are about to come right back in the other direction. There is no need to pop up if they will need to get right back down after 5 yards in order to change direction.

Methods to Improve

Improving quickness into and out of the drill's two directional changes requires the use of edges. Specifically, during a change of direction the athlete should have his weight shift to the outside edge of his inside foot and the inside edge of his outside foot. The outside hand should touch the line at the same time the feet plant on the ground, rather than planting and then reaching out.

In addition to proper weight distribution, shin angles are also critical in the drill's directional changes. Both shins must be parallel and pointing back in the direction the athlete wants to go. This is why cueing athletes to "reach for the line" is a mistake; reaching out will cause the athlete's shins to shift away from the best angle to change direction. Just like in the 40-yard dash, this is an example of trading inches for angles. Shin angle in the pro agility drill will determine thigh position coming out of the cut. A shin that is pointed back in the direction the athlete wants to go will allow him to apply force into the ground with a force vector that projects him in his desired direction. An athlete who moves his feet past the line may appear to be giving up valuable space, but actually he is placing his body in an optimal position to reaccelerate.

PREP LIKE A PRO: PRO AGILITY DRILL

Landow Performance combine prep athletes are taught a general framework for the number of steps they should take throughout the drill. Coming out of their stance, they will take three crossover steps into their first stop, five steps into their second stop, and three steps finishing through the line, totaling 11 steps.

L-DRILL

Purpose

Evaluate quickness and lateral change of direction.

Execution

The L-drill (figure 3.5) is set up with three cones forming a 90-degree angle of two 5-yard lengths. The athlete begins at cone 1. Cone 2 is directly in front of him 5 yards away, and cone 3 is 5 yards directly to the left of cone 2.

Starting in a three-point stance, the athlete quickly

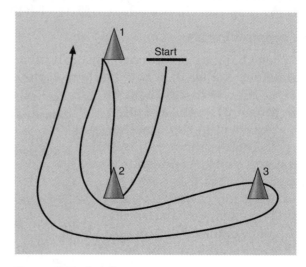

Figure 3.5 L-drill.

sprints forward to cone 2 and touches the line next to the cone with his right hand, returns to cone 1 and touches the starting line with his right hand, then sprints back to round outside cone 2, looping inside cone 3 and back around the outside of cone 2 to finish back through the starting line.

Common Errors

The most common error in the L-drill is the attempt to stay too tight to each cone when making turns. This drill is not intended to look like a receiver making tight cuts in a route with small, choppy steps. Though it may seem like this approach shaves time off the drill, it actually forces players to slow down, whereas rounding the corners opens up the drill by creating more room for curvilinear sprinting. Athletes will also often shift their weight too far outside during the first two changes of direction, resulting in slower changes of direction coming out of both cuts.

Methods to Improve

Whereas in the 40-yard dash, the athlete is primarily concerned with projection for each step to accelerate and cover distance, the L-drill only requires the athlete to move a quick 5 yards from his starting position before changing direction. Therefore, the "trading inches for angles" aspect of the 40-yard dash becomes the opposite: "trading angles for inches" in the L-drill. In other words, an athlete benefits from a stance that backs off the starting line a bit in the former test and crowds the line more in the latter test.

PREP LIKE A PRO: L-DRILL

Since both changes of direction in this drill require a right-hand touch, it is best if combine athletes start with the right foot forward in the stance, even if it feels awkward. This is so they need take only two steps (left foot, right foot) before they can get their left foot and right hand down for their first touch. On their return to the starting line, they will take a slight angle (roughly 3 to 5 degrees) to make their second touch 1 to 2 yards outside where they first started the drill. This allows the drill to open up so that they have a wider angle to round the corner on their first 90-degree turn, giving them more room to use quickness in maneuvering widely around the cones, finishing the drill in a curvilinear fashion like a 200-meter dash sprinter.

60-YARD SHUTTLE

Purpose

Evaluate quickness, lateral change of direction, and speed endurance.

Execution

The 60-yard shuttle (figure 3.6) is set up like a basketball suicide drill. Beginning in a three-point stance, the athlete sprints 5 yards and back, 10 yards and back, and finally 15 yards and back, all in one sequence. At each change of direction, he must touch the line with his right hand.

Common Errors

Far and away the biggest mistake athletes make in the 60-yard shuttle is shifting their weight incorrectly during their turns. If an athlete is too focused on touching the line quickly and then turning to sprint, he will likely reach well outside his center of mass and start to shift his weight to the outside. This forces the athlete to fight against inertia, whereas patience in setting up one's whole body for the turn will result in a better overall outcome. It is also surprisingly common how many athletes fail to finish this test at full speed; the athlete must give all-out effort through the finish line.

Methods to Improve

Luckily, the mechanics involved in this test are already practiced heavily; between the 5-10-5, L-drill, and 40-yard dash, athletes will get plenty of practice in the necessary change of direction and acceleration skills that will allow them to use optimal transitions during the turns on this drill. Therefore, one of the best ways to improve in the 60-yard shuttle is to practice those precise skills while becoming comfortable with the steps needed during each leg of the drill.

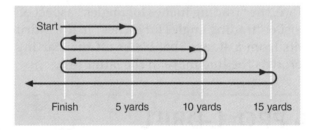

Figure 3.6   60-yard shuttle.

225-POUND BENCH PRESS

Purpose

One of the more publicly glamorized combine tests, the 225-pound bench press has a simple premise: Each athlete gets one attempt to bench press a 225-pound barbell for as many repetitions as possible before reaching failure. At the college and professional levels, for most players this tends to be a test of upper-body strength and endurance.

Execution

To set up for the test, the athlete lies back on the bench with his feet directly under his knees and grips the bar with his hands outside shoulder width. Once he feels in a solid and stable position through his whole body, the athlete gets help lifting the bar off the rack and then sets up with the barbell directly over his chest and with his arms fully extended (figure 3.7a). From this point the athlete must complete as many bench press repetitions as possible until he either fails a repetition or racks the weight. He is allowed to take as much time as he likes between repetitions, as long as he keeps the barbell off the rack without any help—a rule that the athlete can use to his advantage by employing the strategy described in the Prep Like a Pro sidebar.

Common Errors

Lackadaisical setup can severely affect an athlete's performance in this test. Small errors such as taking an overly wide or narrow grip on the barbell, or neglecting to set his feet up properly underneath him, can have a large impact over the course of the test. Sloppy or overzealous bench pressing can also hurt the athlete's official repetition count. A judge assesses each repetition, so athletes who try to pump out their reps too quickly without fully extending their arms at the top may not receive credit for one or more repetitions.

Most athletes simply go all out on the bench press without any strategy beforehand and tire themselves out too quickly. Practicing for this test during training not only improves the athlete's strength and endurance, but it also helps him get a sense of which point in the test would be ideal for him to take quick breaks with the barbell fully extended over his chest. As described in the Prep Like a Pro box, the goal should ultimately be to develop a strategy that works the athlete down a pyramid of decreasing repetitions interspersed with brief breaks.

Methods to Improve

An athlete who learns to anchor himself to the bench will improve his performance during this test. This requires anchoring the feet down into the ground, extending in the lumbar spine, and creating a stacking of the pectorals with the scapulae retracted and depressed. When an athlete creates this position well, the bench press becomes more of a full-body exercise and less purely focused around the arms, shoulders, and chest (figure 3.7b).

Each athlete must find his sweet spot for the bench press grip: one that is not so narrow that it hurts the shoulders or makes the range of motion too long, and not so wide that it becomes a dangerous execution of the lift.

Figure 3.7 225-pound bench press: (a) arms extended; (b) arms lowered.

PREP LIKE A PRO: 225-POUND BENCH PRESS

At the elite level, tactics can greatly affect the number of repetitions produced for this assessment. Athletes must learn to incorporate strategic rest pauses. An athlete finds a point at which his bar speed starts to drop when he can pause, gather himself in a locked-out position so his joints take some of the stress, take one or two good cleansing breaths, then begin performing smaller and smaller clusters of repetitions. Over the course of the test, as bar speed slows again after fewer and fewer repetitions, he will ratchet down from triples to doubles to singles.

For example, a 20-repetition bencher may hit his first 10 repetitions consecutively, then move into clusters of 4 repetitions, 2 repetitions, then 2 again, then 1 repetition, before completing his final repetition. There is no predetermined formula for when or how to ratchet down in repetitions; success in this test requires that athletes experiment during training to find their own optimal clustering strategies.

Conclusion

Every year, the combine tests designed to measure general athleticism become some of the most widely discussed metrics in the weeks leading up to the NFL Draft. These numbers provide teams and fans alike with standardized and objective measurements of players' speed, power, quickness, change of direction, and strength and endurance, among other qualities. They are also the assessments that "check the boxes" for teams, meaning that players must reach a team's baseline performance level in these tests for the team to even consider them. So while the position-specific drills discussed in chapters 4 and 5 are certainly important to a player's combine success, they will do him little good if he has a poor showing in these general athleticism tests.

CHAPTER 4

Defensive Position-Specific Drills

Athletes' combine training plans should include sport-specific preparation, especially at the professional level. NFL combine participants who display an advanced football IQ can impress evaluators during team interviews, and scouts at all levels frequently include positional drill performance observations in their overall player evaluations.

Performance coaches may find these position-specific combine tests overwhelming or intimidating, especially if they lack football playing or coaching experience. However, an athlete's football preparation should not be solely his performance coach's responsibility. Performance coaches should familiarize their athletes with the most common positional combine drills, but these coaches do not need to become football Xs and Os experts, nor should they be overly concerned with understanding each position's finer technical points.

Instead, practitioners should concentrate on making their athletes better overall movers. The focus should be on improving an athlete's key performance indicators, or KPIs: the specific athletic skills and qualities that are most important for that player's position on the field (a concept discussed further in chapter 6). Athletes who invest time in practicing general movement skills will typically be much more successful in positional drills, even if they have not spent a great deal of time practicing those drills.

The NFL combine uses a regular list of position-specific drills each year, allowing athletes to "study" for these tests. Landow Performance combine prep athletes spend most of their Friday morning movement sessions with their position-specific mentors working on these drills. Sport performance coaches without access to football mentors should not be too concerned; at many high school combines, positional drills are either unpredictable or nonexistent.

This chapter highlights some of the most commonly encountered football combine drills for each defensive position group; offensive position groups are covered in chapter 5. Players should become familiar with positional drills and how they are conducted; in doing so, they will practice and refine the overlapping motor skills that will be called on during their combine or pro day drills.

Defensive Backs

The primary KPIs that scouts look for in defensive backs are short-area quickness, acceleration, and top-end speed.

BACKPEDAL AND REACT

Execution

The backpedal and react drill (figure 4.1) is essentially a position-specific 40-yard dash constructed for defensive backs. A lane is created with two cones at the starting line, two cones 10 yards downfield, and two more cones placed another 20 yards further, making a lane totaling 30 yards.

The athlete begins the drill by placing his heels up against the starting line with his back to the finish line. He raises one hand to signal his readiness, then assumes his backpedaling stance. At his discretion, the defensive back begins backpedaling straight back as fast as possible. At 9 yards, he receives a "turn" cue to flip his hips around and sprint for the remaining 20 yards.

Coaching Points

Evaluators look for smooth execution in this drill. However, many players do not understand that it is a timed assessment. They often move much more slowly than they should. Evaluators want to see how well a defensive back covers space; a player's time covering this drill's 30 yards should roughly mirror his 40-yard dash time. Coaches often tell players to be smooth in this drill, which

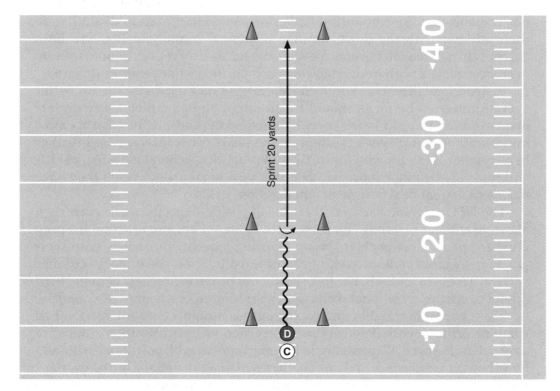

Figure 4.1   Backpedal and react drill for defensive backs.

is certainly a helpful cue, but defensive backs need to show flat-out speed in their backpedal. If an athlete does not perform this drill at maximum speed, it will reflect poorly on his abilities.

W DRILL

Execution

The W drill (figure 4.2) assesses change-of-direction capability in tight spaces. Three cones are placed along the line of scrimmage, with the outer two cones just outside the hash marks and the middle cone directly in between. The athlete begins in his defensive back position at one of the outside cones, facing the coach.

At the coach's cue, the player backpedals straight back. As the player reaches roughly 5 yards in his backpedal, the coach gives another signal to break forward diagonally to the next cone. Once the player is close to the next cone, the coach cues him to backpedal straight back again. He repeats this 5-yard backpedal and diagonal break one more time, and as he closes on the third cone he intercepts and returns a ball thrown at him.

Coaching Points

The W drill's demands are somewhat like the close and speed turn drill, described next, albeit in a smaller space. The W drill can be especially helpful to assess a player's short-area quickness so teams can see how quickly his feet move when he is in too tight of a space to reach full acceleration. Potential slot cornerbacks are identified as players who can change direction and navigate in tight spaces, so evaluators watch athletes closely during the W drill.

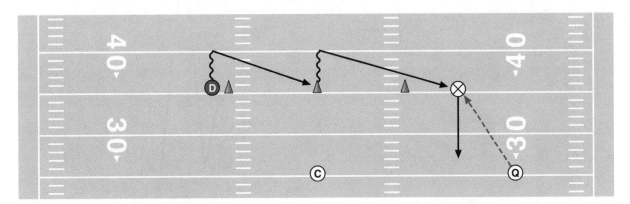

Figure 4.2 W drill for defensive backs.

CLOSE AND SPEED TURN

Execution

Defensive backs must exhibit excellent change of direction ability to succeed at football's higher levels. The close and speed turn drill (figure 4.3) puts an athlete's general movement skills on display. For this drill, the defensive back lines up on the hash mark, directly across from the coach as if in man coverage. The throwing quarterback is located on the opposite hash, also at the line of scrimmage.

All aspects of the drill occur at the coach's signal. Starting at the line of scrimmage, the athlete backpedals when the coach signals the snap. At the coach's next signal, the player plants and drives back toward the line of scrimmage as if closing on the ball. A third cue from the coach tells the player to make a speed turn away from the coach, at an angle toward the sideline. After his speed turn, he must locate the quarterback's ball in the air and make an interception, then change direction again to return the interception.

Coaching Points

This drill is an excellent assessment of acceleration, deceleration, and change of direction in multiple planes of movement. The athlete must be able to backpedal, decelerate, reaccelerate forward, decelerate once more, and make an efficient bridging movement to reaccelerate at an angle.

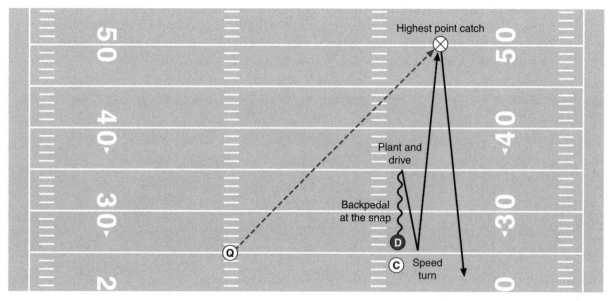

Figure 4.3   Close and speed turn drill for defensive backs.

Linebackers

The top KPIs for linebackers are lower-body explosiveness, acceleration, and change of direction. These drills reveal how well a linebacker can swivel his hips and change directions, then reaccelerate and close on a position.

PASS DROP AND HIP ROTATION

Execution

To demonstrate their pass coverage abilities, linebackers must be able to move well in space. To simulate a zone coverage, the player will begin directly in front of the coach. At the coach's cue, the linebacker drops into a crossover run moving backward at a 45-degree angle. After the player reaches a depth of roughly 5 yards, the coach will point the ball in the other direction.

When the linebacker sees the coach move the ball, he reacts by planting his outside foot, then flips his hips to transition his drop. He still uses crossover steps, now dropping back at a similar 45-degree angle in the opposite direction (figure 4.4). The coach will give two more signals to change direction by moving the ball back and forth, with the player quickly responding to drop in the signaled direction. Then the coach will pull the ball in toward himself, at which point the player makes one last plant step to break on the ball and catches a ball thrown to him as he sprints forward.

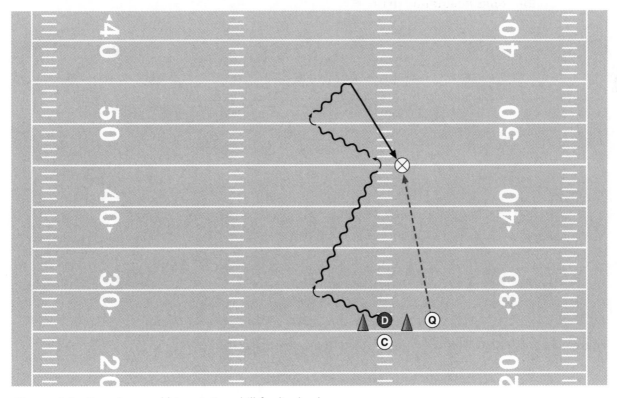

Figure 4.4 Pass drop and hip rotation drill for linebackers.

PASS RUSH DRILL

Execution

The pass rush drill is conducted for both outside linebackers and defensive linemen at the NFL combine. The drill is set up with a mirrored layout so that players can complete one repetition each on the left and right sides. A coach is situated directly between the hashes, holding a ball or a snapper stick (a football attached to a stick) to establish a line of scrimmage. One starting cone is placed at each hash, aligned evenly with the ball (figure 4.5).

For his first repetition, the player assumes his pass rushing stance at the left-side cone. One standing heavy bag is situated across the line of scrimmage from the player and slightly to his right; these tall, cone-shaped bags contain a heavy spherical rubber bottom, which helps them pop back up to an upright position after being hit. The coach will move the ball to signal the start of the drill, at which point the player executes his get-off from the line of scrimmage. He clubs and rips through the first bag and then through a second bag placed 4 yards behind the first. After clubbing and ripping past the second bag, he turns the corner and sprints to his right to flatten out his path to the quarterback. The rusher sprints all the way through double cones placed on the opposite hash to finish the drill.

For his second repetition, the rusher now lines up at the right hash, with the ball to his left. As he comes off the line from the right side, the rusher will club and swim around the first bag as well as the second bag (placed 4 yards behind the first). He now flattens his pursuit to the left, finishing through the double cones to end the drill.

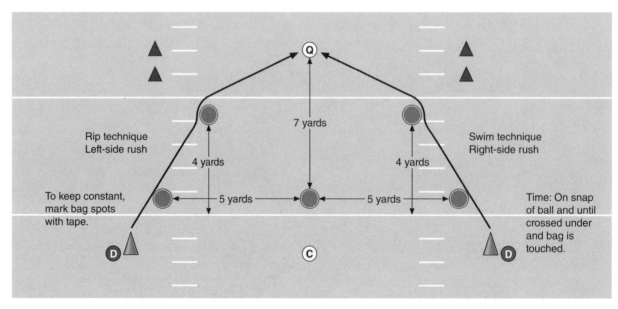

Figure 4.5   Pass rush drill for outside linebackers and defensive linemen.

FOUR-BAG SHUFFLE DRILL

Execution

The linebacker begins in a two-point stance, next to a cone placed 2 to 3 yards behind and to the left of a series of four football agility bags (figure 4.6). These bags are a trapezoidal shape, roughly 4 feet long and a foot tall. The agility bags are lined up in a parallel sequence, with 2 to 3 yards between bags.

The player faces in the coach's direction throughout the drill. At the coach's signal, he sprints at an angle toward the inside edge of the bag closest to him. Still facing forward, he moves left around the first bag's top edge, then back-pedals between the first and second bags toward the bottom of the second bag. He moves around the bottom of the second bag to its left side, then transitions back into a forward sprint between the second and third bags. At the top of the third bag, he maneuvers around the top of the bag into another backpedal between the third and fourth bags.

As the linebacker moves around the bottom of the fourth bag and reaches the fourth bag's left side, he transitions into a lateral stepover across the middle of each bag. Still facing forward, he steps over the bag one foot at a time, leading with his right foot and following with his left foot. He quickly repeats this lateral stepover sequence across all four bags until he steps back across the bag closest to his initial starting position.

Now back on the right side of the bag closest to his starting cone, the player quickly positions himself behind the bag, then shuffles left in a straight line behind the series of bags. As he shuffles across, he bends to slap each bag with both hands. As he reaches the leftmost bag and contacts it with his hands, the player sprints around the left side of the bag at a 45-degree angle through the designated finish line. This is a timed drill that displays the linebacker's short-area quickness, bend, change of direction, and lower-body explosiveness.

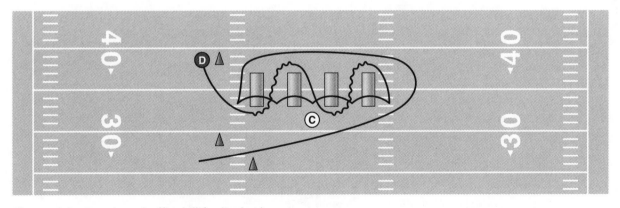

Figure 4.6   Four-bag shuffle drill for linebackers.

Defensive Linemen

In defensive linemen, coaches and evaluators like to see bend, lower-body explosiveness, and upper-body as well as lower-body strength. The pass rush drill from the linebackers section is also conducted for defensive linemen.

FOUR-BAG AGILITY DRILL

Execution

This drill uses the same agility bag setup as the four-bag shuffle drill for linebackers. The trapezoidal-shaped bags are lined up parallel to each other, with 2 to 3 yards between bags (figure 4.7). The defensive lineman starts the drill lying between the middle two bags, with his whole body on the ground in a push-up position. His chest lines up with the midpoint of the bags.

The player faces the coach until the very end of the drill. At the coach's cue, the lineman pops up onto his feet and steps over the bags to his right, leading with his right foot and following with his left. Once his right foot contacts the ground outside the rightmost bag, he moves back in the opposite direction, stepping to his left and stepping over all four bags laterally.

Once the player steps laterally over all four bags moving to his left, he begins a sprint and backpedal weave around the bags, moving back to the right. He maneuvers around the front of the bag he just stepped over and continues his backward and forward zigzag in between the bags. He clears the bottom of the last bag and sprints toward the coach. The coach gives a signal for the lineman to react and cut, at which point the lineman plants his foot and turns his back to the coach, sprinting out to the hash to finish the drill.

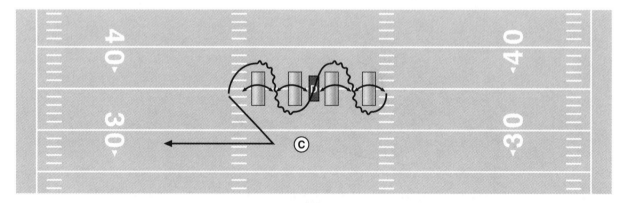

Figure 4.7 Four-bag agility drill for defensive linemen.

THREE-MAN BAG DRILL

Execution

The three bags used in this drill are the standing heavy bags used in the pass rush drill. These bags are spaced out evenly between the hashes, with one trapezoidal agility bag placed in each gap (figure 4.8). Typically, coaches or players will hold the stand-up bags to create more resistance.

The lineman starts on the left hash, directly opposite a coach with a ball placed on the line of scrimmage. As soon as the coach moves the football, the lineman explodes out of his stance to strike the first stand-up bag with both hands. He then moves laterally along the line of scrimmage. He stays low to slap the agility bag to his right, then strikes the next stand-up bag, continuing the slap-strike sequence for one more of each bag. Once he contacts the outermost stand-up bag, the athlete reverses the sequence, moving laterally back to his left. After striking the stand-up bag at the left hash, he finishes the drill by sprinting left around the bag through the finish line roughly 5 yards past the bag.

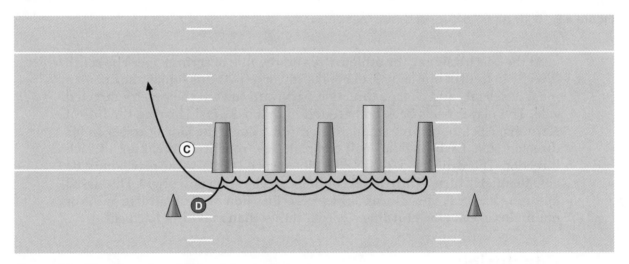

Figure 4.8   Three-man bag drill for defensive linemen.

BODY CONTROL DRILL

Execution

Change of direction and pursuit are both key aspects of a defensive lineman's skill set. The body control drill measures both, as well as lower-body explosiveness and accelerative burst. The defensive lineman begins the drill in a position-specific three-point stance between two cones at the starting line, directly in the middle of the field (figure 4.9). Two 8-yard lanes of cones are set up, with one placed just outside each hash and beginning roughly 2 yards past the starting line. The coach begins roughly 5 to 7 yards directly in front of the lineman.

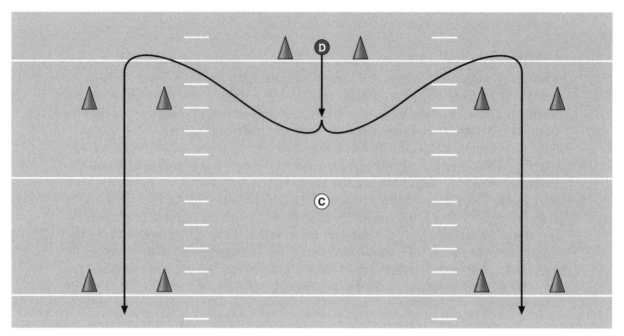

Figure 4.9 Body control drill for defensive linemen.

At the coach's signal, the athlete fires off the line of scrimmage. The coach directly in front of him signals to break right or left. At this signal, the lineman must decelerate and change direction backward toward the coach's directed side. The player peels back and around to that side, just clearing the line of scrimmage before turning again and sprinting down the lane of cones on his directed side. Each lineman will complete one repetition breaking in each direction. This drill also assesses curvilinear speed because the player must be able to quickly turn a corner and continue accelerating downfield. Discussed more in chapter 8, curvilinear ability describes how well an athlete gains or maintains speed when turning a corner rather than making a hard cut.

Conclusion

The performance coach is ultimately responsible for teaching the general movement skills that transcend the requirements of any single position. For example, a defensive back who can sprint and backpedal cleanly, flip his hips around, and use T-steps as a movement bridge will generally be able to perform drills well. When a high school or pro day combine uses positional drills the player hasn't seen before, he is much more likely to succeed in these drills if he has built a foundation of strong fundamental movement capabilities. When a defensive back starts getting out of his break faster over the course of training, this improvement positively affects his performance in any defensive back drill. Chapter 5 discusses the position-specific drills for offensive players.

CHAPTER 5

Offensive Position-Specific Drills

Chapter 4 stressed the importance of adding guided football-specific preparation to the athlete's schedule, regardless of whether he plays offense or defense. Players training at their high school or college often will seek out their football position coaches to work on football skills and combine positional drills, whereas some private training facilities bring in current and former professional players to mentor combine preparation athletes. Players invited to NFL rookie minicamps or organized team activities (OTAs) will have to learn their new playbooks quickly, so it is important for them to incorporate football's tactical and technical aspects into their pre-combine studies.

The performance coach's chief aim should not be to create a better football player, but to create a quality athlete. If coaches can train their athletes to be more efficient movers and familiarize them with expectations for the common positional drills, football coaches at the next level will inherit better athletes who have a higher capacity to improve in their sport.

Sport-specific practice and study should be included on the offensive side of the ball. Receivers and quarterbacks should be familiar with route trees, above all else. Offensive linemen should focus on refining body position, both in their stances and during basic blocking footwork. Scouts look to see whether a lineman can get into a deep hip, knee, and ankle bend position in his stance, displaying a good balance point, solid anchoring, and proper heel position.

Ultimately, an athlete's success in these drills comes less from specific drill rehearsal and more from sound underlying movement skills. Positional drills are founded upon general locomotion skills (acceleration, change of direction, top-end speed), so building these general skills will vastly improve the athlete's performance in all positional drills—like the athletic equivalent of upgrading a race car's brakes, steering, and engine so that it will drive better on any course.

Quarterbacks

The majority of NFL combine quarterback drills evaluate players' throwing ability in three-, five-, and seven-step drops. Scouts search for quarterbacks who can display arm strength, timing, and touch on a variety of throws to wide receivers, tight ends, and running backs. This section explains three of the most important routes.

OUT ROUTE

At each step up in the level of competition, throwing windows and their respective margins for error shrink. Elite quarterbacks can create space in coverage by throwing a receiver open, which requires both excellent accuracy and well-rehearsed timing with the receiver. The out route (figure 5.1) provides an excellent example of how technically sound and in-sync the wide receiver and the quarterback must be in their timing to successfully complete the route. As the two have most likely been relative or complete strangers before the combine, never having had the luxury of practicing with each other, this becomes all the more difficult to pull off on testing day.

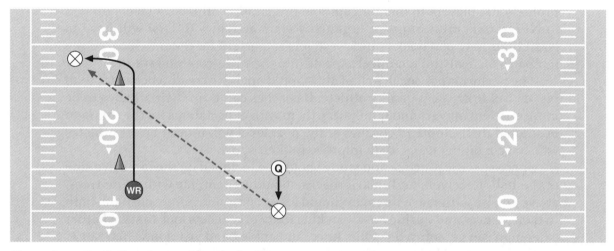

Figure 5.1   Football evaluators often look at the out route to evaluate timing capabilities between quarterbacks and wide receivers.

NINE (GO) ROUTE

For quarterbacks, the ability to hit a receiver streaking down the field on a nine or go route (figure 5.2) is fundamental, albeit difficult to develop. It displays throwing touch, arm strength, and ball placement, all at once. Receivers will be expected to know this route and to show their speed carrying ability as they try to separate from the defender.

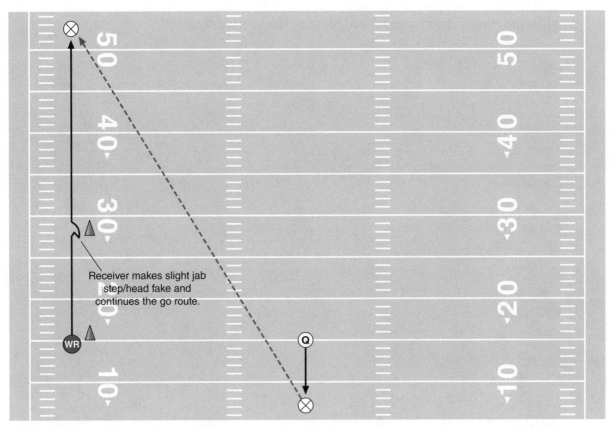

Receiver makes slight jab step/head fake and continues the go route.

Figure 5.2 The nine, or go, route (the nine denotes its number in the route tree) tests a quarterback's deep ball throwing ability and his receiver's capacity to stretch the field.

POST-CORNER ROUTE

Wide receivers and quarterbacks entering the professional ranks are expected to be comfortable and skilled in executing the post-corner route (figure 5.3). This pattern consists of a double move, with the wide receiver making a cut like in a post route, immediately followed by a cut back out toward the pylon. Quarterbacks are expected to be able to lead the receiver by throwing a pass that gives him ample time to run underneath it. It takes a combination of arm strength, touch, and a sound judgment of the receiver's speed.

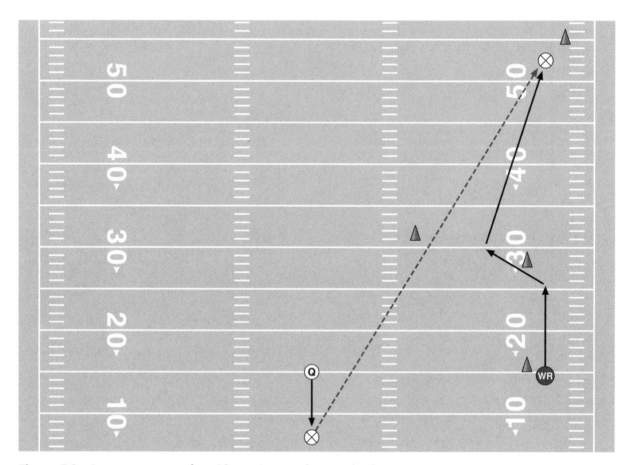

Figure 5.3   Post-corner route for wide receivers and quarterbacks.

Running Backs and Fullbacks

Running backs and fullbacks are expected to have exceptional lower-body strength and explosiveness, as well as acceleration and short-area quickness. The most important drills for this group will show those qualities, but running backs are encouraged to show what makes them unique. Christian McCaffrey memorably performed position drills with the wide receivers as well as the running backs to display his versatility.

OFF-TACKLE REACTION

Short-area quickness is a major KPI for running backs because they must move well and explosively within narrow spaces. The off-tackle reaction drill (figure 5.4) requires the running back to smoothly take a handoff cut, then make a quick change of direction based on a coach-issued visual stimulus.

A quarterback sets up at the line of scrimmage with a football, while the running back lines up in his position stance 5 yards behind the quarterback and 3 yards over to his left. At the quarterback's snap of the football, the running back moves right and takes the handoff as if running an outside zone play. He corners around a cone to his left, then runs over a parallel series of four large trapezoidal foam agility bags.

The coach stands with a heavy stand-up tackling dummy 3 yards directly past the last bag. As the running back finishes stepping over the agility bags, this coach quickly jabs the dummy toward the running back's right or left side. The player must quickly read the stimulus, then react by making a cut to change direction away from the would-be tackler. Once the player cuts, he corners around a cone 5 yards to the side of the tackling dummy.

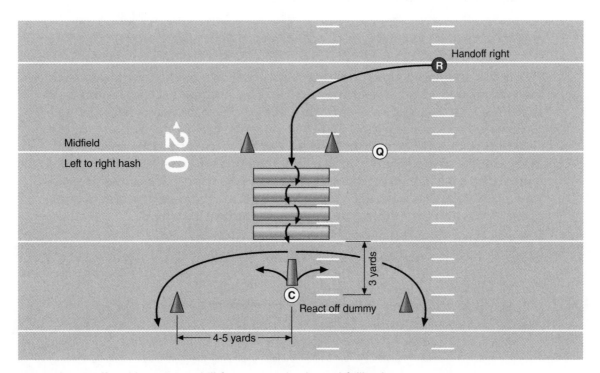

Figure 5.4   Off-tackle reaction drill for running backs and fullbacks.

BLAST READ

The blast read drill (figure 5.5) is nearly identical to the off-tackle reaction drill in both setup and execution. However, in the blast read there are no agility bags to maneuver over after receiving the handoff and making a reactive cut to avoid a tackling dummy. The quarterback starts the play 9 yards away from the heavy blue stand-up tackling dummy and makes a handoff exchange with the running back.

The running back sprints through a pair of cones set up 4 yards before the dummy, then makes a reactive cut away from where the coach directs the dummy. After making his cut, the running back sprints around a cone 4 to 5 yards wide of the dummy, then turns upfield and sprints.

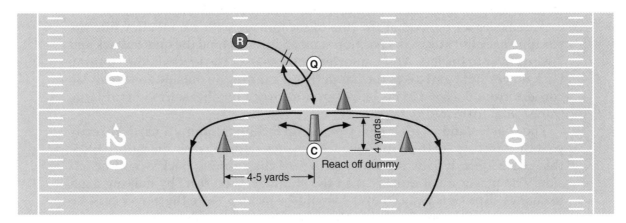

Figure 5.5   Blast read drill for running backs and fullbacks.

FIND THE BALL

Two cones are placed along the same yard line, with one on or outside each hash mark 10 to 12 yards apart (figure 5.6). The running back starts the drill at the left cone facing downfield, while the quarterback starts with the ball 10 yards behind him and directly between the hashes. At the drill's start, the running back sprints directly to his right, catching a pass from the quarterback in the middle of the field. Upon reaching the opposite cone, he will ditch the football, turn back, then catch another pass as he sprints back across. He will turn again at the first cone, ditch the second football, then sprint across to catch one last pass and turn upfield until he hears the coach's whistle.

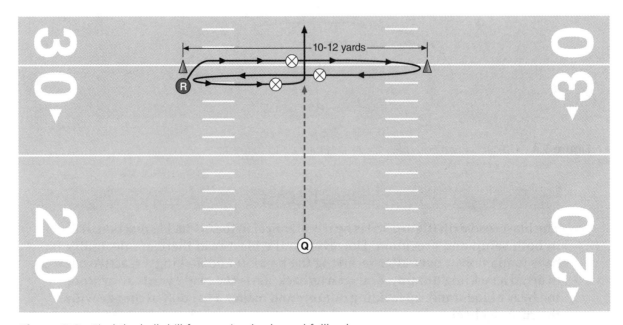

Figure 5.6   Find the ball drill for running backs and fullbacks.

Wide Receivers

Much like defensive backs, wide receivers need lower-body explosiveness, sprinting acceleration, and top-end speed, all in spades. Unlike defensive backs, however, receivers are expected to display these skills both in their route-running ability and in their execution of positional drills.

GAUNTLET

The receiver starts facing quarterback number 2 (figure 5.7). To start the drill, he flips 180 degrees to face quarterback 1 and catches a pass from QB 1, then drops the ball and flips back again to catch a pass from QB 2. As soon as he catches this second pass, he drops the ball and sprints the width of the field across the designated yard line.

Five more QBs are spaced across the field on alternating sides, each QB 5 yards back from the receiver's running path. They alternate throwing passes to the wide receiver as he sprints across the field. First he turns to his left, securing the pass and then dropping the ball as he continues sprinting. He catches four more passes, turning back to his right, left, right, and left again. After catching the final pass from his left, the receiver tucks the ball and turns to sprint upfield along the sideline.

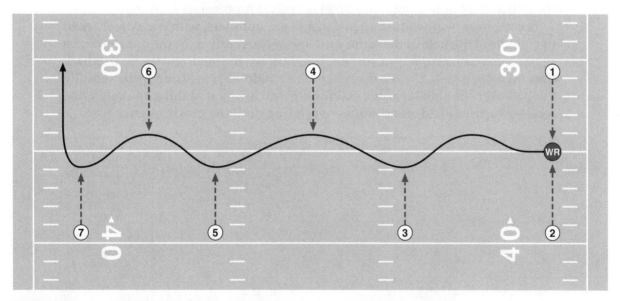

Figure 5.7 Gauntlet drill for wide receivers.

SIDELINE TOE-TAP

The sideline toe-tap drill (figure 5.8) aims to gauge a receiver's ability to maintain body control and make difficult catches in tight spaces. The player lines up at the numbers with a coach directly across from him and a quarterback roughly 7 yards behind the wide receiver. At the coach's signal, the wide receiver takes a jab step and then opens back toward the quarterback while sprinting toward the sideline. The quarterback lofts in a pass near the sideline; the receiver secures the ball with two hands, "walking the chalk" by getting both feet down barely in bounds.

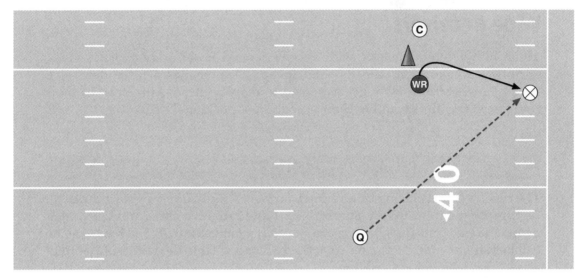

Figure 5.8   Sideline toe-tap drill for wide receivers.

OVER-THE-SHOULDER ADJUST

The over-the-shoulder adjust drill (figure 5.9) gauges the simple, albeit difficult, skill of adjusting speed and position to catch a ball thrown over one's shoulder. With the prevalence of back-shoulder throws in the NFL, manipulating body position and maintaining hand-eye coordination to "high point" the ball (catch the ball at the highest point possible) is critical for receivers.

The receiver begins lined up just inside the numbers, with a quarterback in the middle of the field at the same yard line as the receiver. At the quarterback's signal, the receiver runs a seam route straight down the field, and the quarterback fires off a deep pass; the receiver then must maintain his stride while locating the ball over his shoulder and making the catch. Upon making the catch, the receiver turns upfield and continues sprinting until the coach's signal.

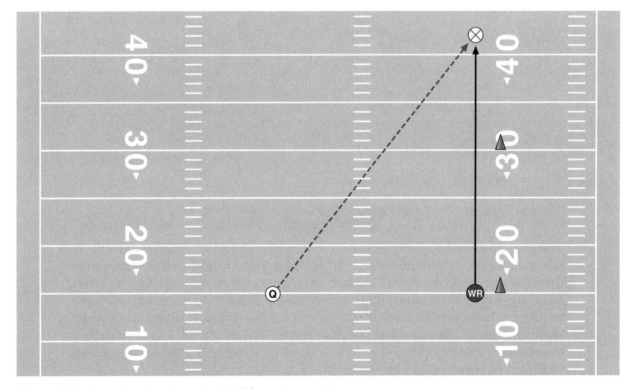

Figure 5.9   Over-the-shoulder adjust drill for wide receivers.

Tight Ends

Tight ends are asked to do quite a lot in today's game, lining up all over the field to block and catch. This need for versatility makes lower-body strength and explosiveness a tight end's most vital qualities, along with acceleration and change of direction. In addition to the blocking drill listed here, most tight ends are expected to run the routes depicted earlier in this chapter.

BLOCK EXPLOSION

Bend, overall strength, and lower-body explosiveness are KPIs described in chapter 6 that are put on display during the block explosion drill (figure 5.10). The tight end lines up in his football three-point stance directly across the line of scrimmage from a coach or player holding a blocking pad. At the coach's signal, the tight end fires out of his stance with short, quick, powerful steps, striking the bag with both hands and driving the bag holder backward until the coach's whistle.

Figure 5.10   Block explosion drill for tight ends.

Offensive Linemen

Any offensive lineman will proudly tell you that his position group has "the real athletes" on the field. This would not be an outrageous claim, either, since offensive linemen need a rare mix of size, lower-body strength, short-area quickness, and the ability to bend well (discussed further in chapter 6). The combine drills for this group are designed to test all these skills along with position-specific footwork.

PASS PROTECTION MIRROR DRILL

The pass protection mirror drill (figure 5.11) is a great change-of-direction drill that emphasizes bend and short-area quickness as well as position-specific footwork and reactive capabilities.

The offensive lineman starts in his stance at the line of scrimmage, with a standing player across from him serving as the rabbit or mirror. At the coach's signal, the offensive lineman pops up into his pass protection footwork and takes lateral steps while trying to keep the mirror player directly in front of him. The mirror player runs back and forth to try to shake the offensive lineman. Each repetition lasts for approximately 16 seconds. The drill can indicate a lineman's ability to maintain bend throughout changes of direction.

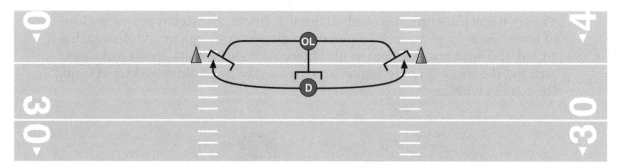

Figure 5.11 Pass protection mirror drill for offensive linemen.

LONG PULL

Offensive linemen who can pull and quickly get out in space to make blocks are highly valuable, especially as football continues to evolve and get faster. Although pulling in football is limited to guards and tackles, the long pull drill (figure 5.12) can also indicate a center's athleticism.

The lineman begins in his football three-point stance at one hash mark, facing downfield. The coach directly across from him signals for the lineman to immediately pull back out of his stance and sprint down the line of scrimmage toward the other hash, rounding a cone placed at that hash to turn upfield. As he turns upfield, the lineman angles back inside the hash toward a coach placed directly between the hashes. This coach gives the player a signal to cut back outside toward the hash again and finish the drill sprinting.

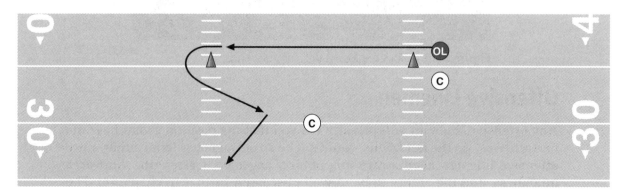

Figure 5.12 Long pull drill for offensive linemen.

HIP ROTATION DROP

Evaluators at the college and pro levels want to know what an offensive lineman's hip fluidity looks like and how his hips move in the transverse plane. For the hip rotation drop (figure 5.13), a 10-yard-wide lane is marked off with two parallel rows of four cones. Cones in each row are placed 10 yards apart, forming a 30-yard-long lane. The lineman begins the drill at the start of the lane facing backward toward a coach and starts chopping his feet in place.

The coach points a football in one direction, and the lineman swivels his hips that way and begins to shuffle down the lane while keeping his eyes fixed on the coach. At the first 10-yard interval, the coach points the other way, and the lineman flips his hips all the way across, still shuffling but now leading with the opposite foot. He is commanded to swivel his hips three times. To finish the drill, the coach cues the lineman to turn another 90 degrees and begin sprinting downfield in the direction he has just been shuffling.

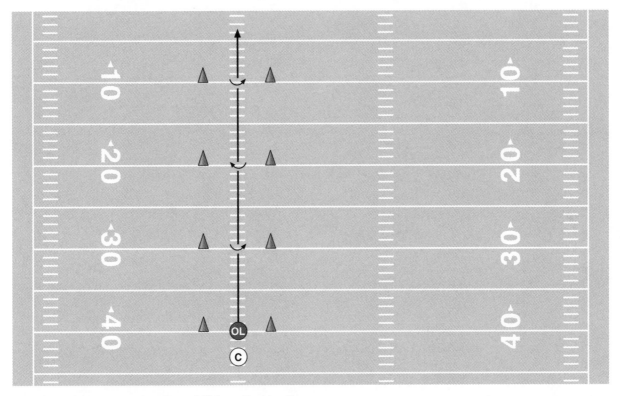

Figure 5.13   Hip rotation drop drill for offensive linemen.

Conclusion

Performance coaches are general physical preparedness specialists, first and foremost. If possible, all tactical and technical football instruction should be outsourced to an expert who can mentor athletes through their sport-specific preparation. Landow Performance uses former professional players and coaches to mentor combine prep athletes in their football-specific preparation for their upcoming job interviews. These pro-level veterans instruct athletes in their position's finer technique points as well as relating what to expect from coaches running the drills.

With the burgeoning of football combines at different competitive levels, players might encounter any, all, or none of the position-specific drills described in these chapters. Many high school combines choose not to include positional drills at all. These events often focus purely on general athleticism testing, or they replace positional drills with 7-on-7 tournaments. College scouts watch 7-on-7 games with an eye for the same general movement skills the position-specific tests would have assessed. Regardless of the particular drill or contest, evaluators are looking to see how well players execute fundamentals.

From a coach's perspective, prioritizing basic strength and general movement skill development is much more useful for a high school athlete than trying to predict what, if any, drills the player may face at his combine. Chapter 6 discusses how to combine and analyze insights from player intake testing and then use that information to tailor the athlete's training plan.

CHAPTER 6

Analyzing Data and Developing a Training Plan

The athlete intake information gathered according to chapters 1, 2, and 3 can prove exceptionally useful in deciding how to coach individual athletes during combine training. Awareness of factors such as athlete vitals, active and passive ranges of motion, and active dynamic warm-up performance can affect micro-level decisions throughout the preparatory process.

Most high school athletes require a basic, clean-cut approach to weight room programming during combine training. Coaches should use the evaluation methods appropriate for their athletes to gain overall context about them, but it will not greatly affect the high schooler's training plan.

When planning a combine preparation training cycle for elite athletes, advanced metrics such as eccentric utilization ratio and modified reactive strength index can offer deeper insight into a player's training needs. Using these tests, coaches can see the extent to which a player can use his stretch-shortening cycle and decide whether to shift some of the volume load in his workout program to favor strength-speed or speed-strength.

Force–Velocity Profiling

At the elite level, athletes have already garnered a high enough training age to be prepared for more advanced training strategies, such as the contrast method or velocity-based training (VBT). Because these athletes are better developed than their younger counterparts, they need specifically directed programming to realize maximum training adaptations.

Muscular contraction force and velocity have an inverse parametric relationship, which is a fancy way of saying the muscle's shortening speed will slow down as it tries to contract against a heavier external resistance. Such a trade-off makes logical sense; one can pick up a 10-pound dumbbell faster than a 75-pound dumbbell. A.V. Hill, an English physiologist who won a shared Nobel Prize in 1922 for his work studying muscle mechanics, was among the first to find that muscle contraction velocity and external force magnitude do not exhibit the linear relationship one might expect.

Instead, a graph of these variables (figure 6.1), with force as the Y axis and velocity as the X axis, displays a parabolic relationship. As velocity nears 0 m/s, a muscle's force capability is at its highest because it has maximum time to develop force. Then, as velocity increases along the X axis, force dips rather sharply and then begins to plateau.

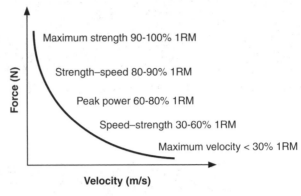

Figure 6.1 Strength qualities positioned along the force–velocity curve.

Stretch-Shortening Cycle (SSC)

To explain the parabolic force–velocity relationship, Hill proposed that muscle exhibits a three-element model of dynamic action. In addition to the muscle's contractile elements (CE), the series elastic component (SEC) and the parallel elastic component (PEC) contribute to the muscle's force production (Hill 1938); these elastic contributions occur primarily via the stretch-shortening cycle (SSC).

Put simply, the SSC is any muscular sequence in which an eccentric (or lengthening) contraction is immediately followed by a concentric (or shortening) contraction. Two primary neuromuscular mechanisms comprise SSC action: the elastic and neural components (Komi 1984).

The muscle membrane itself comprises the PEC; within the muscle tissue, stretch receptors called muscle spindles recognize the muscle's change in length and communicate to the brain about how hard the muscle should contract to overcome its lengthening. Meanwhile, the SEC consists of tendons and connective tissue, with Golgi tendon organs (GTOs) sensing the magnitude of the force placed on the tendons. If the GTOs determine this force is too great for the tendons to handle, the Golgi tendon reflex relays a protective nervous system signal to relax the muscle. The product of the excitatory muscle spindle signal and the inhibitory Golgi tendon reflex will ultimately determine stretch reflex, or the absorbed elastic energy that can be employed during the SSC. Proper training shifts the force–velocity curve, making the athlete more effective on the field (figure 6.2).

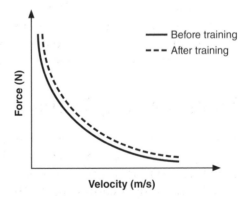

Figure 6.2 Athlete improvements along the force–velocity curve following a periodized resistance training plan.

Along with contractile factors such as muscle recruitment (the central nervous system's ability to call on multiple motor units to generate force) and rate coding (the frequency of action potentials sent to these motor units), the PEC, SEC, and their respective proprioceptive mechanisms combine to create the SSC.

Strength Qualities Along the Curve

Human muscle's tendency to produce a certain level of force at a specific velocity has enabled researchers and coaches to chart and describe different types of strength as they relate to athletic movement. Two of the main velocity ranges Landow Performance combine athletes train during their brief preparatory window are strength-speed and speed-strength, which straddle the strength and velocity ends of peak power production.

A wide array of exercises can be used to train these different strength qualities. When deciding how much volume the athlete should receive at a given velocity (e.g., strength-speed loading vs. speed-strength loading) during his training cycle, coaches can refer to SSC-related metrics such as eccentric utilization ratio.

Eccentric Utilization Ratio (EUR)

To plot an athlete's current profile along the force–velocity curve, coaches can analyze the ratio between the athlete's countermovement jump (CMJ) and non-countermovement jump (NCMJ) height with hands on hips. The CMJ is a classic vertical jump; the athlete begins in a tall standing position and lowers into a squat position, immediately reversing direction to jump as high as possible while using his arms to create momentum. The NCMJ, however, requires a pause in the bottom position, so that the athlete's first movement is a concentric jump without any eccentric dip beforehand.

The pause in an NCMJ removes the effect of the SSC, which uses the elastic components of muscles and tendons to create stored elastic energy. If an athlete begins to contract his muscles concentrically just before the stretch, he can use this energy like a released rubber band to help him generate more force as he contracts. The elongated amortization (stopping) phase of an NCMJ causes this stored elastic energy to dissipate, so concentric muscle action alone will determine his jump height. Therefore, an athlete should be able to jump higher during a CMJ than during an NCMJ (figure 6.3) due to the SSC's contributions during the countermovement.

The relationship between an athlete's CMJ height and NCMJ height is known as the eccentric utilization ratio (EUR). This metric displays an athlete's elasticity, or his ability to use his SSC in force production. Genetics partially determines an athlete's elastic capabilities; muscle fiber type percentages and Achilles tendon length have both been shown to help athletes develop more late eccentric force during SSC potentiation (Hunter et al. 2015). However, both plyometric training (Fouré et al. 2011) and various types of resistance training can drive adaptive improvements in various SSC components and enhance an athlete's elasticity (Cormie, McGuigan, and Newton 2010).

Regardless of the jump testing strategy used during athlete intake, practitioners should use the same method for both CMJ and NCMJ to determine the most accurate possible EUR figure. Methods range in accuracy and cost, but whether an athlete's jumps are measured on a force plate or by making chalk marks on a wall, he should perform both his CMJ and NCMJ tests in the same manner.

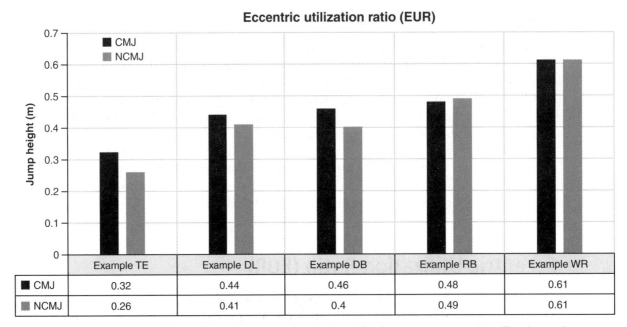

Eccentric utilization ratio (EUR)

	Example TE	Example DL	Example DB	Example RB	Example WR
■ CMJ	0.32	0.44	0.46	0.48	0.61
▓ NCMJ	0.26	0.41	0.4	0.49	0.61

Figure 6.3 An example of hypothetical CMJ to NCMJ ratios (also known as eccentric utilization ratio, or EUR) a coach may observe during athlete intake.

Modified Reactive Strength Index (RSImod)

Similar to EUR, the modified reactive strength index (RSImod) describes an athlete's quickness in switching from eccentric to concentric muscular contraction (Young 1995). Whereas the classic version of RSI uses a depth jump, RSImod is a safer version that provides similar data using a standing countermovement jump instead. RSImod is calculated as the ratio between countermovement jump height and jump takeoff time, and it offers another dynamic tool for assessing SSC capability.

Although RSImod is most commonly measured using a force plate, such equipment is cost prohibitive for most coaches. Recently, new measuring equipment and inexpensive mobile applications have reduced the barrier to entry for gathering this data without major sacrifices in measurement quality; at least one mobile app has already been studied and found to be a reliable and valid assessment tool for determining RSImod in comparison with a force plate (Haynes et al. 2019).

Training age is an important aspect to consider in force–velocity profiling. Even though it may be helpful to understand a high school athlete's elasticity, this should not greatly affect his training because he needs a different type of stimulus at this point in his development. Looking back to Istvan Balyi's LTAD model described in chapter 2, high schoolers are most likely in either the Learn to Train or the Train to Train phase, whereas players leaving college for the professional ranks are typically in the Train to Compete or the Train to Win stage of their careers. High schoolers generally need only simple, straightforward strength training to continue making tremendous performance gains. College players are more physically mature and have accumulated more training volume, so they are prepared for a more advanced type of training.

PREP LIKE A PRO: REACTIVE STRENGTH INDEX (RSI) USING FORCE PLATE MEASUREMENTS

During the Landow Performance intake process, combine preparation athletes undergo an additional assessment with dual force plates. To complete the test, an athlete drops from a 20-inch box, landing with one foot on each force plate, then tries to quickly rebound back off the force plates and jump as high as possible. This test creates helpful plyometric-related data for coaches. Another metric that can be drawn from this depth jump is time to stabilization (TTS), or the time required at ground contact for the athlete to fully stabilize his body weight. TTS can be helpful in understanding an athlete's dynamic postural stability during a jump landing (Ross and Guskiewicz 2003).

In addition to ground contact time and jump height, the dual force plates can measure the percentage of asymmetry between the athlete's right and left sides during both the eccentric and concentric portions of the depth jump. Therefore coaches can know not only an athlete's reactive strength, but also the extent to which he favors a particular side during eccentric and concentric portions of the assessment.

Determining Key Performance Indicators (KPIs)

All combine general athleticism and positional drills are intended to display one or more athletic qualities. These qualities are all displayed on the football field, but to varying extents depending on position groups. Key performance indicators, or KPIs, are the most pertinent attributes for a specific football position.

For example, wideouts and defensive backs need to be able to stretch the field with top-end speed, so scouts place a premium on the full 40-yard dash time for these positions. Meanwhile, running backs need more short burst accelerative speed, so evaluators place more emphasis on a running back's 20-yard split. To be clear, both the 20-yard time and the 40-yard time are important metrics for all of these position groups. KPIs seek to prioritize these metrics based on the most desirable attributes for a position group. Players should strive to perform well in all combine tests, but practitioners should know which tests are most closely scrutinized for their athletes' individual positions.

KPI Definitions

Key performance indicators are the lifeblood of the football scouting and analysis field. The terms for various KPIs form an unofficial universal language that helps everyone—from NFL general managers to college coaches to ESPN draft analysts—to describe a player's physical toolbox as they see it.

Bend

In football parlance, "low man wins" describes the role leverage plays in one-on-one physical struggles. This expression generally refers to an athlete's pad level relative to the ground, but low pad level should not come at any cost.

Bend is a qualitative term referring to a player who has the ankle, knee, and hip range of motion required to drop his pad level and cut to change directions. He must also be able to extend and project force out of a bent position.

In evaluating linemen, scouts refer to knee benders and waist benders to describe where a player's bend comes from. Knee benders are the players who exhibit proper bend, although this bend primarily comes from ankle range of motion. A waist bender athlete often has restricted ankle dorsiflexion and cannot achieve the shin angle he needs to drop his hips, so he tries to drop his pad level by hinging at the hips, causing him to produce force from suboptimal joint angles. Range of motion restrictions at the ankle and hip can also present a long-term knee injury risk.

Although range of motion measurements and FMS scores during athlete intake can help coaches to determine an athlete's bend, this KPI is predominately qualitative. Scouts assess bend when they watch positional drills and the pro agility (5-10-5) drill. They look specifically for where the athlete's bend comes from and whether there are joint range of motion restrictions that could pose a performance issue at the next level. Thus, coaches should pay special attention to how athletes perform the active dynamic warm-up in chapter 1. The warm-up serves as a daily screen to see where joint ROM is limited and where an athlete may compensate to try and create extra range.

Upper-Body Strength

Upper-body strength tends to be more important for players in the trenches such as offensive and defensive linemen and tight ends. These players must be able to initiate and resist physical challenges by producing immense upper-body force. At the NFL combine and pro days, the 225-pound bench press is the primary upper-body strength assessment, although for most athletes at the elite level, the test measures strength endurance. Combines or college camps for high school players sometimes use either the 225-pound bench press test or the same test at 185 pounds, and at this level the test tends to measure maximum strength.

Lower-Body Strength

Though there are no direct lower-body strength assessments at most combines and pro days, several drills and tests provide indirect measurements. The vertical jump and standing broad jump indicate an athlete's lower-body strength in the corresponding force vectors (vertical and horizontal). One-repetition maximums in back squat and power clean are closely correlated with vertical jump performance (Nuzzo et al. 2008).

Change of Direction

For most positions, each play during a game requires movement in all three planes: sagittal, frontal, and transverse. Players must be able to accelerate and decelerate in both the sagittal and frontal planes, and they often use transverse plane bridging movements to transition back into acceleration. Coaches and scouts pay close attention not only to the quantitative values from change of direction tests such as the 5-10-5 drill and three-cone drill, but also to the movement strategies an athlete uses in all drills.

Change of direction is closely associated with bend and acceleration. Athletes must have the strength and joint ranges to create optimal body shapes during multiplanar movement. They also must be able to efficiently accelerate from each change in direction.

Lower-Body Explosiveness

Lower-body explosiveness is a KPI for all positions. Linemen and tight ends need more strength, and skill positions need more speed, but lower-body explosiveness is an indicator for both. The vertical jump, broad jump, and 20-yard split of the 40-yard dash are good demonstrations of lower-body explosiveness.

Top-End Speed

Coaches and scouts want to see how well all players accelerate. For wide receivers and defensive backs, the ability to carry speed over a longer distance is vital to on-field success. As discussed in chapters 3 and 9, the best top-end speed measurement occurs during the latter half of the 40-yard dash.

Although 40-yard dash times are assessed for all position groups, several position groups (especially linebackers and defensive linemen) are judged more for their 10- and 20-yard splits in the 40-yard dash. These athletes rarely need to cover a long distance, so evaluators are more concerned with their ability to pick up speed over a shorter distance.

Curvilinear Speed

Change of direction requires deceleration and reacceleration in multiple planes of motion, whereas acceleration and top-end speed refer to straight-ahead sprinting. Curvilinear speed, however, is the ability to turn a corner while maintaining or gaining speed. Curvilinear running is crucial for tight ends and wide receivers because several passing routes require a tight turn while sprinting instead of decelerating, cutting, and reaccelerating.

Edge rushers also must display curvilinear running ability because beating an offensive tackle on a speed rush (especially from a wide 9 outside alignment) requires the rusher to quickly turn a corner and close in on the quarterback, a skill symbolized in the classic hoop drill used in football practices at all levels. Several other positional drills display curvilinear running, but the L-drill is the most common combine assessment for the skill.

Acceleration Burst

The ability to display a burst in acceleration overlaps strongly with lower-body explosiveness, which is best demonstrated in the vertical jump and broad jump. However, variables involved in an accelerative burst are more complex. As discussed in chapter 7, an athlete must be able to apply great amounts of force in a short time using optimal joint angles and in the proper direction. To accelerate optimally, he needs to exhibit the four Ps: posture, position, placement, and patterning. An athlete could jump out of the gym but still lack the skill to properly burst out of a stance or a change of direction. He must combine lower-body explosiveness with proficient acceleration technique to display this KPI.

Short-Area Quickness

Overlapping strongly with change of direction, short-area quickness describes a player's ability to move within a 5- to 10-yard box and is critical for most positions. For linemen, football coaches like to describe short-area quickness as the ability to operate in a phone booth with excellent footwork. Another prime example of short-area quickness is a quarterback's ability to sense pressure and climb the pocket or avoid a sack. While most field-based combine drills involve short-area quickness to some extent, it is best displayed in drills like the pro agility (5-10-5) and L-drill.

KPIs by Position

Each key performance indicator is valuable to players, but the point of making them keys is to prioritize what's most vital for a player. Table 6.1 shows the relative priority each KPI carries within a given position group, denoted by check marks. The marks range from one to five; a box with five marks denotes a KPI that is critical to performance at that position, whereas a box with one mark indicates the KPI is much less relevant to success at that position. Certain KPIs, like lower-body explosiveness, are valued highly across the spectrum of positions; others, such as top-end speed, vary widely in importance by position group.

Building the Training Plan

Coaches who follow all the athlete intake testing steps in chapters 1 through 3 (including careful observation of active dynamic warm-up performance) will be armed with an arsenal of information. Making sense of all this accrued testing data, interview information, and qualitative observation can seem overwhelming. However, most of this data is intended to provide context for better understanding the athletes. This information may guide certain programming decisions and coaching cues, but it will not greatly affect many athletes' training plans. Especially for athletes with a younger training age, testing will guide the micro decisions rather than the macro ones.

Data-Informed, Not Data-Driven

The testing, observations, and interviews completed in chapters 1 and 2 become even more valuable when used along with EUR and RSImod, and this assembled information can indicate helpful tweaks for an athlete's training plan. An athlete's warm-up performance, assessed joint ranges of motion, and ROM deficits can illuminate his areas of need and inform the selection of mobility- and stability-based assistance exercises. EUR and RSImod values can indicate the proportion of strength-speed versus speed-strength training elite athletes should receive.

The Landow Performance combine training periodization strategy generally uses a weight room load and velocity scheme targeting strength-speed at the beginning of the preparation window. Then, over the course of the training cycle, coaches will adjust loading to move down the force–velocity curve into

Table 6.1　Key Performance Indicators (KPIs) by Position

	Bend	Upper-body strength	Lower-body strength	Change of direction	Lower-body explosiveness	Top-end speed	Curvilinear speed	Acceleration burst	Short-area quickness
QB	✔	✔✔	✔✔	✔✔✔✔	✔✔✔	✔✔	✔✔✔	✔✔✔✔	✔✔✔✔✔
WR	✔✔	✔	✔✔✔	✔✔✔✔	✔✔✔✔✔	✔✔✔✔✔	✔✔✔✔✔	✔✔✔✔✔	✔✔✔✔
RB	✔✔✔	✔✔✔	✔✔✔✔✔	✔✔✔✔	✔✔✔✔✔	✔✔✔	✔✔	✔✔✔✔✔	✔✔✔✔✔
TE	✔✔✔✔	✔✔✔✔	✔✔✔✔✔	✔✔✔✔	✔✔✔✔✔	✔✔✔	✔✔✔✔	✔✔✔✔	✔✔✔
OL	✔✔✔✔✔	✔✔✔✔	✔✔✔✔✔	✔✔✔	✔✔✔✔	✔	✔	✔✔✔	✔✔✔✔✔
LB	✔✔✔	✔✔✔	✔✔✔✔	✔✔✔✔✔	✔✔✔✔✔	✔	✔✔	✔✔✔✔✔	✔✔✔✔
DB	✔✔✔	✔	✔✔✔	✔✔✔✔	✔✔✔	✔✔✔✔✔	✔✔	✔✔✔✔✔	✔✔✔✔✔
DL	✔✔✔✔✔	✔✔✔✔✔	✔✔✔✔✔	✔✔✔	✔✔✔✔✔	✔	✔	✔✔✔✔	✔✔✔✔

a speed-strength range at the proper time. It may sound counterintuitive to take weight off the bar as combine training progresses; however, most of the assessments in combines and pro days are measurements of speed and explosiveness. As training progresses toward testing day, bar speed should start to become a higher priority. More details on the use of velocity-based training (VBT) are covered in chapters 10 and 11.

Generally speaking, an athlete's strength forms the foundation for his power output, while his power capacity provides the basis for speed improvements (Bompa 1996). Improving one of these athletic qualities will raise the trainable capacity of the next quality further along the force–velocity curve; this concept is known as phase potentiation (DeWeese et al. 2015). Working along the force–velocity curve logically requires training the force-dominant qualities before moving to velocity-based ones.

Force–velocity profiling helps indicate which areas of the force–velocity curve have the most room for improvement. When an athlete's EUR and RSImod values indicate that he is more elastic, then he will typically spend more time training with higher loads; his testing indicates that he is more deficient at the curve's force-dominant end, so he needs more training saturation in strength-based qualities. Conversely, an athlete who displays an EUR favoring his NCMJ will benefit from more exposure to high-velocity training. Both athletes will begin their preparation windows working in similar areas along the force–velocity curve, but their profiling helps to determine when their training loads should begin moving down the curve into higher-velocity training.

Once athletes have reached the speed-strength portion of their training, emphasis must be placed on moving the bar as fast as possible. Elastic-dominant athletes who have spent more time working with heavier loads should now work on using their newly acquired strength with the elasticity that already comes naturally to them.

Training Age and Training Priorities

Programming modifications based on EUR and RSImod are intended primarily for elite athletes of a high training age. Most high school athletes should not use elite-level programming strategies that involve speed work in the weight room. Due to their younger training age, high schoolers' central nervous system capabilities are usually not developed enough to derive quality adaptations from advanced speed-based exercises. Instead, novice trainees will benefit more from developing technical proficiency in strength exercises.

High school athletes simply need to accumulate basic training volume and should spend most of their combine preparation training cycle in the strength and strength-endurance realms to reap maximum training benefits. Even exceptional high school athletes who can physically handle higher-level training concepts will still be better off in the long run if they wait to use these advanced methods until they are more physically developed within the LTAD model.

Conclusion

Coaches should always try to give athletes the best individual training stimuli. An athlete stands to benefit more from training his weaknesses than training his strengths, especially during a short training window such as combine preparation. Evaluating these weaknesses helps target the areas that could lead to the greatest gains for combine day.

Aside from the bench press (which will be discussed in more detail in chapter 10), almost none of the weight room training during Landow Performance combine preparation begins at the very top end of the force–velocity curve (maximum strength). There simply isn't enough time in this training window to work through all strength qualities, so coaches must prioritize the velocity ranges most important to each player's development. The tools in this chapter help coaches to pinpoint these velocities and further customize training programs as needed.

Coaches and athletes are well served by looking at the data and trying to improve relevant metrics. But perhaps the best training investment they can make (for performance in the combine and beyond) is spending time and effort to learn and rehearse general locomotion patterns. The next chapter on movement training is not about hard data; it is about learning to better solve movement problems in space and to better execute movement patterns. A better mover becomes a better athlete, and a better athlete can become an even better football player.

PART III

General Movement Skills Training

CHAPTER 7

Acceleration

Simply defined, acceleration is the rate of change in an object's velocity. In sprint-based field sports, acceleration is arguably the most important athletic ability. Football players rarely reach true maximum velocity during a game due to the constant changes of direction required. A player's movement goal during each change of direction is to find the most efficient way to get back to acceleration. This constant need to accelerate, decelerate, change direction, and then reaccelerate makes each linear burst vital to a player's success both on the field and during combine tests and positional drills.

Rate of force development (RFD) is one of the most discussed metrics in acceleration training. RFD is understood to be the magnitude of the force a muscle or joint can produce in the early phases of muscle contraction (typically measured within bandwidths of 0-200 milliseconds). Most muscles take longer to reach maximum voluntary contraction than sprinting ground contact time allows, so the athlete's ability to develop as much force as possible while contacting the ground is crucial to sprinting speed (Aagaard et al. 2002).

Research has noted that field sport athletes who accelerate well exhibit shorter ground contact times than those who do not (Murphy, Lockie, and Coutts 2003). Therefore, conventional wisdom dictates that the quickest athletes can produce equal or greater force than their slower peers within a shorter time span, making RFD integral to athletic success. Researchers have discovered that the maximum relative force an athlete can develop during a countermovement jump takeoff—which occurs during a mean period of 121 ms—is the single best predictor of how fast he will run the first 2.5 meters of a sprint (Young, McLean, and Ardagna 1995).

RFD is a trainable characteristic that can be improved through a variety of resistance training methods (Aagaard et al. 2002; Haff and Nimphius 2012). Those strength and power development methods will be discussed in more detail in part IV because they contribute a great deal to improving sprint times. However, coaches' acceleration training priorities often begin and end with RFD, omitting technique work entirely.

There is much more to maximizing an athlete's accelerative ability than developing his RFD. Sprinting follows a two-part technical model: The athlete begins his sprint in pure acceleration, and as he speeds up his running style naturally converts to top-end speed (also known as maximum velocity) technique. Coaches should understand proper sprinting biomechanics and know how to teach them.

Building a Faster Football Player

Acceleration is a specific motor skill with an ideal mechanical execution. A football player may not know how to accelerate properly, even if he runs a fast 40-yard dash. If you lined up a group of athletes for a race, the vast majority would begin to cycle their legs almost immediately out of their starting positions; even the fastest among them will almost never display the proper technical acceleration model unless they've learned and practiced it or have found it by accident on their own. Knowing this should be encouraging to coaches because it means that these athletes can become even faster.

An athlete's first pure acceleration steps should look different than his true top-end speed strides, with a gradual evolution occurring from the former to the latter as he speeds up. In the Landow Performance model, these qualities are trained separately so that athletes can master each and then learn to blend the two.

Football players should become masters of acceleration, but sadly they often aren't adequately trained in the skill. Many coaches simply make their athletes run a heavy volume of sprints to become faster, but this workload can worsen their movement technique. A conditioning approach comprised of distance runs or repeat sprints and suboptimal recovery periods will promote an uneconomic cyclical acceleration style reminiscent of top-end speed mechanics. Training this way may improve athletes' speed endurance or speed reserve somewhat, but it will never truly optimize their athletic abilities. However, when athletes train using the correct (and most efficient) sprint mechanics, it will also improve their conditioning in the long term.

RFD is a necessary training goal, but simply running more sprints without learning and practicing acceleration's technical model will only ingrain bad habits. An athlete who trains to produce more force will generally become faster, but if he still produces that force with suboptimal motor patterns, he will not reach his full potential.

Sport performance practitioners should see themselves as general physical preparation specialists, with the goal of helping athletes to master movement techniques. Any coach who can help football players to master general locomotion strategies will help create better athletes; better athletes can become even better football players, and they certainly perform better at combines.

Areas of Improvement

There are four major ways an athlete can achieve faster acceleration: He can produce more force, create force in less time, use ideal joint ranges in force production, and direct that force in the proper direction.

More Force

Perhaps the most logical way to affect acceleration velocity is to improve the total force an athlete can apply into the ground. Studies have shown that propulsive impulse (relative to athlete body weight) accounts for over half of the variances in athlete sprint velocities (Hunter, Marshall, and McNair 2005). In Division I football players, maximum squat strength relative to body weight displays statistically significant correlation to 40-yard sprint times and 10-yard sprint times (McBride et al. 2009).

Faster Force

Time spent repositioning the limbs has been found to be less related to sprinting velocity than time spent on the ground (Lockie et al. 2012). By definition, an athlete who can apply the same amount of force while spending less time on the ground will be a faster sprinter.

Optimal Range of Motion

Close study of sprinting kinematics has found that even during acceleration, there are sub-phases characterized by distinct differences in foot, knee, and hip angles (Nagahara et al. 2014); finding optimal postures and joint angles at these step-to-step stages helps athletes to follow the ideal technical model and improve their sprinting speed.

Directional Force

Researchers examining body position in sprinting have found that, regardless of performance level, athletes accelerating with forward body lean exhibit lower but more forward-oriented force magnitudes, thereby achieving higher levels of acceleration (Kugler and Janshen 2010). Directional force will be explored further in the biomechanics section of this chapter.

To succeed in the 40-yard dash test, athletes must be able to accelerate well. A poor first few steps will make it challenging to record a good time in the assessment. This chapter addresses linear acceleration in sprinting, explaining the technical model of human acceleration biomechanics and providing coaches with the best drills and cues to help athletes unlock their fastest 40 times.

Biomechanics of Acceleration

Football is completely different from track and field, so coaches should not try to make their football players run exactly like sprinters. However, certain *sprint qualities* are relevant to football. Sprinters help to provide coaches with a technical model for the coordinative, rhythmic, and elastic elements of pure athletic movement. This model can be applied to help football players become better performers in combine testing.

Newton's Laws and Linear Sprinting

In 1687, Isaac Newton published his magnum opus, *Philosophiæ Naturalis Principia Mathematica*, a three-book series that helped define what we now know as classical mechanics. Within its incredibly dense volumes, the *Principia* contains what Newton termed his "Axioms, or Laws of Motion," now commonly known as Newton's laws of motion.

In describing his Law I, Newton explained, "Every body perseveres in its state of rest, or of uniform motion in a right line, unless it is compelled to change that state by forces impressed thereon" (Newton, Motte, and Chittenden 1850). Known today as the Law of Inertia, Newton's first law plays a role in acceleration biomechanics that will be explained shortly. For now it is important to note that an athlete must have a force pushing his body to begin moving from a stopped position, and he will subsequently need less and less of that force as he gathers speed.

Newton's Law II states that "the alteration of motion is ever proportional to the motive force impressed; and is made in the direction of the right line in which the force is impressed" (Newton, Motte, and Chittenden 1850). Newton's description may seem overly complex, but the concept is foundational to sprinting. This second law, often termed the Law of Acceleration, means that to increase his speed horizontally, an athlete must have a force propelling him in that direction.

The necessary propelling force is described in Law III, which states, "To every action there is always opposed an equal reaction: or the mutual actions of two bodies upon each other are always equal, and directed to contrary parts" (Newton, Motte, and Chittenden 1850). Known in common terms as the Law of Reaction, Newton's third law dictates that in order to accelerate, the athlete needs the ground to push him forward, and he needs to push back against the ground to create an opposing force to propel him horizontally.

In accordance with Newton's laws, researchers have found that the strongest predictor of sprint velocity in acceleration is relative horizontal impulse, or the amount of force applied horizontally into the ground over time in the opposite direction of the athlete's intended movement. The fastest sprinters show the greatest horizontal impulse in acceleration and enough vertical impulse to generate the flight time required to reposition their limbs (Hunter, Marshall, and McNair 2005).

Acceleration Versus Top-End Speed Mechanics

The major observable distinction between acceleration and top-end speed is a difference in mechanics. After the athlete starts his sprint, each accelerative step (figure 7.1) evolves gradually as he gains speed, progressing from a forward-back leg movement toward a purely cyclical leg action occurring at maximum velocity.

During his first few steps of pure acceleration, the athlete should use a pistonlike leg action with a forward body lean. With this approach, he overcomes inertia (Newton's first law) and gains propulsive horizontal force from the ground (second law) by applying horizontal force back into the ground (third law).

Forward body lean is needed to aim the ground's responsive force in the desired direction (forward). The athlete leans forward so that he can more effectively push back rather than down. The athlete creates an alternating piston motion with his legs, punching forward and driving back to create the most force possible to overcome inertia. Ideally the athlete should create roughly 90-degree angles in his hips and knees relative to his torso angle. These landmarks allow him to generate the greatest possible torque into the ground.

Figure 7.1   *(a)* First and *(b)* second steps in acceleration's pistonlike action.

Newton's first law necessitates a transition in mechanics as velocity increases. Eventually the athlete will be unable to continually lean forward without falling on his face, and his leg action will apply less and less accelerative force. With each step, his torso angle changes, and the backside recovery portion of his leg mechanics shortens and becomes more cyclical. Since the athlete's inertia is now directed in Newton's uniform motion rather than in a state of rest, he needs less horizontal force to continue moving as he reaches maximum velocity; instead, he needs to apply more vertical force to allow time for backside recovery as his legs cycle faster.

Arm Mechanics

Arm mechanics should remain mostly uniform throughout sprinting's acceleration and top-end phases. The glenohumeral joint serves as the primary axis for arm swing to maximize momentum. Some coaches cue athletes to keep their elbows at 90 degrees through the backswing; such a technique may work for jogging, but it is incorrect for sprinting. Like a pendulum, the athlete's arm movement should be long on the backswing to generate more force. The athlete's elbow should change angles within each arm swing, flexing to less than 90 degrees on the forward swing and then extending to greater than 90 degrees (but typically not fully lengthened to 180 degrees) on the backswing. He should bring his hand to about chin level as his arm swings forward, and then aim his hand past his hip as his arm swings backward. This elongated backswing helps to encourage knee and hip extension on the opposite side, whereas an athlete who stays too short on his arm swing will tend to create short and choppy steps.

When viewed from a sagittal or straight-on perspective, the athlete's arms should adduct as they swing forward, moving in closer toward his midline.

He will then abduct or widen his arms to a natural shoulder width during his backswing. If he keeps his arms too wide on his forward swing, the added rotational force will begin to add unnecessary torque and rotate his trunk as he sprints.

Coaches should cue athletes to drive their arms back, rather than forward. Forceful backward arm swing will naturally place a stretch on chest tissue, thereby potentiating an elastic rebounding effect for the arm to swing forward again.

From a biomechanical perspective, a longer lever generates more force, whereas a shorter lever moves faster around an axis. In sprinting, the arm lever's rotational momentum is best minimized moving forward to rotate faster and maximized moving backward to rotate more forcefully. The added horizontal force moving behind the athlete will help project him forward, primarily because his longer arm backswing lever is designed to match his contralateral, or opposite leg, extension.

As his upper arm swings forward about his shoulder axis, a narrowing elbow angle creates a shorter and faster lever to economize the SSC response he created with a long backswing lever. The resulting lever is easier to swing forward, making it more like a directed reflex matching the contralateral lower limb's punch forward.

The Four Ps

During both acceleration and top-end speed training, all Landow Performance athletes learn the four Ps: posture, position, placement, and patterning. These are foundational concepts for understanding and practicing quality movement patterns.

Posture

Posture—the collective organization of the head, shoulder, trunk, hip, knee, and ankle—drives biomechanical efficiency in acceleration. Landow Performance coaches constantly remind athletes of their posture with the phrase, "posture is priority." If an athlete doesn't begin a drill or a sprint with correct posture, he will not be able to find that posture once he starts moving.

Athletes should learn how to organize their joints from top to bottom and develop an awareness of how proper posture ought to feel. Football players often find holding posture to be a major challenge, especially if they have never been taught how to correctly align their bodies and generate stability. For these athletes, foundational acceleration drills such as marches and skips become especially vital in restoring postural integrity.

Joint position dictates muscle function; an athlete who cannot hold posture in acceleration will invariably exhibit poor joint positions and use suboptimal muscular recruitment patterns, leading to movement inefficiency and possibly injury.

Position

Within the framework of acceleration posture, there are optimal joint angles an athlete should try to achieve during acceleration. Legendary coach Dan Pfaff often talks about the concept of "acceptable bandwidths" within technical movement models (Pfaff 2019). No athlete will perfectly replicate the ideal acceleration model for every single sprint, but if he falls within the guidelines of proper joint position, he will be successful. In the case of sprinting, coaches and researchers who have dedicated their careers to studying athletic movement have observed that the best sprinters create a specific position on the front side of the hip axis, which gives them ideal leverage to generate torque into the ground.

The biomechanical nature of sprinting dictates that body position should change as an athlete accelerates and transitions into maximum velocity sprinting. At the outset of acceleration, the athlete's body should have a more angular position relative to the ground, with an imaginary straight line running through his ear, shoulder, hip, knee, and ankle. He will naturally begin to transition to a more upright position as he reaches his maximum velocity, but to accelerate most efficiently he should angle his body forward to apply his force more horizontally into the ground. This will propel him forward in accordance with Newton's second law of motion, which dictates that to move forward, he must push backward.

The athlete's thigh position relative to the ground will begin to change with each stride as he gains velocity. As a rule of thumb, his thigh should remain roughly perpendicular to his torso throughout the sprint. Thus, at the beginning of acceleration, the athlete's forward body lean causes his thigh to angle toward the ground when it hits the proper landmark. As he transitions into top-end speed mechanics, his torso will rise vertically, eventually positioning his thigh more parallel to the ground.

This principle of thigh position flies in the face of speed training dogma that many coaches learn early in their careers. The commonly used sprinting cue to "drive those knees up high" is rarely germane to the technique changes needed. Too much knee punch during the initial steps will create an excessively high thigh position, causing suboptimal horizontal impulses into the ground. From a timing perspective, a thigh position that is too high will cause the initial stride to take too much time, forcing the athlete to take shorter and shorter steps.

Placement

As discussed earlier in this section, horizontal propulsion is the key to excellent acceleration. Once an athlete has created the ideal joint positions, the next step (literally) requires correctly placing his foot into the ground to produce maximum force. An athlete should place his striking foot underneath or slightly behind his hips, depending on the phase of sprinting. In early acceleration, his foot should strike behind his hips to push back into the ground, thereby creating a greater horizontal impulse. As he gains speed and gradually transitions into a more upright posture for top-end speed, he will strike more directly underneath the hips to produce more vertical force. If he strikes the ground in front of his hips, he will create a braking force and place excessive stress on his hamstrings, especially during his top-end speed phase. The finer points of top-end speed technique are discussed in chapter 9.

The striking portion of the foot poses another vital placement consideration. Coaches often teach their athletes to run on their toes, which creates multiple problems. An athlete who strikes the ground with his toes while sprinting will not be able to optimize the elastic capabilities of his foot and lower leg. When used properly, this elastic component—an eccentric stretch on the muscles and tendons that creates stored elastic energy—can provide a rebounding force and improve sprinting speed. Coaching athletes to run on their toes will encourage them to reach in front of their hips with each foot strike to "feel" for the ground as a proprioceptive reflex, as if they are walking down a flight of stairs. This can place excessive strain on the hamstrings and lower leg, possibly even leading to injury.

The back portion of the ball of the foot is the proper foot contact point during sprinting. The back portion is especially ideal; athletes can run mostly on their toes while thinking that they are striking on the balls of their feet because they can feel the front part of the ball on ground contact.

Landow Performance coaches teach athletes to prepare for the ground by dorsiflexing their striking foot in midair; this is called creating a loaded, stable foot. This approach is preferred over a relaxed or unstable foot strike. A relaxed foot must move through full triplanar pronation as it strikes, thereby increasing amortization (or time spent on the ground). A locked foot allows an athlete to develop elastic tension in his ankle complex more quickly, thereby minimizing amortization. As an analogy, consider the difference between dropping a hard rubber lacrosse ball and an overripe tomato on the ground.

Perhaps most importantly, when a loaded foot strikes the ground it provides a more stable position for the athlete's most powerful joint forces—his hip and knee—to produce more force. Many practitioners view sprinting as a full triple-extension movement (requiring full extension of the hip, knee, and ankle), so they coach athletes to focus on plantar flexion. However, sacrificing an optimal surface for powerful hip and knee extension merely to favor ankle plantar flexion is shortsighted.

The first three Ps (posture, position, and placement) dictate the spatial aspects of acceleration. But acceleration is defined at the beginning of this chapter as the rate of change in velocity over time. Timing is therefore just as important as any other aspect of acceleration. The patterns in which an athlete executes his sprint technique are time-based, and they must be addressed as a component of the technical model.

Patterning

There should be a rhythm and smoothness to how an athlete runs; the Landow Performance model refers to this concept as *patterning*. An athlete may try to execute ideal posture and positions during a sprint, but if his timing is off, the entire movement is affected. Patterning is one of the easiest issues to diagnose because a poorly timed movement pattern looks wrong to even the greenest coach.

Acceleration patterning problems can occur for several reasons. Perhaps the athlete is spending too much time in ground contact or moves his arms and legs arrhythmically. Regardless of the issue, the first culprit a coach will often spot is improper thigh position or foot placement because these will immediately indicate that timing is off.

Many of the drills in this chapter are intended to improve an athlete's patterning in acceleration. The chief word to associate with patterning is *rhythm*. Rhythmic patterns of movement create a smooth and relaxed tempo. The more relaxed an athlete is at the right times during a sprint, the more elastic he becomes. Strategic relaxation and its subsequent stored elastic energy increase movement efficiency and speed. Athletes who remain rhythmic and relaxed while sprinting can maximize their use of this elastic energy.

Acceleration Drills

Early in their careers, many young coaches who train athletes for speed want to start with the most intense and exciting drills. But as they come to better understand the human body's complexity, we hope they will place more emphasis on simpler reinforcement drills such as marches and skips. Though these drills may not look exciting on social media, they create the necessary foundation for more advanced acceleration work. To use a mathematics analogy: Why should a coach teach calculus to an athlete who hasn't mastered basic addition and subtraction? Coaches should prioritize drills that reinforce basic posture, positions, and placement. Putting athletes through more advanced drilling is a waste of time when they can't properly execute these fundamentals.

Coaches should develop an eye for the four Ps—posture, position, placement, and patterning—and recognize when an athlete needs to regress to basic marches or skips. Furthermore, even if the athlete has mastered a specific drill, this does not mean he no longer needs to practice the drill. Skills must be constantly reinforced and rehearsed in the same way that seasoned PGA Tour golfers constantly practice their swing fundamentals. Even the All-Pro NFL players who train movement skills at Landow Performance regularly practice marches and skips as their "driving range drills."

PVC A-MARCH/A-SKIP

The athlete performs these two drills while holding a PVC rod or dowel over his shoulders, thereby allowing him to focus on posture and lower-body movement before introducing his arms into drills.

PVC A-March

Execution

The PVC A-march is a basic acceleration drill, but it is also one of the most useful because it helps to create postural awareness. The athlete stands tall, with his feet hip-width apart, shoulders back, and eyes straight ahead. He grips the PVC rod at a comfortable (but not excessive) width and holds it behind his neck along his upper trapezius and shoulders like the barbell for a back squat, keeping the rod in place but not actively pulling or bending it.

While maintaining perfect upper-body posture, the athlete steps forward, flexing his hip and knee to lift his knee, heel, and toe (figure 7.2*a*). His lifting foot should be directly underneath his knee, actively dorsiflexing as his thigh lifts. He punches his knee and foot straight forward into position, rather than cycling his heel up toward his rear end before extending his knee to bring his foot forward (figure 7.2*b*). The athlete's down leg should remain tall with his hip fully extended, while his down foot stays flat on the ground. This flat-footed

Figure 7.2   Correct posture and leg angles for the PVC A-march: *(a)* lift knee, heel, and toe; *(b)* extend leg to drive straight down underneath the hips.

bottom leg position helps him to learn proper balance between pronation and supination while on the ground.

When the athlete returns his lifted foot to the ground, he should not try to land on the ball of his foot in this drill. In acceleration drilling, ground strike location along the foot should match the drill's degree of movement speed. When humans walk, we heel strike; when we jog, we strike on the midfoot; when we sprint, we strike on the ball of the foot. Since the PVC A-March occurs at walking speed, heel strike is necessary.

The PVC A-march is completed at a slow, controlled pace for 10 yards. The athlete walks back to the starting line between repetitions as active rest. He completes 3 to 5 repetitions per set.

Coaching Points

The coach observing this drill can notice how well athletes hold posture and find positions. Based on any issues or asymmetries, the coach can develop further lines of inquiry. For example, perhaps an athlete's toe is dropped as he lifts his leg; this could be due to a lack of awareness, a neuromuscular issue, or a prior injury, among other possibilities. An athlete who struggles with actively dorsiflexing his lifted foot should continuously work toward achieving dorsiflexion.

PVC A-Skip

Execution

Athletes should work on the A-skip using a PVC rod or dowel before jumping into the A-skip drill itself. Skipping with a PVC rod allows the athlete to work on posture and removes arm movements from the exercise. The drill can also serve as a movement screen for coaches. An athlete's arm swing can obscure his trunk movement during drills, so adding the PVC will reveal how well he can maintain segmental stability in his trunk while moving.

Assuming the same starting position as in the PVC A-march, the athlete now performs the same knee-up, toe-up, heel-up actions with a double-bounce skipping rhythm (figure 7.3). Because of the slightly increased tempo, he strikes flat footed with a weighted emphasis on the balls of his feet, striking the ground underneath

Figure 7.3 Correct posture and leg angles for the PVC A-skip.

or just behind his hips. Athletes should learn and practice this drill's cadence and rhythm. Even though they won't be sprinting at this tempo, the ability to coordinate movements in a relaxed manner will quickly reveal general patterning skill. Coaches will easily hear the difference between a rhythmic sound and an arrhythmic one as athletes strike the ground.

The athlete completes the drill for 10 yards, walking back to his starting position between repetitions for active rest to keep quality high throughout the drill. He performs 3 to 4 repetitions per set.

Coaching Points

The PVC A-skip emphasizes posture, position, placement, and patterning. The drill's timing requires the athlete to get his foot back down promptly rather than allowing it to float. Practitioners should not coach athletes to drive hard into the ground during this drill. Instead, encourage knee and hip extension.

Coaches should observe the angles their athletes create during an A-skip. Ideally, they should see 90-degree angles in the hip and knee, as well as ankle dorsiflexion, because these angles create the greatest leverage for torque.

A-SKIP

Execution

This drill is the same as the PVC A-skip, except that the athlete puts away the PVC rod and adds arm swing to his skip (figure 7.4). This change is simple, but it is much easier said than done. The athlete must perform a coordinated contralateral (opposite) arm and leg movement, meaning that his right arm swings forward as his left leg punches forward, and then his right arm swings back as his left arm moves forward and his right leg lifts. Athletes who are new to movement training may find it particularly challenging to do this skip with correct posture, position, placement, and patterning.

Arm swing should occur at the glenohumeral (shoulder) joint. The arms and legs move contralaterally (opposite) in smooth rhythm without hunching the shoulders. Posture should be maintained throughout the drill—the athlete should not lose

Figure 7.4   Correct posture, arm swing, and leg angles for the A-skip.

initial spinal position by dropping his chin or breaking at the waist.

The athlete completes the drill for 10 yards, walking back to his starting position between repetitions for active rest to keep quality high throughout the drill. He performs 3 or 4 repetitions per set.

Coaching Points

The A-skip can be counterintuitive and challenging for many athletes, so coaches must limit the number of cues they give. Telling an athlete to fix parts of his skip midway through the repetition may cause another part of his technique to lapse; frustration can mount because there are too many things to think about. Coaches should instead provide athletes with one specific technical point to focus on before each skip repetition.

Athletes who consistently find great positions in marching drills may still struggle mightily with the A-skip, probably due to the A-skip's patterning component and to the greater postural stability demands it places on the athlete. Many athletes find it helpful to begin each repetition bouncing lightly on both feet in place, as if they are jumping rope; this double-bounce helps them to establish a rhythm before starting the drill, rather than trying to immediately begin skipping from a standing position.

WALL DRILL: MARCH AND 1, 2, 3 COUNT

The coach should find a solid surface, such as a wall or railing, for the athlete to lean against. To set up for wall drills, the athlete leans forward and places his hands on the surface. He aligns his body at a 45-degree angle with his arms fully extended, hips forward, and legs straight (figure 7.5a). His weight is distributed between his hands and the back portion of the balls of his feet, with his heels off the ground. Both feet remain actively dorsiflexed throughout the drill.

The rest of the athlete's body displays proper posture and positioning, forming a straight line from ear to ankle and mimicking an ideal 45-degree body lean in acceleration. The athlete may not have the necessary trunk stability and lower-body explosiveness to hold this acceleration angle when he actually sprints, but the wall drill allows him to feel how his lower body should operate while he is leaning forward while challenging him to hold posture. His chin remains tucked, his gaze fixed between his hands throughout the drill.

Figure 7.5   Wall drill: *(a)* proper initial setup; *(b)* posture and position at the end of each wall drill leg exchange.

Wall Drill March

Execution

The first wall drill exercise is performed at a marching tempo. The athlete assumes the starting posture with his legs together. Next, he simultaneously flexes his right knee and hip, keeping his right foot dorsiflexed and low to the ground while he moves it forward. As described in the biomechanics section, he should simultaneously flex both his hip and his knee to roughly 90 degrees each, aligning his thigh roughly perpendicular with the rest of his body while his right foot is dorsiflexed (figure 7.5b).

After finding this forward position, the athlete concurrently extends his right knee and hip to push his dorsiflexed right foot back to its starting position on the ground. He then performs the same forward-back movement with his left leg, alternating legs at a slow enough tempo to ensure that he can find the optimal degree of movement at his hip, knee, and ankle while maintaining postural stability in the rest of his body. He will continue this interchange at a controlled marching tempo for roughly 10 seconds according to his coach's discretion, resting between repetitions.

Coaching Points

Some athletes have better postural awareness than others, which means one could need more exposure to wall drill marches than his peers to learn how to hold the correct body posture while angled against the wall and moving his legs. Athletes new to this drill can struggle with placing their feet consistently, finishing repetitions with their feet up to several inches away from their starting position on the ground. Holding posture in wall drill marches should be the athlete's primary focus, with the leg punch/drive position coming with additional repetitions.

Wall Drill 1-Count

Execution

The next iteration of wall drills involves a reactive 1-count, or a single exchange of the legs. After assuming the starting position against the wall, the athlete creates a static position with his right leg forward—his knee, toe, and heel are all lifted to form 90-degree angles at his hip and knee perpendicular to his trunk, while he maintains perfect posture and position in the rest of his body. His right foot is dorsiflexed.

On the coach's command, the athlete quickly drives his right leg back to the ground to fully extend it, landing on the ball of his dorsiflexed foot with his heel off the ground. As the athlete extends his right leg down and back, he simultaneously punches his left leg up and forward to create the same 90-degree positions that his right leg just displayed. At the coach's next cue, the athlete drives his left leg down and back while punching his right leg up and forward. The athlete continues quickly exchanging punch and drive positions in the legs at the coach's cue for 5 or 6 repetitions per set.

Coaching Points

The coach should observe and manually correct the athlete's leg angles and body position between repetitions while the athlete is still engaged with the wall. These adjustments allow the athlete to feel correct positions and try to re-create them on the subsequent repetition.

Wall Drill 2-Count

Execution

The next progression for the wall drill is a 2-count. The starting position and exchange movement remain the same, except now the athlete executes a double exchange at his coach's command. This means that if the athlete begins the drill with his right leg up and forward, he will perform two exchanges in quick succession so that his right leg is up and forward again at the end of the repetition. He reacts to the coach's cue for each repetition, completing 5 or 6 repetitions for one set for each leg as the starting leg.

Coaching Points

The coach should be aware of the athlete's tempo, ensuring that the athlete makes his double leg exchange quickly, but not so quickly that his patterning sacrifices the drill's desired posture, positions, and placement. (Athletes often short-change the double exchange, creating a shallow first thigh punch in attempting to quicken their pace.) The athlete freezes after each 2-count repetition, so his starting forward foot remains forward to start each repetition.

Wall Drill 3-Count

Execution

Last in the wall drill progression is a 3-count, or triple exchange. On the coach's cue, the athlete switches his forward leg three times. If he starts a repetition with his right leg forward, he finishes it with his left leg forward, and vice versa. The coach cues each 3-count switch, for 6 repetitions per set and 1 set with each leg starting forward.

Coaching Points

Landow Performance coaches progress athletes through this drill according to each person's skill level and stability, adjusting the sets and repetitions as well as the rest intervals to accommodate fatigue and keep drill quality high.

PARTNER-RESISTED A-MARCH/A-RUN

This drill requires the use of a Bullet Belt or similar type of equipment to hold the athlete in forward body lean while he marches. It may be helpful to think of the partner-resisted drills in this book as moving wall drills with an arm swing, first performed at marching speed, then at running speed. With the athlete's coach or partner standing behind him and holding the strap as a counterweight, the athlete secures the belt around his waist just above his hips. Similar to taking away a PVC rod for A-skips, moving away from the wall to partner-resisted A-marches and A-runs requires the athlete to incorporate an arm swing into his drill technique.

After securing his belt and confirming that his partner is ready to provide counterweight, the athlete leans forward while maintaining correct posture with a neutral chin. From this starting position, the coach should be able to draw an imaginary line straight through the athlete's ear, shoulder, hip, knee, and ankle. Unlike wall drills, in partner-resisted drills the athlete should lean forward only at an angle he can maintain throughout the drill without losing posture. Stronger athletes may take a more aggressive lean, whereas weaker athletes need to stay more upright. The athlete creates this lean from the ground rather than bending forward at the hips or trunk.

The partner or coach holding the belt plays a critical role. This partner must not only provide a counterweight to enable the athlete to maintain his lean, but he also needs to move forward with the athlete at a smooth, controlled pace in sync with the athlete's tempo. A strong resistance from the partner encourages the athlete to create an angle and apply a force that will move him forward, but too much resistance will cause the athlete to create compensatory movement patterns. A partner who does not do this job correctly will upset the drill's rhythm and timing as well as the athlete's positioning.

In partner-resisted acceleration drilling, athletes commonly make the mistake of creating trunk lean through trunk flexion instead of ankle dorsiflexion. To help athletes to avoid breaking at the hips, coaches can cue them to keep their hips pushed forward to neutral (but not extended) position. Some athletes also find it beneficial to pretend they are leaning forward to look over a fence.

Partner-Resisted A-March

Execution

With weight on the balls of both feet, the athlete maintains his lean and begins a contralateral (opposite arm, opposite leg) marching pattern, punching one knee forward as the other leg drives back into the ground while using the arm swing technique described in the biomechanics section of this chapter (figure 7.6). Aside from his moving limbs, the athlete's posture should remain intact throughout the drill. His feet should remain dorsiflexed throughout each punch-drive movement.

The athlete completes an A-march for 10 yards moving out, then switches out of the belt and holds it while his partner completes a 10-yard repetition moving back to the starting line. Each athlete completes 3 or 4 A-marches for a single set. If the coach is holding the belt, the athlete gets rest intervals similar to those he would get if he had an active partner.

Coaching Points

As the athlete marches forward at a smooth, controlled tempo (faster than a PVC A-march, but not rushed to the point of becoming arrhythmic or sloppy), the coach watches the athlete's heel path during each leg movement. Athletes commonly bring their heels up toward their rear end while marching, thereby reducing their drive angle efficiency. The coach should cue the athlete to bring his foot further forward. The athlete punches his knee forward as if he is trying to break an imaginary pane of glass, then drives back into the ground behind him.

Partner-Resisted A-Run

Execution

The setup, body lean, posture, arm swing, and leg angles for the partner-resisted A-run are the same as for the A-march. For this drill, the athlete now moves his arms and legs at a running tempo instead of a marching pace. Drill tempo may vary from person to person depending on skill level and relative strength.

Figure 7.6   Partner-resisted A-march: *(a)* setup; *(b)* execution.

The partner or coach holding the belt should treat the A-run similarly to the A-march. His goal is to hold the athlete up and move at a pace that maintains the athlete's starting body lean throughout the drill. His resistance should force the athlete to push back into the ground but should not prevent the athlete from moving forward. Meanwhile, the athlete should focus on his posture, position, placement, and patterning rather than trying to pull his partner forward like a sled or a parachute. This drill is about practicing the four Ps, and it should look like a smoothly moving wall drill with fast-paced leg action and arm swing.

The athlete completes an A-run for 5 yards moving out, then switches out of the belt and holds it while his partner completes a 5-yard repetition moving back to the starting line. Each athlete completes 3 or 4 A-runs for a single set. If the coach is holding the belt, the athlete gets rest intervals similar to those he would get if he had an active partner.

Coaching Points

Although the patterning of this drill is not quite the same as an unresisted sprint, it begins to approach that level of tempo. An athlete who can pattern well during a resisted A-run will generally be able to do the same in true acceleration.

TWO-POINT ACCELERATION START

Execution

Landow Performance combine preparation athletes typically use a two-point starting stance to practice acceleration. This position is more applicable to football and to sport in general. Although three-point stances are certainly common in football, they are much more sport-specific and do not fully mimic the starting position for a 40-yard dash. In competition, football players start from a true three-point acceleration stance only during their combine and pro day testing. Accelerating out of a three-point stance is more difficult, so the two-point start is meant to groove acceleration pattern acquisition and build relative strength that can then be transferred into the three-point start during 40-yard dash preparation. Athletes who struggle with other drills should still practice two-point starts because sprinting can often help them work through problems that don't make sense to them in drilling.

To set up in a two-point stance (figure 7.7), the athlete stands tall with both feet together at the line and his toes pointed straight ahead, emphasizing posture. He brings his right foot back behind his left and opens his back foot out to the right side so that his toes point to the right with his heels meeting at a 90-degree angle. From here, he keeps his left foot in place and pivots his right foot on his toes to swing his right heel out and bring his feet parallel again but now a foot's width apart. He wiggles his right foot

Figure 7.7   Setup for acceleration from a two-point stance.

along the ground another 6 to 8 inches back, based on comfort level and limb length. (Athletes with long legs should lengthen the distance between their front and back feet to accommodate their dimensions.)

From this starting foot position, the athlete loads onto the ball of his front foot, lowering his hips and leaning his trunk forward without losing spinal integrity. His two-point stance should distribute roughly 75 percent of his body weight on his front foot and 25 percent on the back foot. He splits his arms in opposition with his legs, bringing the arm opposite his front leg forward to a comfortable level while his other arm moves back.

As the athlete loads into position, his shin angle shifts forward so that his knee moves out neutrally over his toes. The angle of his front shin is critical to an effective start. In accordance with the biomechanics section from earlier in this chapter, the athlete's shin angle will determine the direction in which he puts force into the ground as he starts. An athlete can create more horizontal force with a more horizontal shin angle.

Ankle mobility is the main factor that limits shin angle because an athlete must create passive dorsiflexion to move the shin forward without improperly shifting weight onto the toes. The athlete should certainly strive for positive shin angle; however, he must not try to project at a more aggressive angle than his body can hold during acceleration. In addition to ankle mobility, lower-body explosiveness and relative strength determine the athlete's ability to hold a steep body lean as he accelerates.

From this loaded two-point stance, the athlete focuses on pushing off both legs, orchestrating his movements to make everything happen at once. He drives his forward leg back aggressively into the ground behind him while punching his back leg forward as if trying to break an imaginary pane of glass with his knee. As his legs split, his arms split in the opposite direction.

During an acceleration training session, Landow Performance athletes typically perform 10-yard starts from a two-point stance for a widely varying number of repetitions and sets, depending on where they are in the training cycle. A slow walk back to the starting line between repetitions provides active rest. They usually complete 3 or 4 repetitions per set, with two minutes between sets. The number of sets varies based on the day and the week within the combine training window.

Rest intervals should be ample, regardless of the day or week, in order to keep drill quality high. Once an athlete starts showing fatigue, his coach should cut drilling for the day. Movement skill acquisition is predicated on quality of execution, so if the athlete continues to work under fatigue, he will begin to compromise the adaptations gained from movement training.

Coaching Points

The first two or three steps are the most important for a coach to watch in a two-point acceleration start. Video analysis allows coaches and athletes to closely examine technique and identify areas for improvement.

THREE-POINT ACCELERATION START

Execution

As described in the 40-yard dash section in chapter 3, the optimum three-point stance trades "inches for angles," sacrificing distance from the finish line to create more optimal acceleration shin angles. Beginning with both feet together at the starting line, the athlete brings one foot and then the other back to move himself a full foot's distance from the starting line. His back foot moves back one more foot's length, then he spreads his feet to hip width. After sliding his back foot back another 3 or 4 inches, he kneels while keeping his toes on the ground. His lead arm aligns outside his back knee with the crease of his elbow aimed forward and his hand placed on the starting line. He raises his hips above his shoulders to move three quarters of his weight forward, bringing his up arm to hip height of his lead leg (figure 7.8).

Just like the two-point start, the three-point start requires orchestration of limb movements to violently split the arms and legs. The athlete maintains acceleration technique for a duration natural to his skill level, lower-body explosiveness, and relative strength. A common distance is 10 to 20 yards from a three-point stance, depending on the athlete's ability to maintain acceleration over distance.

Landow Performance combine training athletes transition into more three-point starts during acceleration sessions as they approach their testing days to prepare for the 40-yard dash, but coaches still use some two-point starts to preserve general acceleration skill. Rest intervals should be long enough to keep drill quality high. The athlete completes repetitions of 10 yards,

Figure 7.8 Setup for acceleration from a three-point stance.

with a slow walk back to the starting line between repetitions for active rest. He completes 3 or 4 repetitions per set, with two minutes between sets. The number of sets varies based on the day and week in the combine training window.

Coaching Points

For a detailed explanation of the three-point stance setup and acceleration start, refer to the 40-yard dash section in chapter 3.

TALL KNEELING ARM ACTION DRILL

Execution

In the same way that the PVC A-march and A-skip drills isolate lower-body action in acceleration, the tall kneeling arm action drill isolates the upper body. This allows an athlete to practice optimal sprinting arm mechanics independently of the rest of his body.

As this chapter's biomechanics section highlights, the athlete's arms should rotate primarily at his glenohumeral (shoulder) joint while sprinting. His elbow should create a short angle in front to bring his hand around chin level close to the body's midline; then his elbow should open at a long angle on the backswing as his hand moves from near midline to just outside and behind the hip.

The athlete begins the drill in a kneeling position on one knee, with his back foot dorsiflexed and his front foot flat on the ground. His hips are in a neutral position, while his shoulders are back with a neutral chin and eyes gazing straight ahead. His coach should be able to draw an imaginary straight line from the athlete's ear down to his knee.

From this kneeling position, the athlete begins a slow, smooth arm swing motion (figure 7.9). At his coach's cue, the athlete ratchets his speed up to 50 percent, 75 percent, and then ultimately 90 percent of his maximum speed. Coaches should not cue the drill to a full 100 percent intensity; this will

Figure 7.9   Tall kneeling arm action drill: *(a)* front view; *(b)* side view.

encourage athletes to try too hard, thereby disrupting the drill's desired arm swing range and rhythm.

At 90 percent intensity, the athlete should focus on driving his arms back, not on bringing them forward. Arm swing's elastic reflex in sprinting means that a forceful drive backward will create a stretch-shortening cycle response in the chest and shoulders to rebound the arm forward. The drill length is the coach's call, but drill duration generally tends to be 15-20 seconds. Athletes take about a 1:1 or 1:2 work-to-rest ratio between repetitions, completing 3 repetitions for one set.

Coaching Points

Coaches should observe this drill from the side to watch athletes' arm swing landmarks (chin angle to hip pocket) and elbow angles (acute moving forward to obtuse moving backward), as well as from a straight-on look to see if athletes move their arms from midline to shoulder width as they swing forward and backward.

PVC ACCELERATION SPRINT

Execution

The PVC acceleration sprint reinforces the need for athletes to finish their backward push against the ground. Without arm movement to mask potential trunk instability or gait imbalances, the athlete must be technically sound in his punch-drive leg technique while maintaining a stable upper-body posture. Most importantly, this restriction in available limbs forces the athlete to

Figure 7.10   PVC acceleration sprint drill: *(a)* setup; *(b)* sprint.

fully project his hips and will cause him to fall over if he cycles his lower legs during the sprint.

During a normal sprint, an athlete who cycles his legs in acceleration recovery or does not finish his backward leg push can hide these issues by using his arms to counterbalance. With a PVC rod on his shoulders, the athlete who exhibits these errors has no counterbalance and will nearly fall flat on his face.

Setup for this drill is exactly like the two-point acceleration start, except the athlete holds a PVC rod on his shoulders (figure 7.10*a*). The athlete sprints for 10 yards (figure 7.10*b*), walking back slowly to the starting line between repetitions for active rest. He completes 3 or 4 repetitions per set, with two minutes' rest between sets. The number of sets varies depending on the day and week within the combine training window.

Grooving the Skill

Acceleration is a technically difficult skill that requires significant time and repetition to learn and master. Coaches should be cautious in cueing athletes during drilling. Bombarding an athlete with multiple simultaneous coaching cues will only confuse him.

Even if an athlete displays multiple technique problems at once, he will correct them more efficiently if he can focus on cleaning them up one at a time. The coach's job during acceleration drilling is to assemble a mental hierarchy of exhibited errors to prioritize the athlete's areas of focus. Athletes do not need constant verbal feedback; in fact, they often learn better if their coach gives them a few repetitions to figure things out in between verbal cues.

Tables 7.1 and 7.2 (on pages 112 and 113) outline basic acceleration training programs for both novice and elite athletes.

PREP LIKE A PRO: RUN ROCKET

At Landow Performance, combine prep athletes use an acceleration training device called the Run Rocket (figure 7.11). This contraption is designed to provide a consistent, adjustable resistance throughout the acceleration phase of an athlete's start. It serves as a more explosive bridge between partner-resisted A-runs and two-point acceleration starts, allowing the athlete to focus on finishing his push into the ground while aligning with angular landmarks.

The Run Rocket helps the athlete to hold a more aggressive body lean than he would be able to with an unresisted start, but the resistance should still be low. This drill should be like the sprinting equivalent of putting a weighted doughnut on a baseball bat. If the athlete cannot hold his body position while using a Run Rocket, he should regress to simpler drills.

Landow Performance coaches use this device for multiple protocols: full sets of Run Rocket–only repetitions followed by unresisted starts or Run Rocket and unresisted run contrast sets in which each Run Rocket repetition is followed by an unresisted two-point acceleration start.

Figure 7.11   Run Rocket device for acceleration training.

Table 7.1 Acceleration Training Program for a Novice Athlete: Monday, Weeks 1 to 4

MOVEMENT SKILLS SESSION		WEEK 1		WEEK 2		WEEK 3		WEEK 4	
	Exercise	Sets × reps (intensity)	Rest	Sets × reps (intensity)	Rest	Sets × reps (intensity)	Rest	Sets × reps (intensity)	Rest
Active dynamic warm-up (chapter 1)	General movement prep								
	Walking series								
	Ground series								
	Standing series								
Acceleration training (chapter 7)	Wall drill (1-count, 2-count, 3-count)	2×4 each side	60 sec	2×4 each side	60 sec	1×4 each side	60 sec	None	NA
	A-skip	1×2 (10 yd)	WB	1×2 (10 yd)	WB	1×2 (10 yd)	WB	1×2 (10 yd)	WB
	Resisted A-march	1×2 (10 yd)	WB	1×2 (10 yd)	WB	1×2 (10 yd)	WB	1×2 (10 yd)	WB
	Resisted A-run	1×3 (5 yd)	WB	1×3 (5 yd)	WB	1×3 (5 yd)	WB	1×3 (5 yd)	WB
	Two-point acceleration start*	1×2 (10 yd)	120 sec each rep/180 sec each set	2×2 (10 yd)	120 sec each rep/180 sec each set	3×2 (10 yd)	120 sec each rep/180 sec each set	2×2 (10 yd)	120 sec each rep/180 sec each set
	Three-point acceleration start*	3×3 (15 yd)	120 sec each rep/180 sec each set	3×3 (15 yd)	120 sec each rep/180 sec each set	3×3 (15 yd)	120 sec each rep/180 sec each set	None	NA

WB = walk back

* Rest = 180 seconds between sets plus an additional 60 seconds for every 10 yards sprinted

Table 7.2   Acceleration Training Program for an Elite Athlete: Monday, Weeks 1 to 4

MOVEMENT SKILLS SESSION		WEEK 1		WEEK 2		WEEK 3		WEEK 4	
	Exercise	Sets × reps (intensity)	Rest	Sets × reps (intensity)	Rest	Sets × reps (intensity)	Rest	Sets × reps (intensity)	Rest
Active dynamic warm-up (chapter 1)	General movement prep								
	Walking series								
	Ground series								
	Standing series								
Acceleration training (chapter 7)	A-skip	1×3 (10 yd)	WB	2×3 (10 yd)	WB	2×3 (10 yd)	WB	1×3 (10 yd)	WB
	Resisted A-march	3×2 (10 yd)	WB	1×2 (10 yd)	WB	1×2 (10 yd)	WB	1×2 (10 yd)	WB
	Resisted A-run	3×3 (5 yd)	WB	3×2 (5 yd)	WB	3×2 (5 yd)	WB	2×3 (5 yd)	WB
	Two-point acceleration start*	3×3 (10 yd)	120 sec each rep/180 sec each set	3×3 (10 yd)	120 sec each rep/180 sec each set	3×3 (10 yd)	120 sec each rep/180 sec each set	2×3 (10 yd)	120 sec each rep/180 sec each set
	Three-point acceleration start*	None	NA	2×3 (10 yd)	120 sec each rep/180 sec each set	3×3 (15 yd)	120 sec each rep/180 sec each set	2×2 (15 yd)	120 sec each rep/180 sec each set
	Overhead throw	2×3 (8-12 lb)	60 to 90 sec	3×3 (8-12 lb)	60 to 90 sec	3×3 (8-12 lb)	60 to 90 sec	3×1 (8-12 lb)	60 to 90 sec

WB = walk back

* Rest: 180 seconds between sets plus an additional 60 seconds for every 10 yards sprinted

Conclusion

Coaches and athletes should place major emphasis on acceleration work during combine preparation, as well as during the off-season in general. Acceleration is the foundational movement skill in sprint-based field sports such as football. Developing a football player's acceleration technique will not only boost his marks in combine tests such as the 40-yard dash but will also vastly improve his game-day performance on the field once the season starts.

Acceleration is perhaps the most fundamental general movement skill, but even an athlete who accelerates well would have a tough time succeeding in football if he lacked the ability to quickly decelerate and then redirect his sprinting in another direction. Football players need to efficiently transition between different movement planes to perform successfully at a combine or on the field. Chapter 8 addresses this skill, which is generally known as agility.

CHAPTER 8

Agility and Deceleration

Football, like all other field-based repeat sprint sports, is ultimately governed by locomotion. A highlight-worthy catch, for example, may be credited to the player's incredible hand–eye coordination—but his catching ability is ultimately less important than the movement skills he uses to put himself in a position to make the play.

These movement skills are collectively referred to as the athlete's *multidirectional ability*: his aptitude in moving forward, backward, side-to-side, and rotationally as needed to achieve his desired movement tasks. But moving well in all three cardinal planes is not enough; the athlete's level of *agility*—his ability to change directions in response to external stimuli—is the true difference-maker.

Agility requires the athlete to notice and interpret a relevant visual or auditory cue, then make snap decisions about where to go and how best to get there. For example: A defensive back who jumps a route to break up a pass on a critical third down was able to recognize something in his opponent—perhaps a specific formation, or a motioning receiver—thanks to preparation in film sessions and practices. Just anticipating the play is not enough; he must be able to move his body quickly and efficiently enough to make the play. Sloppy general movement mechanics could prevent an otherwise smart and talented player from reaching the next level because all the football IQ in the world cannot make up for poor agility.

With other factors being equal, players win their positional battles by creating slightly better leverage, or taking a marginally better step, than their opponents. To become more agile and win these battles, a player needs to train his multidirectional ability on a nuts-and-bolts level, then practice using his movement skills in gamelike scenarios. This involves learning how to efficiently manipulate his center of mass during a cut (figure 8.1), thereby reducing his movement time and energy cost.

When an athlete learns and uses better locomotion strategies than his competition, it can make a major difference both on the field and in combine testing. One could compare this to old computer software competing against newer and better versions. Quality, focused training of smaller movement components can help an athlete to upgrade his movement "software," while his peers who run through an ever-changing gauntlet of agility drills continue to exhibit bugs.

Teams at the college and professional levels search for players who can demonstrate agility skills quantitatively (with excellent testing times) and qualitatively (subjectively assessed). Although this book focuses mainly on football combine preparation, agility training is the same for any sport or event. The sport-specific goals and stimuli may be different, but the underlying movement mechanics are universal.

Figure 8.1   Change of direction (COD) skill levels are primarily determined by how well the athlete can control and position his center of mass relative to his base of support.

Biomechanics of Agility and Deceleration

Every human movement is a learned skill, and the finer motor tasks associated with football are complex. However, all these sport-specific tasks are underpinned by general locomotion patterns. The humans who achieve success in a given movement skill generally display similar tendencies in their approach, and research-based technical models have emerged from these trends. Athletes stand to improve most when they first learn discrete movement skills, then practice responding to external stimuli by assembling these skills into a cohesive pattern to achieve a movement goal (such as a linebacker visually recognizing the ball carrier's change in direction, and adjusting his own movement path to reach the ball carrier as quickly as possible).

Players are constantly blending these different types of locomotion, but it would be wishful thinking to assume that an athlete has developed a movement pattern correctly just because his strategy gets him to the target quickly. Most football players—and athletes in general—will exhibit some dysfunctions or asymmetries. These are usually revealed through movement compensations or recruitment pattern adjustments that the athlete makes to cover for inhibited muscles or joints. These compensations usually occur subconsciously or unconsciously, so athletes' movement mechanics can benefit greatly from a coach's eye.

Terminology

Movement skills are often misunderstood because of their subtle categorical differences. *Agility* is difficult to define in words, although several authors have proposed frameworks for describing agility and its related skills. Although making semantic distinctions may not get everyone's blood pumping like running a 60-yard shuttle does, it's important to define the agility-related terms discussed in this chapter because of their complex, interconnected relationships.

Sometimes athletic qualities such as change of direction (COD), agility, multidirectional ability, speed, and quickness are mistaken as synonyms. In fact they are distinct, interrelated descriptions of an athlete's movement capabilities. For example, a change-of-direction drill is not always an agility drill per se; a fast athlete isn't always a quick one, and agility encompasses multidirectional ability, yet the reverse isn't necessarily true.

A distinction must first be made between two terms that are sometimes used interchangeably: *multidirectional ability* and *change of direction* (COD).

Change of direction is an elusive term to define simply because it encompasses multiple skills and their application in a wide array of contexts. Scholars generally define COD as an athlete's quickness in decelerating and then reaccelerating in another direction, and often in a different plane of motion. The National Strength and Conditioning Association (NSCA) defines COD as "skills and abilities needed to change movement direction, velocity, or modes" (DeWeese and Nimphius 2016). Thus, one could think of COD as the nuts and bolts of agility.

Many practitioners and researchers use *change of direction* interchangeably with *multidirectional ability* in speech or writing. In this chapter, *multidirectional ability* describes an athlete's skill in navigating all directions and planes of movement. COD can be used in the same sense as multidirectional ability to describe movement quality or, in a narrower context, to describe skill in a smaller-scale movement, such as the ability to make a specific type of cut or transition.

Changes of direction occur constantly in sprint-based field sports, and with varying degrees of intricacy. The athlete's task sequence could be simple, like sprinting for 10 yards, making a sharp 180-degree cut, then sprinting right back to his starting point. But situational demands could require a much more complicated string of movements, such as shuffling left for three steps, decelerating, turning and sprinting to the right, decelerating, then crossing over into a sprint aimed 45 degrees back and to the left.

Some of the NFL combine's general athleticism tests measure different combinations of sprinting, deceleration, change of direction, and maneuverability; however, they are not agility drills per se. (Even though one of them, the pro agility drill, even has the word *agility* in its name.)

Understanding Agility

Agility is expressed as "a rapid whole-body movement with change of velocity of direction in response to a stimulus" (Sheppard and Young 2006). Therefore, agility *is* change-of-direction ability, but the major distinction is the stimulus–response aspect; the change of direction now includes a reactive component, which requires the "constant integration between perceptual cognitive ability and physical movement throughout the game" (Spiteri et al. 2015).

If *change of direction* can describe either specific skills or COD ability in a closed or isolated setting, then *agility* is the integrated application of movement skills within an open environment to achieve a desired outcome. An agile athlete "is able to control the individual components and manipulate the degrees of freedom of the movement to meet the demands of the situation" (Spiteri and Nimphius 2013).

Agility certainly includes sprinting ability, especially acceleration. An athlete could be skilled in using the most efficient possible frontal plane locomotion and bridging movements, but if he cannot accelerate well, then he is not truly agile. Several of the NFL combine's general athleticism tests (chapter 3) and position-specific tests (chapters 4 and 5) assess an athlete's agility, yet they are not necessarily as valid in determining his pure COD skill. Many agility and COD assessments are biased to sprinting ability, meaning that an attempt "to truly measure one's ability to decelerate and subsequently reaccelerate in a new direction is often tangled within one's ability to perform straight line running" (Nimphius et al. 2013). A better sprinter, the logic follows, could stop and cut like he is caught in quicksand, but then accelerate like a bolt of lightning; if he can accelerate well enough, it effectively masks sloppy and inefficient changes of direction because he still records a good time on agility tests.

Training Deceleration

The inclusion of the word *deceleration* in the chapter title was a conscious choice, intended to emphasize the skill's importance. If acceleration means speeding up, then deceleration means slowing down. Perhaps this simplicity is what causes many coaches to neglect training in deceleration; they contend that if the athlete is strong enough to absorb the forces of deceleration, he is competent without giving the skill itself much practice.

However, deceleration is a neuromuscular skill that requires practice and coaching. Assuming an athlete's decelerative competence would be a major mistake for any coach. Overreliance on connective tissue instead of the neuromuscular system when "hitting the brakes" is like driving on a mountain road by using the guardrail instead of the steering wheel: It will result in serious wear and tear, and possibly injury.

Effective acceleration maximizes propulsive forces and minimizes braking forces; therefore, effective deceleration demands the opposite. Muscle work shifts from primarily concentric action during acceleration to more eccentric action while decelerating.

To accelerate, the athlete shifts his center of mass (COM) over his ground contact point into a 45-degree anterior lean, striking on the ball of his foot during each stride. Then, as he decelerates, the athlete reverses his body lean back to above or behind his feet; he now contacts the ground heel-to-toe with a partially flexed knee.

Strength and conditioning practitioners tend to focus heavily (with good reason) on strength training in the weight room. Effective training programs designed for long-term athletic development (LTAD) promote strength adaptations such as increased muscle mass, neural drive, and tendon stiffness, among others. These neuromuscular and connective tissue improvements are vital to building a robust athlete who can decelerate safely and effectively. But such physical adaptations do not guarantee that he can perform the skill properly even at full strength, let alone under fatigue during a game or testing event.

Combine preparation specialists can also fall prey to this trap because their reputation is largely based on how much they can reduce players' 40-yard dash times. This test receives the bulk of scout and fan attention, so practitioners who train athletes for this event tend to focus mainly on concentric force production. The practitioner's duty, however, is to serve the athlete's best interests; decelerative ability translates to other combine drills, and especially to football itself.

Lateral Deceleration: The Hockey Stop

Efficient frontal plane change of direction depends on how well an athlete can perceive and manipulate his center of mass relative to his base of support. Multidirectional ability depends primarily on several small, but critical, details: the athlete's weight distribution on his feet, the angle of his shins relative to the ground, and his ability to bend at the hips and to dissociate his hips and trunk.

When a shuffling athlete needs to stop, he should do it strategically. In this case, his weight should lean back toward his inside foot, away from the direction he is traveling. In this the athlete uses gravity to aid in his deceleration. He shifts his center of mass (roughly around his belly button area) unevenly over his base to help fight against his own moving inertia. For example, if a player shuffling to his left suddenly decelerates, his weight should be favored over the outside edge of his inside foot, in this case the right edge of his right foot. The athlete initially uses the left edge of his right foot to push left laterally, then anchors on the outside (right) edge of that same pushing foot when he decelerates. The ending position resembles the angled position of a hockey player making an abrupt stop on the ice, so coaches often informally call this technique "the hockey stop."

Maneuverability

Athletic changes of direction can include more than abrupt cuts and sharp angles. An agility-related term, *maneuverability* (Nimphius 2014), describes how well an athlete maintains velocity during a wider change of direction (figure 8.2). A running back's wheel route, for example, takes a winding path; he briefly sprints upfield, then curves sharply out toward the sideline and banks hard back inside once more to sprint straight down the field.

The L-drill (chapter 3) is a phenomenal closed maneuverability drill due to its emphasis on curvilinear

Figure 8.2 Curvilinear sprinting, or rounding a corner while maintaining or gaining sprinting speed, is also referred to as *maneuverability*.

sprinting. Certain positional drills (e.g., route trees, outside pass rush) also stress maneuverability in a sport-specific context.

Strength Qualities in COD

Research examining strength's integral role in COD ability has found that the stronger subjects examined were "able to produce a significantly faster post-COD stride velocity and greater vertical and horizontal braking force, vertical propulsive force, vertical braking and propulsive impulse, angle of peak braking and propulsive force application, increased knee flexion and hip abduction angle when compared to weaker subjects" (Spiteri et al. 2013).

That is not to say, however, that strength does not also play an important role in developing agility. Improving an athlete's rate of force acceptance (RFA) requires building strength in all three muscle action phases: concentric, eccentric, and isometric. The latter two qualities are especially important in RFA. Researchers note that athletes who perform faster in change-of-direction tests also tend to exhibit greater eccentric and isometric strength, allowing them "to complete the direction change within a significantly shorter braking time enabling a faster transition into the propulsive phase of the movement, [while] increasing propulsive force application" (DeWeese and Nimphius 2016). A stronger athlete will, by nature, display better COD ability than a weaker peer with comparable technical skills.

PREP LIKE A PRO: COD DEFICIT

Researchers have developed a variable to evaluate athletes' change-of-direction ability relative to sprinting speed. The individualized metric, known as *COD deficit*, describes how much time one-directional change adds to a pure sprint over an equivalent distance. Contrasting the athlete's performance in linear sprinting with change-of-direction drills effectively removes sprinting from the equation and evaluates an athlete's COD skills in isolation.

Perhaps contrary to common belief, scientific explorations of COD deficit have revealed that athletes who are "capable of sprinting faster in a linear course and performing better in strength-power tests often have challenges in transferring these superior abilities to specialized COD maneuvers…. [T]hese findings are in line with previous research, suggesting that the development of COD performance depends almost exclusively on specific training means" (Loturco et al. 2018). Thus, a training program focused solely on lifting weights will not maximize agility development. Movement skill training is just as important for combine testing success as strength and power work, if not more so.

Teaching Locomotion as a Language

Many football combine tests can be rehearsed down to the smallest detail, but the true question is whether a football player can apply these skills in the ultimate open environment: a game during which he will need to make split-second movement decisions by reacting to what he sees.

The football combine drills that best display true agility are those in which an athlete reacts to a designated coach or scout's signals to make a change of direction (for more details, refer to the positional drills highlighted in chapters 4 and 5). These are the combine's most open drills, where scouts and coaches analyze how well players can solve reactive movement problems that mimic position-specific demands. To prepare for these demands, players should approach movement training as if they were learning a second language.

Conceptually, movement training has many similarities to learning a second language. One might argue that this is not so because athletes can already move. But for most athletes, the challenge is learning to move *optimally*, to use the best possible technique given a specific scenario and the athlete's own anomalies.

The Landow Performance movement coaching model draws heavily from second language development pedagogy because learning to move well in all three planes (sagittal, frontal, transverse) closely resembles the process of acquiring a second language.

New language students typically begin by studying simple vocabulary, verb tenses, and grammar. Next, they rehearse these basic components as teachers begin testing their ability to combine language chunks into sentences. The goal is to progress to free-flowing conversations in which students must operate in varied contexts using their linguistic tools.

Closed Versus Open Drills

Similar to the language student, an untrained athlete should be taught correct posture, position, placement, and patterning for individual movement patterns (e.g., a first acceleration step, or a lateral shuffling deceleration). These micro-level skills serve as the building blocks for macro-level agility development, in much the same way that a new language learner uses syntax and grammar to begin creating sentences. The coach can then gradually increase the level of complexity by introducing change-of-direction drills that use preplanned routes and strategies.

As another example, consider closed versus open movement drills. In a closed drill, the athlete is provided with a preplanned movement strategy meant to help him learn the skill gradually in a controlled environment. As the athlete's ability improves, his coach begins making drills more open—that is, the athlete must move in reaction to external stimuli. This added challenge marks the transition from pure change-of-direction training to agility training.

Some of the drills in this book distill a movement's posture, position, placement, and patterning into small chunks. But the progressions are designed so that athletes must ultimately learn to assemble these chunks into movement paths.

The Landow Performance movement coaching strategy mirrors language learning philosophies that stress the need to acquire "intensive" knowledge that is "held unconsciously and can only be verbalized if it is made explicit. It is accessed rapidly and easily and thus is available for use in rapid, fluent communication" (Prabhu 1987).

During a well-coached movement training session, athletes groove quality basic movement patterns into their nervous systems. These patterns in isolation are athletic movement's intensive knowledge; they form the toolbox from which a football player works to solve movement problems on the field.

Studying intensive language knowledge allows one to "acquire both a rich repertoire of formulaic expressions, which caters to fluency, and a rule-based competence consisting of knowledge of specific grammatical rules, which cater to complexity and accuracy" (Skehan 1998). In combine testing (and in football), successful performance coaches will first establish intensive movement knowledge for athletes and then give them the autonomy to use that framework much like an oral examination in a language class.

Agility research categorizes a training session's difficulty by contextual interference (CI), which describes the degree to which a drill's difficulty increases as two or more tasks are integrated. Agility progressions can be described as low CI or high CI, depending on task complexity; some researchers recommend allowing novice athletes to work on simple movement patterns in isolation with low-CI drills, then adding and combining other movements to increase contextual interference (Holmberg 2009).

Second language learning researchers stress the importance of learning formulaic expressions. According to Skehan (1998), those learning a second language need "a rich repertoire of formulaic expressions, which caters to fluency, and a rule-based competence consisting of knowledge of specific grammatical rules, which cater to complexity and accuracy." If movement is indeed a language-like mode of human expression, then coaches could consider fundamental locomotion skills to be the formulaic expressions of movement, taught with basic drilling such as wall drills, shuffle progressions, and so on.

Aiming for Unconscious Competence

Any athlete or language learner's motor skill development progress can be charted along four stages. *Unconscious incompetence* is the earliest stage, meaning that one performs the skill wrong while not understanding how it should be correctly performed. At this level the athlete looks clueless and cannot comprehend what his coach wants.

Conscious incompetence is the next developmental stage for motor skills. The skill is still being performed incorrectly during practice, but the athlete now knows what he is supposed to do. When an athlete begins displaying competence but still needs to concentrate on technique while performing the skill, he has entered the *conscious competence* motor skill development phase.

If the athlete continues to receive good coaching and practices the skill with effort and intention, he will eventually reach *unconscious competence*. At this point, he can execute a skill consistently, to near perfection, and without a conscious thought. Second language learners aim for unconscious competence as well. Like second language learners, young athletes must practice movement's intensive knowledge to improve their athletic ability. They should aim to build enough confidence in their movement skills that they can navigate contextual interferences with unconscious competence.

Shuffle Progression

Shuffling (like sprinting) may seem a relatively straightforward task for football players, as they have all shuffled before in practice, workouts, and (for most of them) games. But two football players might look completely different in their shuffling technique due to unconscious anomalies in posture, position, placement, and patterning. Athletes need to learn a clear strategy for moving in the frontal plane before they learn to change direction in the frontal plane.

Successful shuffling begins with a good athletic position. Landow Performance coaches teach athletes the commonly accepted athletic position standard. When finding an athletic position (figure 8.3), the player moves his feet to roughly shoulder width apart and points his toes straight ahead, lowering his hips down and back to roughly quarter-squat depth. His back remains flat with his chest and eyes up, and his hands remain free at his sides.

To shuffle most efficiently, the athlete pushes off the inside edge of his trailing foot for each step, then places his lead foot down to quickly gather his inside foot and push again (figure 8.4). In order to shuffle to his right, for example, the athlete pushes off the right edge of his left foot to laterally extend his left leg and project his body sideways to the right. As his right foot makes landing contact on the ground, the athlete immediately draws his left foot back underneath his midline to push once more.

Figure 8.3   Setup in an athletic position.

Figure 8.4   Shuffling: *(a)* push off inside edge of trailing foot; *(b)* inside foot gathers under athlete for next shuffle.

LATERAL SQUAT PUSH

Coaches would be wise to instruct athletes in the skill of shuffling before delving into their foot placement and weight shift during shuffling changes of direction. The lateral squat push drill does this, serving as the frontal plane equivalent of an A-march.

Starting in a low athletic stance, the athlete waits for a predetermined visual or auditory cue from the coach. At the coach's signal to step left, he immediately lifts his left foot and moves one step to his left by extending his right leg, placing his left foot on the ground, and immediately bringing his right foot back underneath him (figure 8.5). The athlete has now restored his original athletic stance, but he is shifted one step to his left.

Figure 8.5 Lateral squat push: *(a)* left foot lift; *(b)* right leg extension; *(c)* left foot landing while right foot gathers underneath for next push.

This drill helps athletes to better ingrain the correct push–gather shuffling sequence while challenging them to maintain a good bend at the knee and hip throughout. More importantly, it does so without progressing the skill too quickly; some athletes will spend many hours rehearsing change-of-direction drills without addressing the fact that they are shuffling incorrectly in the first place.

The drill can start fully reactive (taking each step on the coach's cue), with the coach allowing the athlete to move at a progressively quicker pace according to comfort level. Drill intensity can continue to increase with competency until the athlete can complete a full-speed shuffle without a breakdown in technique. Complete each 10-yard drill for 3 to 5 repetitions on each side.

FIVE-YARD SHUFFLE TO DECELERATION

This drill targets the specific COD skill of lateral deceleration, a vital but deceptively simple skill. Such plainness can fool coaches into taking deceleration for granted and falling into the trap of overly complex movement sessions.

Some might dismiss the need to repeat easy drills like a five-yard shuffle to deceleration drill, contending instead that more difficult drilling is required to optimally condition the skill. While this is true, athletes also need opportunities to focus purely on the isolated skill of lateral deceleration. Practicing deceleration only within the context of elaborate agility drills will create too much chaos for athletes to hone individual skills.

The athlete begins in an athletic position. At the coach's cue, he shuffles for 5 yards then stops in the lateral deceleration position with his weight shifted over the outside edge of his foot and his shins angling back toward the direction from which he came (figure 8.6). These drills will not look exactly the same for all athletes because of individual differences. The athlete completes 2 or 3 sets of 3 repetitions shuffling each direction for 5 yards.

Figure 8.6   Five-yard shuffle to deceleration: *(a)* shuffle and *(b)* deceleration.

FIVE-YARD SHUFFLE DOWN AND BACK TO DECELERATION

Once an athlete has practiced isolated lateral deceleration, the next progression is to make the drill more dynamic. This drill requires a change of direction followed by an opposite-side deceleration.

The athlete begins in an athletic stance, and at the coach's signal shuffles 5 yards to his right. After 5 yards, he anchors on the outside edge of his inside foot and smoothly transitions into a shuffle back to his left (figure 8.7). After reaching his initial starting line, he decelerates laterally and holds this position briefly. The athlete completes 2 or 3 sets of 3 repetitions facing each way, for 5 yards down and back.

Figure 8.7 Five-yard shuffle down and back to deceleration transition.

SHUFFLE TO REACTIVE DECELERATION

Building the skills of shuffling and lateral deceleration requires careful rehearsal in closed drills. But as an athlete develops competence in simpler drills, he must be challenged with more open drills to continue progressing. The shuffle to reactive deceleration drill could be considered an example of a temporal agility drill, structured for spatial confidence and temporal uncertainty (Sheppard and Young 2006); the athlete's skill execution is preplanned, but he is uncertain of when he will be required to decelerate.

Just like the previous drills, the athlete lines up in an athletic position and, at the coach's cue, begins to shuffle in one direction. Now the athlete continues shuffling until he hears or sees the preplanned cue to stop, at which point he decelerates and holds a stopped position with inside lean. The athlete will check his feet and weight distribution, and make any necessary changes before relaxing to stand up and walk back to the starting line. If the athlete is in between steps when he hears or sees the cue to stop, he does not simply halt in his tracks with his body in a compromised position. Instead, he takes an extra step if necessary to find a better body position and lean. The athlete completes 1 to 3 sets of 2 to 3 repetitions, prioritizing his lateral deceleration technique over how quickly he stops.

SHUFFLE WITH REACTIVE CHANGE OF DIRECTION

This progression's next level of challenge after a reactive deceleration is a reactive change of direction. Now instead of stopping at the coach's cue, the athlete remains continuously shuffling throughout the drill, changing directions at each signal. The athlete starts the drill lined up in an athletic position. At his coach's signal, the athlete begins shuffling in the indicated direction. Then, at random intervals, the coach will give the visual or auditory signal for the athlete to quickly decelerate and start shuffling back the other way. The athlete will remain facing the same direction for the duration of the drill. The emphasis is on quick, smooth frontal plane change of direction. Perform 1 to 2 sets of the drill for 1 to 3 repetitions of 6 to 12 seconds, allowing for ample rest of at least 30 to 60 seconds between reps (depending on the drill's time duration).

Carioca Progression

By their very nature, agility training sessions must include a significant number of decelerations. These repeated high-force eccentric muscle actions, which have been found to create more muscle damage than concentric or isometric muscle actions (Sorichter, Puschendorf, and Mair 1999), add up quickly to fatigue athletes.

This carioca series is an effective way to bring down the physical intensity of an agility workout while still improving movement capabilities. It can serve as a nice flush to the legs for active recovery after all the hard cutting involved in other agility work. These are slightly different variations of similar drills, which is by design: The progression helps athletes better understand how to control their bodies in space. These drills provide an overlapping saturation of the motor skills involved in the target movement.

Carioca drills may not seem pertinent to football combine training, but they are instrumental in teaching the crossover step, a movement strategy players must use for changes of direction in many of their positional drills, especially during execution of the pro agility (5-10-5) drill (described in chapter 3).

The crossover step is a foundational transverse bridging movement, and its complexity makes it hard to master. Decelerating and repositioning one's body to reaccelerate is situation-dependent in sport, based on variables such as speed and weight distribution. Many athletes are taught to simply swing their leg in a wide circle in front of their body, which can result in a plethora of issues over time if the skill is taught incorrectly.

In order to break bad habits and learn the crossover step properly, Landow Performance combine athletes work a carioca progression to build the skill in chunks. The progression includes variants of the classic carioca movement pattern in which the athlete moves laterally, alternating his trailing foot placement in front of and behind his lead foot with each foot contact. Foot strike during this progression should be relatively full-footed, with an emphasis on using the inside edge of the foot for leverage.

CROSSOVER STEP

The crossover step (figure 8.8) could be described as a half-carioca; the athlete's trailing foot moves to his midline before pushing out into the ground. Instead of bringing that same foot back behind his lead foot on the next step—the hallmark stepping pattern of any carioca drill—the athlete instead repeats the crossover step. He does not reach with this step but seeks instead to reach his midline before pushing laterally again.

The athlete stands straight, ready to move in the frontal plane. He keeps his hips square and remains tall as he brings a slightly bent leg across his body and toward his midline, then pushes into the ground away from his body to propel himself laterally to the right, moving at a brisk jogging pace. As the athlete pushes away with his left foot, his right foot contacts the ground for support; the leading step shouldn't be so short as to disrupt the athlete's rhythm or balance or so long that the athlete is reaching out wide with his right foot. The leading leg supports the athlete's weight as the trailing foot moves back into place for another lateral push.

An athlete may open up his trailing foot during the movement, which typically indicates that his hip is opening as he pushes off. This usually occurs when he is overstriding and trying to maximize the push from his trailing leg. The emphasis in this drill should be on fluid movement with minimal hip rotation.

The arms swing front to back contralaterally (opposite-side arm and leg move together) for this and all carioca drills. Just as in sprinting, the athlete's arm swing during these drills will match the rhythm of his feet contacting the ground. Movement variations requiring the athlete's foot to spend more time on the ground will also need a longer arm swing to match up the timing. The athlete repeats the sequence of pushing from his crossover foot rhythmically, taking care to push into the ground instead of merely swinging his leg out into abduction like a peg leg. The athlete completes this drill for 2 or 3 sets of 3 repetitions per side, covering 10 yards per repetition.

Figure 8.8 Crossover step: *(a)* The athlete steps to his midline and *(b)* pushes out against the ground to move laterally.

CARIOCA SMALL STEP WITHOUT ROTATION

As the athlete displays competency and understanding with the crossover step, he can begin to work through the carioca drill progression. The first version of this drill is primarily concerned with foot quickness and placement. Footwork is the same as for the crossover step drill, except in a carioca the athlete alternates strides by taking a crossover step in front of his leading foot and then a cross-under step behind his leading foot (figure 8.9). He sets up in an athletic stance and begins at the coach's cue, moving out to the side while taking quick and precise steps on the balls of his feet and keeping his hips pointed straight ahead. His body should be slowly covering ground laterally across the turf, while his feet make quick and successive carioca repetitions. The athlete completes 2 to 3 repetitions of 15 yards each way for 1 to 2 sets, walking back slowly between repetitions as active rest and taking 60 to 90 seconds of rest between sets.

Figure 8.9 Carioca small step without rotation: *(a)* crossover step in front of leading foot; *(b)* cross-under step behind leading foot.

CARIOCA SMALL STEP WITH ROTATION

The carioca series helps athletes improve their ability to "bridge" between linear and lateral movement patterns. During the crossover step drill and carioca without rotation, the athlete is reinforcing the basic foot pattern of a crossover bridging movement. Adding hip rotation into the small step carioca drill helps further this learning process by involving more of the athlete's kinetic chain.

From an athletic position, the athlete starts to slowly cover ground sideways with the same fast-paced carioca foot contact pattern (crossover step followed by a cross-under step). Now, the athlete's hips should swivel forward and

Figure 8.10   Carioca small step with rotation: *(a)* crossover step in front of leading foot; *(b)* cross-under step behind leading foot.

back with each step: forward with each crossover step, then back with each cross-under step (figure 8.10).

Athletes should display symmetrical rotation on both sides during this drill. Most will have a strongly biased rotation toward the direction in which they are moving instead of achieving a near 180-degree swivel. This lack of hip turn causes them to lose out on the beneficial recoil effect generated by muscles involved in the stretch reflex. The athlete is not overreaching with his step but instead works on how quickly he can rotate and create a "snap" of the hips using elastic energy. This snapping action is what will best influence his bridging ability when changing directions. The athlete completes 2 or 3 sets of 3 repetitions in each direction for 15 yards, walking back between reps for active rest.

CARIOCA KNEE PUNCH WITHOUT ROTATION

The knee is often a fixation in coaching the crossover step. The carioca progression starts by teaching basic foot patterning, then adds in some of the hip coiling and uncoiling action. At the next stage the latter part is removed, with the focus returning once again to foot patterning, with one key caveat: The goal is not just to move with quick feet but to also punch the knee up with each crossover step in the carioca pattern (figure 8.11). The hips remain closed off in this drill, so the athlete does not have to think about too many things at once. He begins in an athletic position and moves at a similar pace as before, but now each crossover consists of punching the knee and driving the foot quickly back down to the ground. The athlete will complete 1 to 2 sets of 2 to 3 repetitions for 15 yards each way, using the walk back to the starting line as active rest.

Figure 8.11 Carioca knee punch without rotation: *(a)* crossover step in front of leading foot; *(b)* cross-under step behind leading foot.

CARIOCA KNEE PUNCH WITH ROTATION (BRIDGING MOVEMENT)

The capstone drill of the carioca progression blends all aspects of the crossover bridging movement that were trained in the first four drills: foot patterning, hip swivel, and knee punch (figure 8.12). This is the most sport-specific of the drills because it allows the athlete to repeatedly practice the crossover step with virtually the same mechanics he would need to transition between different movement planes. The distance remains the same, but now the athlete is moving faster and putting more force into the ground with his crossover step. He performs 1 to 3 sets of 3 to 4 repetitions, traveling 15 yards each direction and walking back between repetitions for active rest.

Figure 8.12 Carioca knee punch with rotation: *(a)* crossover step in front of leading foot; *(b)* cross-under step behind leading foot.

Deceleration Progression

Lateral deceleration, the "hockey stop" described earlier in this chapter, is a critical skill for COD ability. But athletes don't just decelerate when they move side-to-side; they must be able to decelerate from sprinting or backpedaling, too. This skill, linear deceleration, is woefully undertrained and often taken for granted. When athletes are unaware of this skill or how to properly integrate it with other movement patterns, they can decelerate in ways that both hinder performance and endanger long-term joint health.

Practitioners must make sure that athletes do not rely too heavily on passive tissue such as ligaments and bones to decelerate. If a sprinting athlete simply jams his heel into the ground and expects his foot, knee, and hip structures to absorb all his inertia, the wear and tear on his joints will almost certainly lead to some type of injury or pathology. The athlete must be taught how to decelerate and change direction in a safe and efficient manner in a variety of directions.

Athletes can use the deceleration progression in this book to learn and practice the different ways they may need to decelerate while sprinting or back-pedaling. Rehearsing these skills in isolation helps athletes to gain competence and confidence for when the skills are needed in other COD and agility drills.

SUBMAXIMAL ACCELERATION TO BILATERAL DECELERATION

In a classic, isolated linear deceleration, the athlete slows down evenly on both feet and comes to a stop in an athletic position with even feet pointed straight ahead. In this drill, the athlete begins sprinting at a submaximal pace managed by his coach, based on desired drill intensity. At a predetermined point, he begins to decelerate by shifting his type and direction of force application. Instead of pushing behind his center of mass with concentric forces to increase velocity, the athlete now applies eccentric force in front of his center of mass to negate his sprinting inertia. His lean shifts from forward to backward, and his feet now contact the ground in a heel-to-toe fashion (figure 8.13). The athlete completes 1 to 2 sets of 4 to 5 decelerations, with a slow walk back between repetitions as active rest.

Figure 8.13   Submaximal acceleration to bilateral deceleration: *(a)* Athlete runs upright. *(b)* To start deceleration, the athlete leans back and applies eccentric force in front of his center of mass. *(c)* Athlete finishes deceleration in an athletic position.

SUBMAXIMAL ACCELERATION TO SPLIT-STANCE DECELERATION

The split-stance deceleration allows athletes to practice decelerating heavily on one leg to allow for a change in direction. The drill is executed precisely like the bilateral deceleration, with the athlete reaching a pace at which he can safely decelerate, then performing the same heel-toe stepping sequence and ending at the same squat depth; the only difference is that now most of his weight is on one squatting leg, with the other leg behind his hips as in a lunge position (figure 8.14). He performs 2 to 3 repetitions on each leg for 1 to 2 sets, walking back slowly between reps for rest.

Figure 8.14 Submaximal acceleration to split-stance deceleration.

CYCLICAL ACCELERATION TO DECELERATION

The previous submaximal acceleration to deceleration drills are designed to improve skill quality. However, deceleration involves high forces and tissue stress, and it must be conditioned so that the athlete can repeat the skill without sacrificing too much quality under fatigue.

Facing forward, the athlete begins a slow, rhythmic run. At 5 yards, he decelerates into a split-stance position. After establishing eccentric and isometric control in stopping his forward momentum, he remains facing the same direction and immediately begins backpedaling at the same light pace (figure 8.15a). After reaching his starting position, the athlete loads seamlessly back into a split-stance deceleration position with the same foot forward (figure 8.15b). This position is slightly different than the forward-running split-stance deceleration because now to decelerate from a backpedal, his center of mass shifts more forward. The drill allows the athlete to groove proper single-leg deceleration mechanics, teaching him to focus on recruiting the neuromuscular system to complete the task, rather than expecting passive tissue to do all the work. Complete 2 or 3 repetitions per side, and perform each repetition continuously for 15-20 seconds.

Figure 8.15   Cyclical acceleration to deceleration: *(a)* backpedal; *(b)* reverse deceleration position.

CYCLICAL ACCELERATION TO PIVOT

This drill works at the same pace as the cyclical acceleration to deceleration. The difference is that now the deceleration is more transverse in nature, rather than being predominantly sagittal as in the previous drill.

The athlete moves at the same light running pace as in the previous drill. As he reaches 5 yards, he pivots to place most of his weight on the right edge of his right foot, allowing his left hip and leg to swivel around this pivot point so that he is facing to his right (figure 8.16) in the lateral deceleration position (hockey stop) described earlier in this chapter. The athlete then reverses back out of the pivot, backpedals, and decelerates into a split stance with his right foot forward. He completes 2 or 3 repetitions per side and performs each repetition continuously for 15 to 20 seconds.

Figure 8.16   Cyclical acceleration to pivot: *(a)* pivot; *(b)* swivel; *(c)* deceleration.

Types of Transitions

Transverse bridging movements are critical to multidirectional ability because they are the means by which athletes change planes of motion. However, they are not all applicable or advantageous in every context. The most useful transitions are the jab step, rhythm step (or false step), crossover step, and drop step.

The jab step (figure 8.17) is used to reposition the body for acceleration coming out of a cut. An athlete who decelerates while shuffling, for example, will briefly angle his body back inside. To transition out of this decelerated position, he allows his outside foot to pivot slightly and pushes hard off his outside leg while taking a "jab" with his inside foot into a front-side acceleration position. This jab step should match the rest of his body angle, so his silhouette would not look too different than that of sprinting acceleration. The rhythm (false) step (figure 8.18) and the drop step work in much the same way by setting up for a crossover step.

The crossover step (figure 8.19) is the transverse plane bridging movement that completes the athlete's transition between directions or modes of movement. The crossover step can only be deployed effectively when the athlete has a favorable weight distribution and body position. The athlete must use a jab step, rhythm (false) step, or drop step (figure 8.20) to jab his inside foot toward his intended new direction while pushing off his outside leg. Then, as his inside foot drives back into the ground to accelerate, the athlete crosses his outside foot and hip around just like in the carioca knee punch with hip rotation drill. The athlete uses this crossover step to finish turning his body as he reaccelerates out of his cut.

Figure 8.17   Jab step.

Figure 8.18   Rhythm step (false step).

Figure 8.19   Crossover step.

Figure 8.20   Drop step.

Blending Movement Skills

Now that the athlete has learned the basic chunks of movement, he can begin to assemble them. Many drills are possible, all stemming from a strong technical foundation. Described here are some classic COD skills to practice before building more advanced drills. These drills can be performed at different levels of openness depending on what the athlete needs.

LATERAL SHUFFLE TO ACCELERATION

In the lateral shuffle to acceleration, the athlete transitions from a shuffle into a sprint in the same direction (figure 8.21). The athlete shuffles to a predetermined landmark or until he receives a coach's signal, and then he opens with a false or rhythm step to sprint the remaining distance. The athlete completes 2 sets of 4 repetitions in each direction.

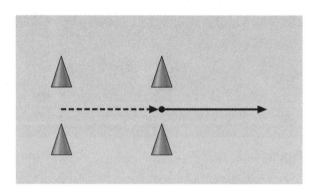

Figure 8.21   Lateral shuffle to acceleration.

LATERAL SHUFFLE TO 45-DEGREE ACCELERATION

For the lateral shuffle to 45-degree acceleration, the athlete shuffles and then opens 45 degrees and sprints either with or against the grain (figure 8.22), meaning that either he keeps his momentum and opens up in the same direction he was shuffling or he fully decelerates and then reaccelerates. The two styles will require different approaches; cutting with the grain allows for less deceleration and more of a rhythm step transition, whereas cutting against the grain is more likely to feature a jab step. The athlete completes 1 to 3 sets of 2 to 4 reps in each direction for the desired drill.

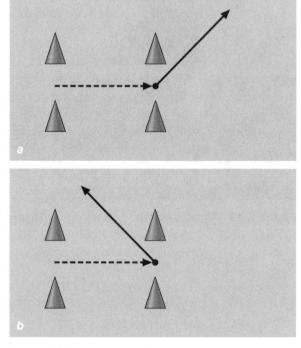

Figure 8.22   Lateral shuffle to 45-degree acceleration: (a) going with the grain; (b) going against the grain.

LATERAL SHUFFLE TO RETURN ACCELERATION

For the lateral shuffle to return acceleration, the athlete shuffles, decelerates laterally, and bridges into linear acceleration, returning along the same line of movement (figure 8.23). This drill can be made more open or closed by making the directional change planned or reactive to suit the athlete's level of competency in the skill. The

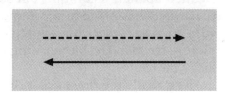

Figure 8.23   Lateral shuffle to return acceleration.

athlete decelerates, takes a jab step, and then takes a crossover step to transition into a sprint back in the direction from which he came. Perform for 1 to 2 sets of 2 to 4 repetitions in each direction.

LATERAL SHUFFLE DROP STEP BACK TO ACCELERATION

In the lateral shuffle drop step back to acceleration drill, the athlete begins with a shuffle before he drop-steps back and accelerates (figure 8.24). This drill challenges the athlete's drop step transition capabilities as he moves laterally when he needs to make the bridging movement into a sprint back behind him. Complete the drill for 1 to 2 sets of 2 to 4 repetitions in each direction.

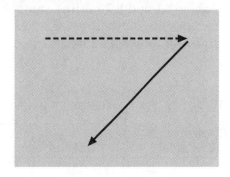

Figure 8.24   Lateral shuffle drop step back to acceleration.

Build Your Own Drills

The beauty of agility drills is that they can be made unique and challenging for athletes while adhering to sound training principles. One could picture these COD drills as forming one giant compass, from which limitless combinations emerge; the only limits are one's own creativity. The only caveat is that drills must feature quality movement patterns.

At the end of the day, it isn't enough to simply understand these movement skills; practitioners must be able to communicate them effectively to their athletes. However carefully worded a coach's cues may be, they are useless if they don't make sense to the listeners. A combination of verbal cueing and physical demonstration can be quite effective, whether a coach displays correct posture and limb positions or actually demonstrates the drills and skills.

Coaches should avoid getting bogged down in trying to correct their athletes' every move. Perfectionism can be useful in small doses, but overly detailed coaching can often hurt athletes' confidence or even worsen their performance.

Sometimes the fastest athletes are best at "cheating" with their movement, meaning that they can use their talent and athleticism to overcome deficient technique. Their movement patterns may be technically incorrect, but they can still get results. Many could make significant improvements if they simply cleaned up their technique, but sometimes those deficiencies are adaptations the athlete has made to accommodate his own traits. In other words, a coach who tries to correct his athlete's every move without looking at the bigger picture could in fact be coaching his athlete to be slower, even if his technique looks better.

The challenge for coaches, therefore, is more than simply understanding and explaining the framework of ideal movement. The coach must also be able to contextualize how individual athletes move, recognizing which "wrong" techniques should be corrected and which should be left alone. Coaching decisions depend on the athlete and his overall movement quality, performance capabilities, injury history, and structural anomalies, among other things. Ultimately, when it comes to training for agility, one must rely on the age-old sports performance training mantra: *It depends*.

Example Training Sessions

Tables 8.1 and 8.2 outline sample agility training programs for a novice and for an elite football player. Agility training would be incorporated into the training week on Tuesdays.

Table 8.1   Agility Training Program for a Novice Athlete: Tuesday, Weeks 1 to 4

MOVEMENT SKILLS SESSION		WEEK 1		WEEK 2		WEEK 3		WEEK 4	
	Exercise	Sets × reps (intensity)	Rest	Sets × reps (intensity)	Rest	Sets × reps (intensity)	Rest	Sets × reps (intensity)	Rest
Active dynamic warm-up (chapter 1)	General movement prep								
	Walking series								
	Ground series								
	Standing series								
Change of direction (chapter 8) and pro agility drill (chapter 3)	Crossover step (tall)	2×4 each side (5 yd)	60 sec	2×4 each side (5 yd)	60 sec	1×4 each side (5 yd)	60 sec	None	NA
	Pro agility drill to first touch	2×3 each side (5 yd)	60 sec	1×2 each side (5 yd)	60 sec	1×2 each side (5 yd)	60 sec	1×2 each side (5 yd)	60 sec
	Pro agility drill to second touch (tall)	2×3 each side (10 yd)	60 sec	1×3 each side (10 yd)	60 sec	1×3 each side (10 yd)	60 sec	1×3 each side (10 yd)	60 sec
	Pro agility drill (full drill)	1×2 each side (20 yd)	120 sec each rep/180 sec each set	2×2 each side (20 yd)	120 sec each rep/180 sec each set	3×2 each side (20 yd)	120 sec each rep/180 sec each set	2×2 each side (20 yd)	120 sec each rep/180 sec each set
	Agility ladder	3 drills × 4 reps each	1:6*	3 drills × 4 reps each	1:6	3 drills × 6 reps each	1:6	2 drills × 4 reps each	1:6

* Work-to-rest ratio

Table 8.2 Agility Training Program for an Elite Athlete: Tuesday, Weeks 1 to 4

MOVEMENT SKILLS SESSION		WEEK 1		WEEK 2		WEEK 3		WEEK 4	
	Exercise	Sets × reps (intensity)	Rest	Sets × reps (intensity)	Rest	Sets × reps (intensity)	Rest	Sets × reps (intensity)	Rest
Active dynamic warm-up (chapter 1)	General movement prep								
	Walking series								
	Ground series								
	Standing series								
Change of direction (chapter 8) and pro agility drill (chapter 3)	Crossover step (tall)	2×4 each side (5 yd)	60 sec	2×4 each side (5 yd)	60 sec	1×4 each side (5 yd)	60 sec	1×2 (5 yd)	60 sec
	Pro agility drill to first touch	2×3 each side (5 yd)	60 sec	1×2 each side (5 yd)	60 sec	1×2 each side (5 yd)	60 sec	1×2 each side (5 yd)	60 sec
	Pro agility drill to second touch (ball)	2×3 each side (10 yd)	60 sec	3×2 each side (10 yd)	60 sec	3×2 each side (10 yd)	60 sec	2×3 each side (10 yd)	60 sec
	Pro agility drill (full drill)	1×2 each side (20 yd)	120 sec each rep/180 sec each set	1×4 each side (20 yd)	120 sec each rep/180 sec each set	3×2 each side (20 yd)	120 sec each rep/180 sec each set	2×1 each side (20 yd)	120 sec each rep/180 sec each set
	Position-specific drills	3 drills × 4 reps each	1:6*	4 drills × 4 reps each	1:6	5 drills × 3 reps each	1:6	None	NA

* Work-to-rest ratio

Conclusion

Agility and its related skills are constantly on display throughout a football game, so athletes should constantly seek to refine their locomotive abilities to cover ground more efficiently. Whether athletes are preparing for a football combine event or an upcoming competitive season, the drills in this chapter can drive major improvements. A separate, major movement quality covered in the next chapter is also relevant both on the football field and in the combine: top-end speed, or an athlete's maximum sprinting velocity.

CHAPTER 9

Top-End Speed

Every aspect of sprinting is a trade-off. The same mechanics that are critical at one stage of the sprint will become a hindrance at another stage. Acceleration is integral to a player's 40-yard dash time, but if he cannot transition out of acceleration technique and into a faster and more efficient stride pattern, he will be unable to carry his speed through the entire 40 yards. Athletes and coaches must work on building the second half of the 40-yard dash, a skill known as maximum velocity or top-end speed; this chapter discusses the biomechanics of top-end speed, as well as how best to train these mechanics.

Biomechanics of Top-End Speed

Linear sprinting is composed of two distinct movement skills: acceleration and top-end speed. They can be emphasized separately in training, but they are still inextricably linked in sprinting performance. As an athlete gathers speed from a state of rest to maximum velocity, he must transition seamlessly between these two skills to match his shifting mechanical priorities.

Acceleration's piston-like punch and drive leg motion lets the athlete spend more time in contact with the ground—which is helpful, since he needs that time to direct force into the ground and overcome the inertia of his stopped or slowed position. As he reaches top speed, however, the athlete must maintain the moving inertia gained. Maximizing ground contact time becomes less important because he has virtually no inertia left to overcome; instead, stride frequency becomes the athlete's new best friend at maximum velocity. He now must be able to turn his legs over fast enough so that his inertia can continue to carry forward at the same speed. The direction of force application shifts as well, as highlighted by the following analogy.

Bike Wheel Analogy of Force Application

Sprinting's technical model dictates that athletes should apply force horizontally during acceleration, then transition to create more vertical force as they reach maximum velocity. To explain the difference in physics, one can imagine a bicycle sitting upside down for repair, with its wheels up in the air.

If the bike mechanic wanted to test one of the wheels by spinning it as fast as possible, he would most likely grasp the tire high along its far side and then powerfully whip the tire horizontally to accelerate the wheel. If he tried to immediately repeat this motion after speeding up the wheel, his hand would likely slow it down. Instead, to keep the wheel spinning fast, he would continuously spike his hand downward along the tire tread in its spinning direction.

Sprinting mechanics are not perfectly analogous to spinning a bike tire, but this example helps to illustrate the transition athletes must make while gaining and then maintaining speed. An athlete who tries to maintain his horizontally directed acceleration mechanics for too long will not be able to move his legs fast enough to continue to apply horizontal force while leaning forward. Instead, he will begin to create braking forces to maintain his balance, or he will simply fall on his face. If the athlete is running a 40-yard dash on national television and in front of NFL scouts, either of these outcomes would be suboptimal, to say the least.

Instead, as the athlete accelerates, his application of force into the ground becomes less horizontal and more vertical. He pushes backward against the ground to propel himself forward, then as he gains speed he pushes down more vertically into the ground to create space for a quick cyclical turnover of his legs at maximum velocity.

Steady Rising

During initial acceleration, an athlete applies horizontal impulse into the ground behind his hips to overcome inertia and propel him forward in accordance with Newton's first and second laws of motion (described in chapter 7). His technique includes a forward body lean, pistonlike leg action, and longer ground contact times to generate optimal accelerative force. But the technical model that benefits the athlete early in acceleration becomes less useful as he gathers speed.

As he gains velocity, the athlete naturally begins bridging into top-end speed mechanics, which are characterized by a more upright body posture and cyclical strides (figure 9.1). One could picture this transition as a slide switch that begins at pure acceleration and slides toward full top-end speed. Within that time span the athlete shifts from acceleration-dominant mechanics to top-end speed mechanics.

As he generates greater velocity, the athlete must direct more of his force vertically to create efficient leg turnover. He cannot continue to lean far forward without falling over. To carry speed, he must decrease ground contact time. Both changes require a vertical body position and a streamlined, cyclical leg action. Applying more force vertically into the ground creates the flight time he needs to quickly reposition his limbs.

Phases of Top-End Speed Mechanics

A top-end speed stride occurs in interrelated movement sequences. Although they overlap each other, defining and understanding each of these discrete movements helps contextualize their role within the mechanical model.

Figure 9.1   Top-end speed mechanics: *(a)* front view; *(b)* side view.

Residual Phase

The residual phase describes the brief time period between ground contact and initiation of back-side recovery. As noted in chapter 7, one of the four ways an athlete can become faster is by spending less time on the ground. Striking the ground directly underneath his hips with a dorsiflexed foot creates a stable surface for putting optimal force in the desired direction. The stiffness of the ankle joint complex helps to employ the athlete's stretch-shortening cycle (SSC) and to minimize ground contact time.

Back-Side Recovery

The initial phase after ground contact is called back-side recovery because it occurs on the back side of the hip axis. The athlete flexes his knee to bring his heel up toward his buttocks quickly and efficiently as his foot leaves the ground. (When an athlete's foot drifts too far back behind his body during back-side recovery, it results in a shorter front-side recovery thigh position.) As he flexes his knee, he also begins to actively dorsiflex his foot, which helps shorten the leg's lever and therefore creates a faster recovery revolution.

Front-Side Recovery

Efficient back-side heel recovery sets up an optimal front-side thigh recovery, in which the athlete's hip flexes to bring his knee and thigh forward into an optimal position to apply force, a landmark of roughly 75 to 90 degrees to his upright body posture. As discussed in chapter 7, the athlete's thigh should maintain this 75- to 90-degree angle with his trunk throughout the transition from acceleration into maximum velocity.

The athlete's front-side thigh position changes its angle relative to the ground only as his body position "climbs" upward during his transition from acceleration into top-end speed. He will "block" his thigh once he finds his optimal angle.

As his thigh flexes into front-side recovery, the athlete's lower limb begins to move his heel away from his hips. His heel remains as close to his hips as possible while initiating front-side recovery and then begins to leave his hips again. Once his knee finds a similar 90-degree position, his recovery phase is considered complete.

Transition and Ground Preparation

At the end of the sprinting recovery phase, the athlete's thigh has found its position and his knee has extended to bring his foot forward, positioning his heel underneath his knee and roughly perpendicular to his thigh (again, within 75 to 90 degrees). This foot should not reach out any further in front of his hip axis before striking the ground or his foot will lose its ideal force application position as his hip begins to extend again.

Once his upper and lower limb find correct recovery positions, the athlete begins elongating his limb to prepare for the ground. He extends his knee and hip simultaneously, elongating his striking lever to lengthen his hamstrings. Ground preparation timing is crucial; at the precise moment of ground strike, the athlete should create a position in which his hamstrings and glutes can co-contract at his leg's longest lever point.

Ground Contact

Top-end speed favors a short ground contact time. This time is optimized if the athlete strikes directly under his hips with an extended knee and hip and a stiff ankle joint complex.

In some coaching circles, casting the foot out in front of the hips is a popular concept. However, an athlete who reaches out with his foot during top-end speed creates multiple problems. First, he cannot apply force at the most optimal joint angles. Reaching his foot forward to pull his hips through would be akin to pulling a wheelbarrow instead of pushing it; the mechanics are simply suboptimal. Second, applying force at this joint position will place an increased stretch on the athlete's gastrocnemius (calf muscle) and biceps femoris (one of the hamstrings), thereby increasing long-term injury risk.

Arm Swing Mechanics

The shoulder should remain the primary axis of arm swing motion throughout the duration of a sprint. The elbow joint plays a role as well, flexing and extending to adjust lever lengths in congruence with lower-body patterning.

Athletes can overcome inertia in acceleration more efficiently when they sacrifice shorter ground contact times and higher limb turnover rates to achieve better levers and more force. The athlete must match his upper-body levers to mirror his lower-body lever patterning. To accomplish this, the arm swing's arc should adjust during sprinting.

Chapter 7 discusses how elbow extension, or arm lengthening during backswing, helps to generate horizontal force and places a greater stretch on the athlete's upper-body SSC. His hand should target hip level during the arm backswing to create a longer lever during contralateral (opposite) lower limb extension, thereby generating a stretch reflex (discussed in chapter 6) to rebound his arm forward. When an athlete narrows his elbow angle during the forward arm swing, he can maximize the elastic energy contributions provided by the stretch reflex his backswing creates in his chest musculature. As his arms move forward, they should aim in toward the body's midline, near chin level.

Top-End Speed Drills

The goal of top-end speed drilling, as in all movement, is to progress from the least chaotic environment possible and work up in complexity. The best sprinting drills focus on simple pattern rehearsal. They distill the technical model into smaller tasks, then allow athletes to assemble those pieces into a cohesive whole.

In the Landow Performance model for top-end speed drilling, athletes rehearse drills such as heel slides and stepovers, which reproduce the recovery and transition phases at walking, jogging, or running speed to familiarize athletes with top-end speed mechanics.

FAST CLAW

Execution

The fast claw drill mimics the top-end speed cycle in a standing and unweighted drill, creating a more isolated and stable environment in which to practice posture, positioning, and placement, with the lack of typical ground force demands encouraging a greater contraction rate.

Correct execution is required for the fast claw drill to display any positive training transfer into improved top-end speed mechanics. To implement this drill properly, a coach must have a keen eye for how fast claws should look and feel.

The drill requires a wall or other stabilizing device like a PVC rod for the athlete to use for balance with his inside hand. The athlete stands tall with his shoulders back, feet hip-width apart, and toes pointed forward, looking straight ahead. He stands with the left side of his body an arm's length from the stabilizing device, with his left hand supported and his right hand on his hip (figure 9.2*a*).

The athlete's inside leg (in this example, his left leg) serves as his standing support leg while his right leg works through his top-end speed stride sequence. He must fully extend through his hip and knee, using his gluteus medius to laterally stabilize his hip and provide the necessary clearance height for his right leg to cycle.

To initiate the drilling sequence, the athlete assumes this starting position and begins to gently let his right leg swing forward and backward just a few small degrees, allowing the ball of his dorsiflexed right foot to brush the ground. At the coach's cue, the athlete reacts by lightly striking the ground underneath his hip with his right foot, then quickly cycles his right heel through the residual, back-side recovery, and front-side recovery phases.

After moving through these initial stride phases, his swinging leg freezes at the point just before his leg starts lengthening to initiate his ground preparation phase (figure 9.2b). The athlete holds this ending position and the coach checks the athlete's posture, adjusting the athlete's limb positions to match the described landmark positions: 90-degree angles (or acceptably close to this) at the hip and knee, with a dorsiflexed foot. After completing 5 or 6 repetitions at the coach's tempo, the athlete completes 5 or 6 repetitions on his other side to complete a full set.

Coaching Points

The fast claw exercise is primarily about practicing back-side heel recovery, but coaches should avoid honing in too much on leg action during the drill. Athletes commonly start to lose posture and dump forward with the upper body; the leg cycle action may look good on its own, but if the athlete's body position is wrong it can engrain bad habits. Coaches should cue athletes to maintain an upright and balanced posture throughout the drill.

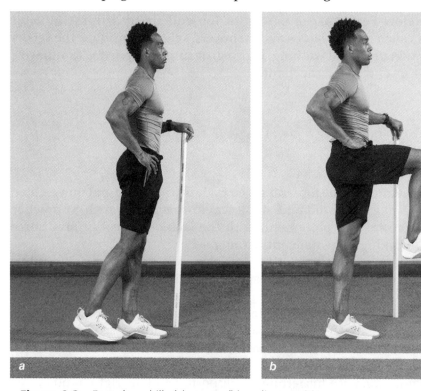

Figure 9.2 Fast claw drill: *(a)* setup; *(b)* ending position.

HEEL SLIDE

Execution

The simplest way to describe a heel slide to someone who has never seen the drill before is that it looks like a perfect hybrid of the common high knees and butt kicks most coaches and athletes have performed.

The athlete stands tall with a relaxed, stable upper body. At a jogging tempo, he simultaneously lifts his thigh up and pulls his heel in toward his rear end, as if he intends to smash his calf and hamstring into each other (figure 9.3).

Figure 9.3   Heel slide: *(a)* first step; *(b)* second step.

Upon bringing his heel all the way up so that his knee raises slightly, the athlete extends his leg again, keeping his foot dorsiflexed to maintain a stiff and stable ground strike. Although the athlete will contact the ground with a mostly flat foot in heel slides (due to the drill's tempo), this should still not result in a full heel strike. The athlete should perform the drill pumping his arms and legs at a running pace, while allowing his body to move forward at a slow walking pace, until he reaches the prescribed distance. The athlete performs 3 repetitions of heel slides per set, covering 10 yards each repetition and walking back to the starting line between reps for active rest.

STEPOVER A-RUN

Execution

The stepover (or dribble, as termed by some coaches) drills build on the heel slide by completing front-side recovery, then cycling through the ground preparation and ground contact phases to strike underneath the hip. During heel slides, the athlete's heels move up and down vertically from the ground to the athlete's hips to mimic back-side recovery. The stepover A-run begins as a heel slide, then evolves: Instead of returning his foot straight back down to the ground, the athlete brings thigh and foot forward for front-side recovery before extending his leg to the ground. The result is a wheeling leg movement that looks similar to riding a bicycle while the arms swing long at the shoulders to match the tempo.

The athlete stands in a tall, relaxed posture. He may either start the repetition in a stepover A-run immediately or begin the repetition with a few steps of heel slides to feel the drill's patterning, then gradually transition into full stepover run cycles while maintaining the same drill tempo and upright body posture (figure 9.4). As with heel slides, the athlete should not be spending much time on the ground. For one set, the athlete performs 3 repetitions of stepover A-runs for 10 yards at a quick jogging pace and walks back to the starting line between repetitions for active rest.

Coaching Points

In putting these phases together into one rehearsal pattern, coaches can give athletes a useful coordinative

Figure 9.4   Stepover A-run: *(a)* first portion; *(b)* second portion; *(c)* third portion. Note: The same mechanics are used for the stepover A-skip.

task that develops body positioning awareness and limb control. The patterning, or rhythmic, aspect of this drill is absolutely critical because it will look horrendous otherwise.

Execution

The stepover A-skip uses the same mechanics as the stepover A-run (figure 9.4) but at a different tempo. The athlete completes the same top-end speed stride phases but in a double-skip rhythm, just like the acceleration A-skip in chapter 7. This modification adds a coordinative task that challenges the athlete's patterning skills. The tempo change also allows the athlete to put more force into the ground with the movement, making it feel more like a realistic top-end speed stride.

The athlete stands relaxed and tall. Depending on preference, he moves either straight into the skip or gets a double-bounce rhythm going on the balls of both feet to establish his tempo before starting to skip. Each skip repetition consists of two bounces: The first bounce allows one leg to move through recovery, then on the second bounce the athlete finishes moving through the transition and ground preparation phases of his moving leg, making a full cycle by the time he hits the ground for a third bounce. The third bounce is the start of the next repetition, with the other leg now moving through back-side recovery and continuing to alternate sides every third bounce. He completes 3 repetitions for 15 yards each, walking back between repetitions as active rest.

FLYING 10S AND 20S

Execution

During a movement training session dedicated to top-end speed, flying 10-yard and 20-yard sprints are helpful drills to isolate and practice maximum velocity technique. To sprint the entirety of a 40-yard dash for every single repetition during the training session would be immensely taxing on an athlete and could result in too heavy a workload. In both versions of this drill, the athlete begins at a start cone and has 20 yards to gradually accumulate speed before reaching the second cone—at which point he sprints as fast as possible for either 10 or 20 yards, then gradually decelerates after passing the third cone. Complete for one set of 1 to 2 repetitions for each distance, resting for three minutes between flying 10s and four minutes between flying 20s.

Coaching Points

For the duration of the 10- or 20-yard flying sprint, the athlete focuses on maintaining an upright body posture, making an efficient backside recovery during each stride to reach optimal thigh position before extending his leg and striking underneath his hips with a locked foot. His strides should be perfectly synchronized with a smooth arm swing.

40-YARD BUILDUP

Execution

Although drills such as 10-yard acceleration starts and flying 10s and 20s give athletes a chance to rehearse isolated portions of the 40-yard dash, practicing the full context of a longer sprint is still important. As was discussed earlier, an athlete's technique evolves over the course of a sprint as he gathers speed, starting in pure acceleration and gradually transitioning to top-end speed. Practicing these skills individually is important, but athletes should also get a feel for how the two naturally blend within a sprint. Sprinting 40 yards at maximum effort carries a high neural cost, however, which is not always desirable during a movement training session.

The 40-yard buildup is an incremental gain in speed, finishing the sprint at a prescribed percentage of the athlete's maximum effort. The athlete begins in a two-point start position (as described in chapter 7). He starts his run at a lighter pace and gradually increases his speed until he reaches the indicated speed. The buildup intensities in this book's programming range from 75 to 85 percent depending on their place within the overall training plan. Perform the drill for one set of 2 to 3 repetitions, resting for four minutes between reps.

Coaching Points

This drill offers athletes the chance to focus solely on their movement quality as they run, rather than worrying about how fast they can run. Practitioners should emphasize maintaining smooth, synchronized technique throughout the sprint. The athlete is running below full speed, but his technique should still resemble that of a normal sprint—though he will not be able to hold his typical angle of body lean during his acceleration phase.

PREP LIKE A PRO: WOODWAY TREADMILL SPRINTS

During their top-end speed sessions, Landow Performance athletes often use curved Woodway treadmills to refine their technique. With its concave design, the treadmill permits the athlete to quickly build to full sprinting speed with lower impact, while coaches can watch his technique as he runs in place. The rubber treads on these machines are manually powered and display speed output, which can make movement sessions highly competitive between athletes.

Example Training Sessions

Tables 9.1 and 9.2 outline sample top-end speed training programs for a novice and for an elite football player. Top-end speed training would be incorporated into the training week on Thursdays.

Table 9.1   Top-End Speed Training Program for a Novice Athlete: Thursday, Weeks 1 to 4

MOVEMENT SKILLS SESSION		WEEK 1		WEEK 2		WEEK 3		WEEK 4	
	Exercise	Sets x reps (intensity)	Rest	Sets x reps (intensity)	Rest	Sets x reps (intensity)	Rest	Sets x reps (intensity)	Rest
Active dynamic warm-up (chapter 1)	General movement prep								
	Walking series								
	Ground series								
	Standing series								
Top-end speed training (chapter 9)	Heel slides	2×3 (10 yd)	WB	2×3 (10 yd)	WB	3×3 (10 yd)	WB	3×3 (10 yd)	WB
	Stepover run	2×3 (10 yd)	WB	2×3 (10 yd)	WB	3×3 (10 yd)	WB	3×3 (10 yd)	WB
	Stepover skip	2×3 (15 yd)	WB	2×3 (15 yd)	WB	2×3 (15 yd)	WB	3×3 (15 yd)	WB
	Straight-leg shuffle	1×3 (5 yd)	WB	3×3 (5 yd)	WB	2×3 (5 yd)	WB	3×3 (5 yd)	WB
	40-yard buildup (to 75%)	1×3 (40 yd)	120 sec	1×3 (40 yd)	120 sec	2×2 (40 yd)	120 sec	1×2 (40 yd)	120 sec

WB = walk back

Table 9.2   Top-End Speed Training Program for an Elite Athlete: Thursday, Weeks 1 to 4

MOVEMENT SKILLS SESSION		WEEK 1		WEEK 2		WEEK 3		WEEK 4	
	Exercise	Sets x reps (intensity)	Rest	Sets x reps (intensity)	Rest	Sets x reps (intensity)	Rest	Sets x reps (intensity)	Rest
Active dynamic warm-up (chapter 1)	General movement prep								
	Walking series								
	Ground series								
	Standing series								
Top-end speed training (chapter 9)	Tall kneeling arm action	1×1 (3-8 sec at 50% speed)	NA	1×1 (3-8 sec at 50% speed)	NA	1×1 (3-8 sec at 50% speed)	NA	1×1 (3-8 sec at 50% speed)	NA
		1×1 (3-8 sec at 75% speed)	NA	1×1 (3-8 sec at 75% speed)	NA	1×1 (3-8 sec at 75% speed)	NA	1×1 (3-8 sec at 75% speed)	NA
		1×1 (3-8 sec at 90% speed)	NA	1×1 (3-8 sec at 90% speed)	NA	1×1 (3-8 sec at 90% speed)	NA	1×1 (3-8 sec at 90% speed)	NA
	Heel slides	1×2 (10 yd)	WB	1×2 (10 yd)	WB	1×2 (10 yd)	WB	1×2 (10 yd)	WB
	Stepover run	1×3 (10 yd)	WB	1×3 (10 yd)	WB	3×3 (10 yd)	WB	2×3 (10 yd)	WB
	Stepover skip	2×3 (15 yd)	WB	2×3 (15 yd)	WB	2×3 (15 yd)	WB	2×3 (15 yd)	WB
	Straight-leg shuffle	1×3 (5 yd)	WB	3×3 (5 yd)	WB	3×3 (5 yd)	WB	2×3 (5 yd)	WB
	40-yard buildup	1×3 (75%)	120 sec	1×3 (85%)	120 sec	2×2 (90%)	120 sec	2×1 (100%)	120 sec

WB = walk back

Conclusion

Ultimately, top-end speed work accounts for only a small portion of the movement training needed to drive optimal performance both in combine drills and in football itself. Coaches must understand the interrelated biomechanics of top-end speed and acceleration, and they must bring the right technical emphasis to each drill in order to see athletes improve. Taking a part–whole pedagogic approach to this movement skill will help build a stronger back half of the athlete's 40-yard dash.

Movement skills are essential to testing successfully at the football combine, but learning and practicing these skills is about more than just trying to do well on a test and improve one's draft stock. It is about upgrading the quality of everything the athlete does on the field. Movement training is about becoming a more skilled and robust athlete and continuing to pursue mastery of movement throughout one's playing career and beyond. Combine preparation cannot all be handled on the field, however. Strength and power underlie the athlete's ability to forcefully express movement skills. A dedicated approach to developing strength and power is needed to prepare athletes for testing day.

PART IV

Strength and Power Development

CHAPTER 10

Training for Strength

Strength is king, or so the common saying goes. Speed, agility, and power are all qualities that rely heavily on strength. Researchers have found an abundance of strong correlations between maximal strength and high-value athletic performance markers (e.g., acceleration, top-end speed, and change-of-direction ability) in a variety of sports and athletes (McGuigan, Wright, and Fleck 2012).

As discussed in chapter 6, an athlete's strength can be plotted along his force–velocity curve, a graph describing the amount of force he can produce at a given speed. Once a coach understands her athlete's strength profile, she can identify which of his strength qualities need the most attention and then train him primarily at those velocities.

In a football combine training context, college players preparing for pro-level combines have a higher accumulated training age than high schoolers, so they need highly specific, advanced stressors to elicit the desired adaptations. These athletes will start in a strength-speed range on the force–velocity curve, whereas novice players simply need saturation in basic strength stressors. This chapter highlights the most important exercises from that menu and explains how to integrate them into the football combine training toolbox.

Exercise Selection

Crafting top-notch strength programming for elite athletes requires precise manipulations of volume, intensity, and frequency. But even if a coach could flawlessly tune these stress variables in a football combine training program, poor exercise choices could diminish that program's effectiveness.

Fundamental multijoint movements, such as the squat pattern, are integral to any successful resistance training program. Increases in maximal squat strength correlate strongly with sprint performance improvements in elite athletes (Comfort, Haigh, and Matthews 2012), and squats are widely viewed as foundational systemic neuromuscular stressors.

Joint position dictates muscle function, so strength development exercises should put the athlete in positions that stress the desired motor units. This requires careful planning and an understanding of each athlete's capabilities and limitations.

Each exercise must serve a purpose in the workout itself, in the current training block, and in the training plan. It may be tempting to view exercises as good or bad, but an exercise's merit ultimately depends on purpose and execution. Any movement can be beneficial or detrimental, depending on how it is executed and who is performing the exercise.

Practitioners can fall into a pattern of training athletes based on their own philosophical biases rather than looking at each situation objectively to determine the athlete's needs. One must plan the training program in relation to the initial athlete needs analysis (chapter 2) and the athlete's stage within the LTAD model.

BARBELL BACK SQUAT

The back squat is described in this chapter, but readers examining this book's included programming will notice that front squats are also prominently involved in Landow Performance combine training. Adjusting bar placement will affect the exercise's primary force vectors.

To begin the barbell back squat, the athlete stands under the loaded barbell in the rack, centering the bar along his upper back; then he grasps the bar with both hands evenly outside the shoulders using a pronated grip. Bringing his hands to the bar creates a shelf of sorts that runs along the athlete's upper trapezius. The athlete then places the middle of the bar along that shelf, allowing him to support the bar without direct contact on his spine.

The athlete unracks the barbell, steps back, then sets up in his squat stance (figure 10.1a) by evenly placing his feet shoulder-width apart or slightly wider (depending on his limb segment lengths and individual preference). This standing position begins and ends each repetition. His feet are symmetrical, either pointing straight ahead or angled out slightly.

After finding his optimal stance, the athlete sits his hips down and back to create a trade-off of levers; his tibias move forward, while his femurs move back and the torso shifts

Figure 10.1   Barbell back squat: (a) start position; (b) squat.

forward slightly (figure 10.1*b*). After he reaches the optimal squat depth for his individual dimensions, he stands up in one smooth, coordinated movement while maintaining stiffness in his trunk and a neutral head position.

The athlete's dimensions may call for unique squatting strategies, so the optimal squat stance and depth can vary by athlete. For an athlete who is severely limited in hip internal rotation, achieving a deep squat position will be extremely difficult; it may even create impinging forces at his hips. Such a limitation is not necessarily a dysfunction, but it must be accounted for.

The kinematics of the squat (and its derivative patterns, such as lunges and split squats) also requires a certain degree of passive ankle dorsiflexion. For athletes who cannot achieve the desired depth due to ankle restrictions, researchers recommend that coaches modify the exercise by placing a solid lift underneath the athlete's heels and that they prescribe supplementary ankle mobility work for the athlete (Schoenfeld 2010). Dorsiflexion (both passive and active) is critical to sprint performance, so squats can improve ankle range of motion (ROM) in addition to developing force production capabilities. Following a 5-repetition warmup set, barbell back squats are performed in this book's training program for 2 to 6 sets of 1 to 5 repetitions, ranging anywhere in weight from 50 to 85 percent 1RM.

STEP-BACK LUNGE

Barbell back squats are fantastic additions to most resistance training programs, but an overemphasis on bilateral squats can hide or even worsen any strength asymmetries between limbs. Step-back lunges allow athletes to modify a traditional squat pattern and make the movement more unilaterally (single-side) dominant.

Beginning in a standing position (figure 10.2*a*), the athlete steps back with one foot to a comfortable distance and lunges into the other leg (figure 10.2*b*),

Figure 10.2   Step-back lunge: *(a)* start position; *(b)* lunge.

finding depth in a pain-free range that keeps his front foot flat and his knee tracking neutrally out over the foot.

Landow Performance combine preparation athletes typically complete this exercise with a loaded barbell on their backs to challenge upper-body postural stability during the exercise. (The setup with the barbell follows the same protocol as the barbell back squat.) At the coach's discretion, step-back lunges can be performed using dumbbells or other loading schemes such as weight vests. Complete the exercise for 2 to 4 sets of 3 to 5 consecutive repetitions, performed one side at a time.

BOTTOM-UP STEP-UP

Bottom-up step-ups are a great exercise for developing unilateral lower-body pushing strength in a range that mimics acceleration. When coached properly, this strength exercise can double as a postural acceleration drill.

Acceleration is a vital skill for combine testing and sport performance, and in a short training window such as combine preparation, the best coaches will take advantage of any opportunities to reinforce their athletes' acceleration posture and positions. In chapter 1, for example, we discussed the importance of cueing active dorsiflexion during many of the active dynamic warm-up exercises, but acceleration skill development can extend even to the weight room.

The athlete stands with a loaded barbell in the barbell back squat position along his upper back (see the barbell back squat exercise description for more detail). At the coach's discretion, bottom-up step-ups can also be performed with dumbbells instead of a barbell. He stands facing a box that is 16 to 20 inches high but can be adjusted based on the athlete's lower limb segment lengths.

He begins the repetition by lifting his left knee and placing his left foot on top of the box; his right foot remains flat on the ground and his right leg stays extended through his knee and hip (figure 10.3a). Next, the athlete loads his weight onto his left foot, driving his left foot into the box to extend his knee and hip. This pushing force lifts the barbell and the rest of the athlete's body up until his left leg is straight.

While his left leg extends, the athlete punches his right foot and knee up into an acceleration A-frame position (figure 10.3b); he makes his right thigh perpendicular to the rest of his body, with his right foot fully dorsiflexed and his right knee flexed at roughly 90 degrees. His finishing position at the top of the box should look just like the PVC A-march drill, except in this scenario the athlete has a barbell sitting on his back instead of a PVC rod or dowel, and his plant foot is up on a box instead of on the ground. After achieving a stable top position, the athlete controls his descent until his right foot reaches the ground, fully completing the repetition.

Throughout the exercise, the athlete's eyes remain focused straight ahead while he maintains an upright posture through his trunk and shoulders. He completes all prescribed repetitions on one side, then switches to the other leg. He should rack or otherwise lower the barbell between sets, ideally with the help of a coach or training partner. Complete the exercise for 2 to 4 sets of 3 to 5 consecutive repetitions, performed one side at a time.

Figure 10.3 Bottom-up step-up: *(a)* start position; *(b)* top position.

BULGARIAN SPLIT SQUAT

Another excellent lower-body pushing pattern, the Bulgarian split squat (also known as the rear foot elevated split squat, or RFESS) is a unilaterally dominant squat with one heavily loaded front foot flat on the ground and the other foot elevated on a raised pad or bench behind the athlete. This setup creates a pattern similar to the step-back lunge, except that the Bulgarian split squat's unique elevated rear foot setup shifts the exercise's physics. In doing so, it requires less dorsiflexion and counterbalances the body, allowing athletes to work into a deeper range than with barbell back squats.

Typically performed with either one dumbbell held in a goblet position or two dumbbells held at the sides, Bulgarian split squats also place an immense proprioceptive challenge on the athlete's heavily loaded front foot, thereby adding bonus balance and ankle stability training to the athlete's strength work.

The athlete starts in a tall standing posture, placing his left foot at a distance from the pad or bench, pointing his toes straight ahead with his feet hip-width apart. He reaches back with his right foot for the bench or pad and, after finding it, takes a moment to find his balance at the exercise's top position (figure 10.4a). Most of his weight is now on his left foot, which remains on the ground.

Maintaining proper upper-body posture, the athlete lowers into a squat on his front leg (figure 10.4b). He bends at his left knee, hip, and ankle until he has reached the desired squat depth. The athlete now drives his front foot into the ground to extend his left leg and raise his body back to the exercise's top position. He completes all the repetitions for one foot while keeping that foot in place, then switches legs and completes all prescribed repetitions on the other side. The emphasis should mainly be on pushing with the front leg, but especially under heavy load athletes often compensate by pushing the rear leg into the pad or bench.

For safety, coaches need to pay attention to their athletes' shin angles at the top and bottom of Bulgarian split squats. The athlete's knee should track out neutrally over his toes. Some coaches may advocate against this. They would prefer that the athlete's lower leg remain more vertical as he descends, contending that if the front knee starts to track forward it will create dangerous shear forces on the joint. While this certainly can happen, in a well-executed Bulgarian split squat the athlete will show a positive (forward) shin angle with the knee tracking forward neutrally. The exercise should be performed for 3 to 5 sets of 5 consecutive repetitions on each leg.

Figure 10.4   Bulgarian split squat: *(a)* start position; *(b)* squat.

BARBELL BENCH PRESS

Described fully in the 225-pound bench press test section of chapter 3, the bench press (figure 10.5) is a key exercise for training upper-body strength and power and is especially important during combine training to prepare for the test. It can be performed using either a barbell or dumbbells, depending on available equipment and individual need.

The barbell version of the bench press is an excellent stressor of the athlete's neuromuscular strength. Dumbbells are also a great choice for the bench press because they can reveal asymmetries in strength and stability between the athlete's left and right sides. In this book's novice program, the barbell bench press is performed on Tuesday workouts for 3 to 5 sets of 2 to 8 repetitions, ranging in weight from 55 to 80 percent 1RM, depending on the scenario. The elite-level program calls for a dumbbell flat bench press on Tuesdays for 4 to 5 sets of 3 to 8 reps and on Thursdays for endurance with a barbell, simulating the combine test.

Figure 10.5   Bench press: *(a)* top position; *(b)* bottom position.

PULL-UP

The pull-up is the most systemic upper-body vertical pulling movement. Landow Performance athletes typically conduct the exercise with a neutral grip. Grasping the bar or handles, the athlete begins in a hanging position with both arms fully extended, then pulls his body up (figure 10.6). A controlled return to the starting position ends the repetition.

Practitioners should look to have their athletes complete pull-ups in their fullest pain-free range. Athletes with adequate strength can add weight if it does not compromise their movement quality. Perform the exercise for 3 to 5 sets of 5 repetitions.

Figure 10.6 Pull-up: *(a)* initial hanging position; *(b)* pull-up.

SINGLE-ARM DUMBBELL ROW

The single-arm dumbbell row requires horizontal upper-body pulling strength as well as trunk stability and coordination. To begin the exercise, the athlete sets up with a dumbbell adjacent to a bench or box of similar height. He takes a staggered stance, bent in both knees with the same leg back as his rowing arm. The athlete's nonrowing arm is straight, with his hand applying pressure into the bench (figure 10.7*a*).

With his back flat and head neutral, the athlete pulls the dumbbell toward his torso (figure 10.7*b*) within his maximal pain-free range, then lowers the dumbbell in a controlled manner. Practitioners should notice if athletes begin to shift their hips or shrug the weight during the exercise. Perform for 3 to 5 sets of 3 to 8 repetitions on each side.

Figure 10.7   Single-arm dumbbell row: *(a)* bottom position; *(b)* top position.

NO-BACK DUMBBELL SHOULDER PRESS

The overhead shoulder press is a fundamental vertical pushing movement. However, the exercise also is highly susceptible to movement compensations as fatigue and load increase. Athletes sometimes begin to arch their spines to turn the lift into more of a chest press, creating dangerous stress on the spinal discs.

To address this issue, and to create an added stability challenge, Landow Performance combine prep athletes perform the dumbbell shoulder press while standing with one foot on the ground and the other foot atop a bench directly in front of the athlete. This helps to keep the hips neutral and to keep stress off the lumbar spine.

As he readies the dumbbells at shoulder level, the athlete places the foot flat on top of the bench (figure 10.8*a*). While maintaining trunk control throughout the movement, he raises and lowers the dumbbells (figure 10.8*b*) through a pain-free range of motion. The exercise is completed for 3 to 4 sets of 3 to 8 repetitions.

Figure 10.8   No-back dumbbell shoulder press: *(a)* starting position; *(b)* press.

BENT-OVER BARBELL ROW

The athlete begins a bent-over barbell row standing upright and gripping the barbell with hands at shoulder width or slightly outside shoulder width, using either a pronated (overhand) or supinated (underhand) grip. To assume the exercise's starting position, he hinges at the hips with a slight knee bend and a flat back. This position will resemble the bottom of a Romanian deadlift (RDL), but likely with more knee bend.

Each repetition begins with the athlete's arms fully extended away from his chest (figure 10.9*a*). He retracts his shoulder blades and pulls the barbell to about chest level (figure 10.9*b*), squeezing primarily in his lats and his middle

Figure 10.9   Bent-over barbell row: *(a)* starting position; *(b)* row.

to lower traps. He then controls the barbell back down to an extended arm position.

Coaches programming bent-over barbell rows should be aware that the exercise creates considerable shearing forces at the athlete's lumbar spine, which ought to be considered in a workout with other exercises that create a similar type of joint stress (e.g., back squats). Complete the exercise for 4 to 5 sets of 2 to 8 repetitions.

CHEST SUPPORTED ROW

The chest supported row is a bilateral horizontal rowing variation performed with dumbbells or a barbell. The only difference between this exercise and the bent-over barbell row is that the athlete now supports his chest on a weight bench set at an incline (figure 10.10); otherwise, his rowing motion remains the same. The chest supported row variation should be used when the athlete needs to remove some of the shearing stress the bent-over barbell row places on the athlete's lower back. In this book's training programs, the exercise is completed for 3 to 4 sets of 5 repetitions.

Figure 10.10   Chest supported row: *(a)* starting position; *(b)* row.

SUSPENSION TRAINER INVERTED ROW

Suspension training systems such as the TRX offer yet another variant for horizontal rows. The suspension trainer inverted row is a unique version of the exercise because difficulty adjustments can be made on the fly with a quick change in body position. The athlete sets the suspension straps at his desired length, then sets up in a backward lean with his arms extended and gripping the handles (figure 10.11*a*). He should either dig his heels into the floor or place his feet on a secure bench or box. If the athlete's body is closer to parallel with the ground, his body becomes a longer lever that is more difficult to lift. Coaches must emphasize the need for a strong and stable posture throughout the movement; the athlete should strive to maintain an imaginary line running straight from his ear down to his ankle. His head position remains neutral as he executes a rowing sequence to pull his sternum up toward the suspension anchor point (figure 10.11*b*). This adds a unique postural instability challenge to

Figure 10.11   Suspension trainer inverted row: *(a)* starting position; *(b)* row.

the rowing movement, giving the exercise a planking quality as well for trunk stability. Complete the exercise for 3 to 4 sets of 5 to 8 repetitions, changing one's body angle to adjust difficulty level.

DUMBBELL INCLINE BENCH PRESS OR ALTERNATING DUMBBELL INCLINE BENCH PRESS

Similar to the dumbbell bench press, the dumbbell incline press (figure 10.12) is an excellent exercise for developing shoulder stability along with pressing strength. Setting the weight bench at an incline, usually 30 to 45 degrees, changes the line of applied force to angle the pressing movement more vertically. This change requires more contributions from the anterior shoulder; most importantly, the incline press trains the athlete's pressing capabilities and shoulder stability at a highly sport-specific plane of movement. The athlete sits on the bench and leans back against the incline, using a spotter's help to get both dumbbells into a pressing position with arms fully extended. From here, the athlete lowers the dumbbells in line with his chest to a comfortable

Figure 10.12   Dumbbell incline bench press: *(a)* lowered position; *(b)* press.

depth, then presses back up to his starting position without the dumbbells hitting each other. The spotter must be prepared to assist the athlete at any point, spotting the athlete at the wrists and not at the elbows. The dumbbell incline bench press is usually performed for 3 or 4 sets of 3 to 5 repetitions.

The alternating dumbbell incline press variation requires the athlete to complete a repetition on one side, while his opposite arm remains fully extended holding the other dumbbell (figure 10.13). Upon completing the repetition, the athlete reverses the process: he holds up the dumbbell he just pressed while completing a

Figure 10.13 Alternating dumbbell incline bench press.

repetition on the other side. He continues alternating sides until all prescribed repetitions are completed; in this book's training program, the exercise is typically performed for 2 to 4 sets of 2 to 5 reps each side.

TEMPO PUSH-UP

Though some may consider push-ups too basic to include in combine training, doing push-ups continuously for a predetermined slow pace can be helpful in building upper-body muscular endurance for the maximum bench press repetition test. In this case the tempo is a three-second controlled lowering (figure 10.14*a*) followed by a one-second controlled push back up to the starting position (figure 10.14*b*). In this book's novice program, the exercise is completed for 8 reps, whereas the elite program uses the same tempo but performs the exercise for 30 seconds instead of repetitions. Both novice and elite athletes complete 3 sets of the exercise.

Figure 10.14 Tempo push-up: *(a)* three seconds to lower; *(b)* one second to push up.

FRONT PLANK OR ISOMETRIC PUSH-UP HOLD IN THE TOP POSITION

Planks are a useful exercise for improving segmental stability in the trunk (often referred to as the core) region of the athlete's body. The plank exercises in this book are designed to challenge trunk stability against different types of joint forces; the front plank forces the athlete to counter against lumbar extension, or arching of the lower back. In both the front plank and isometric push-up hold, the athlete's goal is to maintain neutral position in the head, neck, spine, scapulae, and hips. The only difference is the angle of the plank. Athletes who cannot adequately hold position during the exercise should be regressed to a modified position by lowering their knees to the ground, which creates a shorter plank; their knees, hips, spine, and head alignment must remain neutral.

The front plank exercise in this book's training plan is sometimes called a low plank, in which the athlete holds up his entire weight on his toes and his forearms with elbows directly underneath his shoulders and palms facing up to prevent the athlete from running tension through his arms to compensate in his planking effort (figure 10.15). The athlete's knees remain off the ground, and he keeps his lower body in a line with his torso and head. The top position isometric push-up hold (figure 10.16) requires this same type of lumbo-pelvic and scapular stability as a front plank, but at a slightly different angle and with the arms extended. Front planks in this training program are completed for 3 sets of one 30-second plank.

Figure 10.15 Front plank.

Figure 10.16 Isometric push-up hold in the top position.

SIDE PLANK

The side plank challenges the athlete to stabilize his spine much like the front plank; the only major difference is that here the athlete is preventing spinal lateral flexion (side bend) rather than resisting spinal extension.

Figure 10.17   Side plank: *(a)* setup; *(b)* standard side plank with hips and knees lifted; *(c)* modified side plank with one knee touching the ground.

Setup for the exercise is similar to that in the side-lying straight-leg abduction warm-up exercise in chapter 1: the athlete aligns in a straight line, lying on his side with his ankle, knee, hip, and shoulder joints stacked vertically. He places his bottom elbow directly under his bottom shoulder, with his forearm pointing forward in the same direction as his sternum (figure 10.17a). From here, he raises his hips off the ground so that his only points of contact with the ground are his bottom forearm and the outside of his bottom foot (figure 10.17b). His legs remain fully locked; his hips and trunk all remain in a line, now angling upward as he is propped up on his bottom arm. Legs remain together, but the top leg can be raised if a more difficult variation is needed.

As with the front plank, the side plank can also be modified for athletes who do not have the strength to hold the traditional position. The athlete simply sets up with his knees bent at 90 degrees, so that his body forms a straight line from ear to knee; he lifts his hips off the ground and maintains weight on his bottom forearm and his bottom knee (figure 10.17c). Side planks in this training program are completed for 2 to 3 sets of one 20-second side plank on each side.

DEAD BUG

Bearing a striking resemblance to its namesake, the dead bug exercise looks like a beetle on its back flailing its legs. The setup is like an upside-down version of the quadruped position in chapter 1; the athlete lies back with his legs in the air and his hips tilted posteriorly so that his lower back is flat against the ground. His head is back, and he holds both arms straight up in the air, pointing in the same direction as his sternum (figure 10.18a). Regardless of the variation performed, the dead bug exercise calls on the athlete's anterior trunk muscles to keep his lower back in neutral position; he must resist the lengthened levers of his extending limbs, which threaten to pry his sacrum off the ground into lumbar extension.

The easiest variation in the dead bug exercise progression is to alternate tapping each heel to the ground and then lifting it, while the knees stay bent at a 90-degree angle (figure 10.18b). The athlete can progress from here by adding gradually more knee extension at the end of each repetition (figure 10.18c); once he can control the exercise with alternating fully extended legs, he begins simultaneously extending his contralateral (opposite side) arm with each repetition (figure 10.18d). If the exercise becomes too much of a challenge and the athlete loses lumbo-pelvic stability, the repetition should end, and he should regress in dead bug difficulty or time. Perform for 3 sets of 30 seconds, adjusting based on athlete competence.

Figure 10.18   Dead bug progression: *(a)* starting position; *(b)* variation with knees bent; *(c)* variation with leg extending; *(d)* variation with leg extending in tandem with opposite-side arm.

PHYSIOBALL PLANK HOLD

The physioball, sometimes also called a stability ball, introduces an unstable surface to the otherwise normal front plank described earlier in this chapter. The athlete sets up with his elbows and forearms on the ball, and his toes on the ground with his feet together (figure 10.19). His legs are fully extended, while his scapulae and hip position both remain relatively neutral. He maintains this neutral plank position with steady breathing for 30 seconds, then carefully lowers his knees to the ground. The athlete performs 2 to 3 sets of the exercise.

Placing the elbows up on a physioball during this exercise creates a much greater demand for dynamic mobility throughout the athlete's hips and trunk. This dynamic component adds a significant level of difficulty, so athletes must demonstrate strength and proficiency in the front plank and other planking exercises before graduating to the physioball plank hold.

Figure 10.19   Physioball plank hold.

MONSTER WALK

The gluteus medius serves a pivotal role in stabilizing the hip laterally, but many athletes lack strength in this area. The common tendency to focus training along the sagittal plane (straight ahead) at the expense of frontal plane (side-to-side) and transverse plane (rotational) movements can limit the athlete's ability to control his body in all three planes of movement.

The monster walk variations are designed to strengthen the gluteus medius. Placing a miniband around both legs just above the ankles, the athlete stands tall with hands on his hips and weight shifted back onto his heels (figure 10.20a). His toes point straight ahead and his feet are hip-width apart, putting a mild tension on the band. To begin the lateral exercise, he abducts his right leg, pushing his right foot just outside his right shoulder (figure 10.20b) before letting his foot contact the ground again.

Figure 10.20   Monster walk: *(a)* starting position; *(b)* step to the right; *(c)* back step variation.

He then adducts his trailing left leg toward his right leg, placing his left foot on the ground at hip width. This completes one step. The athlete will continue stepping laterally at a controlled pace for 5 yards, then return 5 yards to his left with the opposite stepping sequence. He repeats this pattern twice, for a total of 10 yards in each direction.

The back step monster walk variation is performed with a slight bend in the athlete's knees. He picks up his right leg, abducting and extending to push the leg back and outside at 45 degrees (figure 10.20c). Once his knee and hip are extended and abducted, his right foot returns to the ground, and he brings his left foot back to meet his right foot at hip width. The sequence is repeated with alternating legs, moving backward 10 yards from his starting position to complete the set.

SINGLE-LEG ABDUCTION

The single-leg abduction exercise offers some of the same lateral hip stability benefits as monster walks, with an added balance component. Placing one miniband around both legs just above the knees, the athlete places both hands on his hips and lowers into a quarter squat on his left leg, holding his right foot off the ground (figure 10.21a). Maintaining balance on his left leg and posture in his upper body, the athlete abducts his right leg (figure 10.21b) as if he were using his hip to push his right knee away from his left. After completing 10 repetitions on his right side, the athlete shifts his weight to his right foot and completes 10 repetitions abducting his left leg. Perform the exercise for 3 sets of 10 consecutive repetitions on each leg.

Figure 10.21 Single-leg abduction: *(a)* starting position; *(b)* abduction of the leg.

BANDED POST T

Many athletes display a hunched-over posture with rounded shoulders and upper spine. Among the potential reasons for this are weak upper back muscles losing control of the scapulae and thoracic spine and too much anterior (forward) training with exercises such as the bench press.

The banded post T exercise helps to restore this postural control, strengthening the muscles tasked with keeping the upper back in neutral position. The exercise requires a light band or elastic cord with two handles attached, anchored at the athlete's sternum level. To perform a banded post T, the athlete stands tall with his arms extended straight out in front of him, holding one handle in each hand with a neutral (thumbs up) grip (figure 10.22a). From this position, he retracts his shoulder blades and then opens his straight arms out to his sides, keeping them at shoulder level (figure 10.22b). Coaches should

Figure 10.22 Banded post T: *(a)* starting position.

ensure that there is not too much upper trapezius involvement, as if the athlete is shrugging his shoulders. The athlete completes his set after performing 10 repetitions at a controlled pace. Complete 3 sets.

Figure 10.22   Banded post T: *(b)* ending position.

SERRATUS STEP-UP

The serratus step-up is an assistance lift for building scapular and shoulder stability, and it targets muscle groups (especially the serratus) that can greatly assist in the bench press test encountered at most football combines.

The athlete sets up in a push-up position with both hands on the ground and one 4-inch box placed between his hands. He then begins a controlled pace of lifting one hand up and in to place his palm fully on the top of the box, just beneath his shoulder (figure 10.23*a*). He follows with the other hand, so that his arms are fully extended with both hands up on the box (figure 10.23*b*). He then walks his hands back to the ground, one after the other, so that he is back in his starting position.

The athlete continues moving up and down off the box in alternating order,

Figure 10.23   Serratus step-up: *(a)* one hand on box; *(b)* both hands on box.

while maintaining a controlled pace with stable posture throughout the rest of his body. In this book's training programs the exercise is performed continuously for 25 seconds, at which point the set is complete.

KNEELING ANKLE MOBILITY

Corrective and mobility exercises are overhyped or underhyped, depending on who you ask. The kneeling ankle mobility exercise deserves all the hype in the world because it targets ankle dorsiflexion range of motion, which we know from earlier chapters is absolutely critical to sprint performance.

To perform this exercise, the athlete begins down on one knee, with his other knee bent and his front foot flat on the ground under his

Figure 10.24   Kneeling ankle mobility.

knee. While in a kneeling position, he guides his shin forward, with his knee tracking neutrally over his toes (figure 10.24). He moves his shin forward as far as he comfortably can with his heel remaining on the ground, feeling a stretch in the back of his (front) ankle and (front) lower leg. The stretch should challenge his muscle and tendon without reaching the point of major discomfort. The exercise should be done for 3 sets of 8 reps on each side.

SUPINE BREATHING

One great way to use a rest interval is to teach athletes to change focus from the sympathetic nervous system to the parasympathetic. The athlete lies on the ground flat on his back and focuses on creating controlled breaths in and out through his diaphragm rather than his ribs. When implemented, the drill is typically performed for three sets of 60 seconds each.

Key Considerations for Combine Strength Training

When it comes to planning strength workouts, the practitioner's primary consideration should be the athlete's training status: novice or elite. Novice athletes should have simple exercise pairings in their workouts, typically around 5 repetitions for most strength exercises. Elite athletes need more complex methods and higher volume.

For combine training, we must take into account the physical qualities that the combine tests and drills demand. Most combines use the barbell bench press to measure upper-body strength, although for many elite players, bench pressing 225 pounds is more a test of strength endurance than absolute strength. For these elite-level athletes, neglecting upper-body strength endurance training will mean suboptimal combine results. Therefore it is crucial for coaches to balance maximal upper-body strength with strength endurance during combine prep. Higher-volume strength endurance work will create more extrinsic (tissue) stress, which requires a longer recovery period. The Friday lift is a good candidate for this type of training because athletes will have the weekend to recover physically before resuming training on Monday.

Conclusion

Strength exercises are foundational to a training program's effectiveness, even in preparation for a specific one-time event such as a football combine. These exercises are intentionally simple. Athletes must receive adequate saturation of a training stressor, especially during this narrow training window. Too much exercise variability from week to week will only limit the athlete's potential for training gains. Chapter 11 is dedicated to power exercises, although readers will find exercises from this chapter located throughout the book's novice and elite training programs in chapter 12. Some of these exercises can shift from being strength-dominant to more power-dominant when they are programmed at a specific volume and intensity, whereas others are used as assistance exercises throughout the training cycle. All of them are staple exercises that athletes should learn and practice.

Training for Power

Several high-priority athletic qualities need to be trained during combine preparation: endurance, strength, power, and speed. These qualities build upon each other over the course of training, but if we narrow them down to those that are most vital to testing day performance, power sits at the top of the list. *Power* describes work done over time, and it is a vital physical component in both combine testing and sport performance.

A football talent evaluator might have to pore over files collected about thousands of athletes to determine which ones deserve a closer look. With only limited testing information available for these players, the evaluator would be best served by focusing on those with the best raw power scores. As mentioned in chapter 3, the vertical jump and broad jump are gold standard tests that help football scouts to quickly determine athletic potential, along with the 10-yard and 20-yard splits in the 40-yard dash. Power is a strong predictor of speed, and the athletes who put up better numbers in power testing also tend to be the faster athletes (Cronin and Hansen 2005).

Balancing Mass and Acceleration in Combine Training

The classic force equation from Newton's second law is written as $F = m \times a$. This equation denotes that we calculate a force using the mass of an object or body in motion, multiplied by its rate of acceleration. We are interested in this equation as it pertains to an athlete's ability to produce and withstand forces in competitive sport and combine testing scenarios. During a vertical jump, for example, the athlete's takeoff force is defined as the product of his body's mass and the rate at which his mass accelerates off the ground. To produce more force during his jump, the athlete could accelerate the same mass faster off the ground, move a heavier body mass at the same rate of acceleration, or do both by moving more body mass faster.

The value of F in the $F = m \times a$ equation (force is classified in units of Newtons) is less important to most strength and conditioning practitioners than developing a working knowledge of how to best manipulate the equation's other two variables (mass and acceleration) during training to maximize that value. Some strength coaches become overly concerned with how much weight someone can lift. They emphasize mass over acceleration, making our force equation read more like $F = M \times a$. Absolute strength does serve as the foundation for other physical qualities, and it has its place in training, but too much focus on training this end of the force–velocity curve will fail to produce the maximum possible performance gains for elite athletes. Football players do not have much time to generate force in their sport; chapter 7 describes the need in sprinting acceleration to produce as much force as possible within a fraction of a second. A football player could train at a very high percentage of his one-repetition maximum (1RM) for the duration of his combine training and make impressive strength gains, but if he cannot translate that added strength into a greater rate of force development (RFD), he will see less improvement than he might have hoped for.

For superior athletic development, we must flip the emphasis around so it reads $F = m \times A$, placing more emphasis on movement velocity as the training cycle progresses. This does not make absolute strength unimportant; one must train both ends of the spectrum at the appropriate times.

An important caveat must be given about training age, however. Elite-level football players with more accrued training experience may be prepared to train at power's higher velocity range, but most of their novice-level counterparts will benefit more from staying near the strength end of that spectrum. One must keep in mind that because power is derived from strength, a weak athlete will get little benefit from power training.

High school athletes often are not physically stable and strong enough to handle, for example, the velocity of a barbell coming down into a catch position during a clean, so these exercises can make athletes dangerously vulnerable to joint injuries. Practitioners must first ensure their athletes have developed a foundation of strength and stability before launching them directly into higher-velocity weight room training.

Using the Force–Velocity Curve to Train for Power

The give-and-take between mass and acceleration in the force equation is embodied by the force–velocity curve, initially discussed in chapter 6. This parabolic graph illustrates how much force an athlete can produce within a given time frame. High levels of force can be created at both low velocities and high velocities; a 1RM bench press and a plyometric push-up both involve high amounts of force, despite the disparities in total weight moved (or mass moved, in a physics sense) and time required to move it (also known as its acceleration). These variables determine the exercise's location along the force–velocity curve, which tells us which type of strength quality the exercise trains.

Researchers and practitioners have classified and defined a number of strength quality types along the force–velocity curve (e.g., starting strength, explosive strength) (Mann 2016). Some of these qualities describe a very narrow bandwidth of velocity, whereas *power* can be viewed as a more general term covering the strength-speed and speed-strength areas of that curve. Semantics aside, power means producing high amounts of force at high velocities; it is a useful descriptor that can simultaneously apply to athletes of different training ages.

Knowing the variables involved, we can plot exercises along the force–velocity curve and use them strategically in our training programs, with the intent to influence a desired physical quality at a specific time in the athlete's training cycle. Research has shown that "within a microcycle, power may be trained across the load-power spectrum by varying the barbell load, and this may cause the entire load-power curve to be shifted upward rather than merely elevating one end of the curve (e.g., through strength-oriented training or speed-oriented training)" (Baker 2001).

Although it is not a perfect tool, the force–velocity curve is one of the best available resources to help guide exercise selection over the course of a training program. It can be helpful to classify exercises as either force-dominant or velocity-dominant on a 1 to 5 scale along the curve.

Squats and cleans in the chapter 12 training cycle are prescribed for specific percentages of a 1RM, or a specific measured bar velocity, in order to achieve the exercise velocity athletes will need to train a particular physical quality at that time. Speed squats in this book's elite-level program range up to 75 percent 1RM during the first four weeks of the training macrocycle, but they only build up to 65 percent 1RM during the last four weeks, working down to a maximum of 55 percent 1RM in week 8 (the final week of the taper). In these last few weeks, the trend shifts toward velocity to prime athletes for their testing day.

Power Training Modalities

Power training relies heavily on plyometrics, or exercises that use the stretch-shortening cycle (SSC) and are "aimed at linking sheer strength and speed of movement to produce an explosive-reactive type of movement" (Chu and Plummer 1984). Although achieving this goal seems relatively simple, one can select from an array of modalities and programming techniques to maximize an athlete's power development.

Postactivation potentiation (PAP) is another concept that is critical to elite-level power training. To use PAP in training, coaches can follow a potentiating exercise with a power exercise, creating what is known as a strength-power potentiating complex (SPPC); researchers posit that using potentiating complexes should enhance athletes' training adaptations over more traditional protocols because the PAP effect amplifies the athlete's power output for the training session (Seitz and Haff 2015).

Elastic bands have been studied as an effective training modality; they provide a variable resistance to maintain stress through the movement. Specifically, they increase stress during the movement at a rate that other variable-resistance methods like barbell squats with chains cannot. Bands can also be helpful to decelerate the weight, such as in a speed squat; however, they are not recommended for athletes with a lower training age (Rhea, Kenn, and Dermody 2009).

The PAP method is also best suited for better-trained athletes. Researchers have found that stronger athletes display a faster and greater postactivation response using PAP training methods than their weaker peers (Seitz, de Villarreal, and Haff 2014).

Exercise Selection

The power exercises described in this book are intended for training athletes to produce more force in less time in preparation for a football combine. This chapter describes some of the weight room exercises that can be used as the focus shifts to higher-velocity training.

POWER CLEAN

After finding comfortable positioning for his feet, the athlete squats down low and grips the bar just slightly outside his vertically aligned shins. His chest is up and abs are engaged, with weight set back in his heels.

The athlete begins the first, slower pull, lifting the bar up to knee level (figure 11.1a). His shins remain vertical, and once the bar passes his tibial tuberosity (the bony landmark on the front of his knee, just below the patella) he explosively extends his knees and hips to accelerate the bar (figure 11.1b). As the bar passes his hips, the athlete guides the weight with his arms, keeping the barbell in tight to his body and catching the bar in a front squat position.

The athlete's feet should remain flat during the exercise for long enough to maximize his ability to drive through the ground. If the athlete gets up to his toes before his hips are extended, he cannot continue pushing into the ground to finish hip extension. In this book's elite-level training program, power cleans are completed for 3 to 6 sets of 1 to 3 repetitions, ranging in weight from 50 to 75 percent 1RM, depending on the point in the athlete's training cycle. Barring

Figure 11.1 Power clean: *(a)* end of first pull; *(b)* end of second pull.

some slight variations due to mock combine week and taper week, power clean volume and intensity generally decrease during this program, with the goal of improving bar speed throughout the training cycle.

PREP LIKE A PRO: VERTIMAX

A proprietary system of pulleys and elastic cables, the Vertimax is an excellent tool for those who have access to the equipment (figures 11.2a and 11.2b). It has been demonstrated to significantly improve power for trained college athletes when the tool is used in tandem with more traditional strength and power modalities (Rhea et al. 2008).

Jumping with elastic resistance is different than jumping with, say, dumbbells: The elastic bands are at a shorter length at the bottom of the countermovement, providing less resistance, and they increase in length and tension as the athlete jumps. This dynamic change in resistance can help an athlete to learn how to finish pushing through the ground during a vertical jump because the athlete now has more resistance to push against as he overcomes inertia and gathers speed in his takeoff.

Devices such as the Vertimax provide their heaviest resistance at the peak of the athlete's jump, when the cords are at their longest. This serves to amplify landing forces by pulling the athlete back down to the ground, accelerating his descent. This effect could be helpful when a coach wants to provide a more intense deceleration stimulus during a workout, to challenge athletes' landing capabilities.

Figure 11.2   The Vertimax device provides resistance for jump training.

BOX JUMP

The box jump is an excellent exercise for reducing the landing force of a jump. This is useful for coaches who want to give their athletes more jumps while limiting the effects of repetitive, high-magnitude impacts on the foot, knee, and hip. It can also add a challenge component as long as the box is not so high that the athlete begins to pull his feet up before finishing his jump.

The athlete performs a standing vertical jump (detailed in chapter 3), landing in a flat-footed, bent, and stable position on top of the box (figure 11.3). He then carefully steps down, rather than hopping off the box. In this book's program, box jumps are typically completed for 3 to 4 sets of 2 to 3 repetitions.

Figure 11.3   Box jump: *(a)* starting position; *(b)* finishing position.

STANDING BROAD JUMP

Broad jumps are vital to power training. In addition to being one of the combine tests (see chapter 3), the standing broad jump also trains power production in a horizontal force vector, which is more consistent with sprinting acceleration.

A full description of the standing broad jump (figure 11.4) can be found in chapter 3. Practitioners must be especially careful with the volume and placement of broad jumps in an athlete's training because extreme shearing forces are created at the knees when landing the jump. Both the novice and elite programs in this book include 3 sets of 2 broad jump repetitions during the Monday lift, but only for weeks 5 and 7 of the 8-week training cycle.

Figure 11.4   Standing broad jump: *(a)* starting position; *(b)* countermovement; *(c)* jump; *(d)* landing.

BOX BLAST

The box blast is a vertical jump with one foot elevated on an 8- to 12-inch box and the other foot just outside the box at hip width (figure 11.5*a*). The athlete performs a countermovement (figure 11.5*b*) and jump (figure 11.5*c*), pushing off both feet with the majority of force from the top foot. He then lands with his feet in the starting position.

Box blasts are wonderful for teaching athletes how to attack out of a three-point stance in their 40-yard dash. However, they can also be extremely dangerous for an athlete's foot and ankle. Coaches must first trust that an athlete is coordinated enough to land this complex jump before implementing box blasts in the athlete's training. The exercise tends to be performed for 2 to 4 sets of 2 to 3 repetitions each side.

Figure 11.5 Box blast: *(a)* starting position; *(b)* countermovement; *(c)* jump.

MEDICINE BALL DROP

The medicine ball drop is a unique exercise because it requires triphasic upper-body action performed explosively. The athlete is challenged to quickly slow, stop, and then reaccelerate a falling projectile.

To perform this exercise, the athlete lies flat on his back with the crown of his head aligned near the bottom edge of a 20-inch box. He extends his arms and prepares to catch the falling medicine ball. A partner or coach stands on the box, holding the medicine ball directly over the athlete's waiting hands (figure 11.6*a*).

When the athlete is ready, his partner drops the ball. The athlete catches the ball (figure 11.6b) and chest passes it back up for the partner to catch. Drop height and ball weight are both variables that can be manipulated based on the athlete's level of strength and competence, as well as the desired velocity. The training programs in chapter 12 include the medicine ball drop for 3 to 4 sets of 5 repetitions, using a medicine ball weight appropriate to the athlete's size and relative upper-body power.

Figure 11.6   Medicine ball drop: *(a)* starting position; *(b)* catch.

PLYO PUSH-UP

Setting up in a normal push-up position, the athlete has 4- to 6-inch boxes or risers lined up just to the outside of each hand. He lowers into his bottom push-up position at a controlled pace (figure 11.7a). Once he reaches this position, he pushes explosively through the ground with both hands. He should create enough force to leave the ground, comfortably landing both hands just outside their starting width atop the boxes (figure 11.7b). He then lowers off the boxes one hand at a time to begin the next repetition, taking a moment to reset his posture and body position between reps if necessary. The athlete's body should remain aligned straight from ear to ankle throughout the exercise. Plyo push-ups can be performed for 3 to 4 sets of 2 to 5 repetitions.

Figure 11.7   Plyo push-up: *(a)* lower push-up position; *(b)* hands on boxes.

MEDICINE BALL OPEN ROTATION

Rotary medicine ball throws help to teach and enhance rotational force production and transfer, coming from the ground up through the kinetic chain and into an explosive throw. These throws are performed against a wall either as single explosive efforts with medicine balls designed for reduced rebound or for repeated lower-intensity repetitions to train trunk resilience and endurance.

An "open" orientation means facing the wall in an athletic position, holding the medicine ball in close at hip level and off to one side (figure 11.8a). To execute a repetition, the athlete rotates his trunk to bring the ball just outside one hip, while both feet stay flat on the ground. He then pushes through the ground with both feet, emphasizing the inside edge of his outside foot. He transfers this force through his knees and hips, and as his hips begin to rotate toward the wall, he pivots his back foot. As the athlete transfers maximum force through his kinetic chain to his trunk and upper body, his hands finish releasing the throw forward into the wall (figure 11.8b). The medicine ball open rotation exercise can be performed for 3 to 4 sets of 3 to 5 repetitions on each side.

Figure 11.8 Medicine ball open rotation: *(a)* windup; *(b)* release.

MEDICINE BALL CLOSED ROTATION

The athlete starts the medicine ball closed rotation in an athletic base, holding a medicine ball at hip level, just like the open rotation—except now he faces sideways with his feet running parallel to the wall (figure 11.9a). The intent to transfer force from the ground into the medicine ball should remain the same as in the open rotation throw. The only change is that he is releasing the ball sideways instead of forward (figure 11.9b). This exercise can be performed for 3 to 4 sets of 2 to 4 repetitions on each side.

Figure 11.9 Medicine ball closed rotation; *(a)* windup; *(b)* release.

MEDICINE BALL OVERHEAD THROW

The medicine ball overhead throw (OHT) is a high-velocity throw behind the athlete and over his head. He begins standing tall with his arms extended overhead holding an 8- to 12-pound medicine ball. When he is ready, he hinges at the hips and squats, bringing the ball down toward the ground (figure 11.10a). After reaching his desired bottom position—not quite a squat or deadlift, perhaps some trunk flexion but no rounding in the upper (thoracic) spine—the athlete pushes his feet through the ground and transfers force up through a solid kinetic chain, squatting up and extending his hips as he brings his arms back overhead to release the medicine ball up and behind him (figure 11.10b). The exercise teaches athletes how to produce power from the ground and offers them a very visual feedback mechanism in the height and distance of their throw. In this book's combine training programs, the exercise is completed for 3 to 6 sets of 1 to 2 repetitions; elite-level trainees perform overhead medicine ball throws at the end of acceleration work, whereas novice athletes complete the exercise during their lift.

Figure 11.10   Medicine ball overhead throw: *(a)* bottom position; *(b)* throw.

BARBELL SPEED SQUAT

The barbell speed squat is completed with the same form as a regular barbell back squat (see chapter 10), but with a lighter weight and a greater emphasis on speed. This places the speed squat further toward the velocity end of the force–velocity curve (see chapter 6), making it a useful exercise for power or speed training phases, as well as for the taper before testing or competition.

The lowering or eccentric portion of the speed squat is performed at regular tempo. When the athlete reaches the bottom position of his squat, he explosively extends his knees and hips to return to a standing position as fast as possible without compromising correct squat form. For more details on the barbell back squat, refer to the description in chapter 10.

Because of the speed squat's explosive nature, the athlete's heels may briefly leave the ground as he finishes his squat, but he should not remain on his toes for an extended period of time. Instead, he returns his heels to the ground and resets his squat stance if necessary before beginning the next repetition. In this book's training programs, the barbell speed squat is performed for 3 to 5 sets of 2 to 5 repetitions each, with a weight ranging from 50 to 75 percent 1RM; readers will notice the elite-level training cycle displays a general increase in volume and a decrease in load over the course of the eight weeks (see chapter 12).

DUMBBELL SQUAT JUMP

One of the best lower-body exercises for contrast training is the dumbbell squat jump. It provides a static resistance to overcome as opposed to, say, dynamic resistance such as that provided by the Vertimax device described earlier in this chapter. The dumbbell squat jump is performed using a total dumbbell load equal to 10 percent of the athlete's body weight. Players of different proportions and genetic makeup (e.g., factors such as tendon length and attachment position, among others) may need slight adjustments according to the coach's discretion.

The athlete holds the dumbbells at his sides and performs a countermovement jump while the dumbbells remain at his sides, sticking his landing in a flat-footed quarter to half squat position (figure 11.11). The athlete completes 3 to 5 sets in this book's training cycle for 1 to 3 repetitions each, with a reset back to starting position before each jump. The novice program calls for jumping with 10 percent of the athlete's body weight, whereas the elite program is 5 percent of body weight.

Figure 11.11 Dumbbell squat jump: *(a)* countermovement; *(b)* jump.

SNAP DOWN

The snap down exercise simulates the initial countermovement of a standing vertical jump. The athlete begins by aligning himself as if attempting a vertical jump. He brings his arms high overhead and pulls himself down quickly like he is beginning a countermovement jump (figure 11.12), snapping to his bottom jump position, roughly a quarter to half squat position, depending on his dimensions and RFD capabilities, and holding it. This exercise can be completed for 3 to 5 sets of 2 to 4 repetitions.

This exercise not only benefits the athlete's central nervous system (CNS) but also helps him feel more comfortable with his bottom position during a countermovement. Sets in this book's training program are completed for 2 to 4 repetitions, stopping abruptly and holding at the bottom position, before relaxing and resetting for the next repetition.

Figure 11.12   Snap down: *(a)* arms overhead; *(b)* snap down position.

BACKWARD ANKLE HOP

Backward ankle hops can offer a tremendous benefit to sprinting and athletic performance when implemented correctly. Standing tall with hands on hips, the athlete begins making low-amplitude, reactive jumps off the ground (figure 11.13). His foot stays in a mostly rigid and dorsiflexed position, with the intent of gaining maximal contribution from his lower legs' stretch-shortening cycle (SSC). Rebounding off the ground as high as possible is not the athlete's main goal; rather, he should do so while striving to keep his body stable throughout the exercise. This means he fights his body's tendency to compromise joint positions and sag in posture.

The goal here is not to cover significant ground with each hop; the exercise should be conducted as if hopping in place, but with some of the athlete's momentum carrying him slowly backward over the succession of hops. This exercise places a significant load on the athlete's Achilles tendons, so this added strain must be factored in when programming includes other ballistic movements. The athlete travels backward 5 yards to complete one set.

Workout Structure

Power training places high demands on the athlete's central nervous system (CNS). In order to derive maximum benefit from these exercises, coaches must prioritize by placing the more CNS-intensive exercises earlier in the workout, when the athlete's CNS is less fatigued. This especially applies to the Olympic lifts, such as the power clean, because they require a great deal of learned skill and become more difficult for athletes to execute properly under neural fatigue. Long rest intervals (typically at least 3 minutes) help to keep power output high throughout the workout. Workout volume for novice-level trainees should be lower than that of elite athletes, especially if movement sessions are immediately before an athlete's lift.

Figure 11.13   Backward ankle hop.

Conclusion

Power is one of the most essential qualities to develop when preparing for a football combine—and for the sport of football itself. Power exercises can be spotted throughout the course of this book's training programs, but the coach's goal is to dose these exercises at the desired intersection of force and velocity. Coaches should strategically manipulate these variables during their athletes' training. Chapter 12 explains how to blend this chapter's power exercises with the exercises and drills from earlier chapters to form a cohesive program.

PART V

Training Structure and Programming

Structuring Training Cycles

Once a practitioner has conducted the necessary intake evaluations, assessed the athlete's primary training needs, and determined which exercises and drills to use according to KPIs for success during the testing process, the challenge of writing out a training plan begins in earnest. This road map may include some customizations based on individual athletes' needs, but the approach can remain relatively general because all players are facing the same combine testing parameters. They are all jumping through the same figurative hoops, so most will benefit from the same type of preparation. The training plans laid out in this chapter can be used as a guideline for how to manipulate stress over the course of an eight-week combine training window. Coaches can use these programs as a springboard to develop more individually relevant programs for their own athletes and coaching styles.

Programming and Periodization

Programming is the strategic implementation of training methods and means, with planned fluctuations in volume and intensity. These scheduled variations are called *periodization*. Within the programming process, training is generally described in different time units, or cycles. A microcycle is typically one week long, a mesocycle is traditionally a three- to five-week training block, and a macrocycle can refer to multiple blocks of training spanning as long as one to four years.

To construct training blocks, we must first know how much time is available to hit our target. In most pro day and combine scenarios, the athlete will have six to eight weeks to prepare. The taper takes up 12 days of that window, which leaves little time for the rest of the program. Because of this limited time frame, methods must be totally spot on. Coaching instruction in combine drill specifics and the art behind the testing must be detailed and effective to set up athletes for success.

Building a Combine Prep Training Cycle

In this chapter, we present an eight-week block of training for a hypothetical high school player looking to prepare for camps or combines (referred to here as novice level), as well as a plan for a college player intending to showcase his talents at pro-level combines and tryouts (elite). These eight-week block training programs build in intensity for four weeks, stabilize for one week, and then stair-step down in volume for the next three weeks, which includes the 12-day taper. A mock combine is held during the fourth week.

The training blocks are constructed to maximize a narrow training window. Coaches who have more time could use multiple training blocks, each one ramping up in intensity for three weeks, followed by a one-week deloading period to recover. This sequence would be repeated for multiple blocks, depending on time available.

The major difference between the two sample weeks shown in tables 12.1 and 12.2 is that the novice level does not include some of the more advanced elite activities, such as visuomotor training. Elite and novice athletes are still advised to split up movement and weight room training into separate morning and afternoon sessions, if possible. If a coach feels the need to reduce a novice athlete's training volume, reductions should come from the weight room session. Movement training ought to be prioritized.

Tapering for Combine Success

Working backward from the specific testing date to design the training plan is important because the athlete's taper should begin 12 days out from the actual day of the test. The taper is a plan at the end of a training cycle to maximize the athlete's training benefits. The taper is critical. A training cycle could go almost perfectly, yet if the taper is missed, the athlete will not be at his best, and all his hard work may be down the drain.

During this reduction of volume, it is critical to keep training intensity high. This helps to keep the nervous system primed so that as we reduce

Table 12.1 Sample Microcycle for a Novice Player

Day	Morning	Afternoon
Monday	Acceleration mechanics (quality emphasis)	Lower-body strength (jumps, squats, Bulgarians, etc.)
Tuesday	Multidirectional movement	Upper-body strength
Wednesday	Recovery (foam rolling series, active isolated stretching patterns, barefoot stability, soft tissue therapy)	Off
Thursday	Top-end speed (emphasis on drilling saturation and skill work)	Lower-body strength and power (squats, jumps, etc.)
Friday	Multidirectional drill practice (5-10-5, L-drill, position-specific combine drills)	Upper-body strength (bench press test practice if needed)
Saturday	Recovery: soft tissue work	Video analysis
Sunday	Off	Off

volume, the athlete will start to have more "pop" in his jumps, sprints, and change-of-direction drills. Rest intervals between sets during the taper must be maximal to allow the athlete to fully recharge for the next set and to keep quality as high as possible.

The coach's goal during a taper period is to micro-dose the athlete in exercises with high neural intensity to allow for maximal recovery before the event without the athlete beginning to detrain. Table 12.3 shows an example taper schedule.

Table 12.2   Sample Microcycle for an Elite Player

Day	Morning	Afternoon
Monday	Acceleration mechanics (quality emphasis)	High-effort lower-body speed, power, and strength (jumps, throws, cleans, squats, etc.)
Tuesday	Multidirectional movement (closed and closed-reactive combine drills)	Upper-body strength (225-pound bench press test emphasis)
Wednesday	Recovery (foam rolling series, active isolated stretching patterns, barefoot stability, soft tissue therapy)	Technical work (drills, starts, video analysis) Visuomotor training
Thursday	Top-end speed Throws, jumps, or bounds	Lower-body speed, power, and strength, such as sprints, throws, jumps, bounds, cleans, and squats (including contrast method)
Friday	Combine drill practice (5-10-5, L-drill, position-specific drills)	Upper-body strength (training emphasis rotates between bar speed and muscular endurance overload) Upper-body pulling, scapular stability work
Saturday	Recovery: soft tissue work Auxiliary weight room session	Drill technique, video analysis
Sunday	Off	Off

Table 12.3   Sample Taper Schedule Based on 12 Days Out from Combine

Days from combine	Activities
12	Full warm-up
	1a. Resisted run 3×5 yd
	1b. Acceleration start 3×10 yd
	2a. Resisted run 3×5 yd
	2b. Sprint 2×20 yd
	Medicine ball overhead throw 3×1
	Strength:
	1a. Clean 4×2 65%-70%
	1b. Squat jump 4×2
	2a. Speed squat 4×3
	2b. Vertec or broad jump 3×2
	3a. Bottom-up step-up 4×3
	3b. Side plank 3×20 sec

(continued)

Table 12.3 (continued)

Days from combine	Activities
11	Full warm-up
	Pro agility drill 2×2
	L-drill 2×2
	Position work (light)
10	Full warm-up
	Active recovery
9	Full warm-up
	Acceleration start 3×10 yd
	Sprint 2×20 yd
	Medicine ball overhead throw 3×1
8	Full warm-up
	Acceleration start 1×2 10 yd
	Sprint 1×2 20 yd
	Sprint 1×2 40 yd (85%)
	Strength:
	1a. Power clean 4×2 (60%-65%)
	1b. Squat jump 3×2
	2a. Bottom-up step-up 3×2
	2b. Plank 3×30 sec
7	Full warm-up
	Pro agility drill 1×2
	L-drill 1×2
	Strength:
	Last 225-pound bench press test
6	Full warm-up
	Active recovery
5	Full warm-up
	Acceleration start 2×10 yd
	Pro agility drill 1×1
	L-drill 1×1
4	Full warm-up
	Pro agility drill 1×1
	L-drill 1×1
	Power clean 4×1 (65%)
3	Full warm-up
	Acceleration start 2×10 yd
	Pro agility drill 1×1
	L-drill 1×1
	Medicine ball overhead throw 3×1
2	Full warm-up
1	Day of combine

Macrocycle Examples

This chapter contains two example eight-week training macrocycles. These two programs are designed to address two levels of football combine athletes: novice for potential future college players and elite for prospects at the professional level. This status is primarily determined by an athlete's training age and physical maturity, so not all players are expected to fall neatly into one category or the other.

Each week has four training days (listed here as Monday, Tuesday, Thursday, and Friday). Each training day includes both a movement skills session and a weight room session. It is recommended that the day's movement and lifting sessions be performed back to back as written. If an athlete needs a reduction in training volume or must skip a workout, movement sessions should be prioritized over lifting sessions.

Listed next to each exercise are the sets, repetitions, and intensities for each week of the program, followed by rest between sets. Some of the exercises in a workout may be grouped together into "pairings," denoted by a number and letter. For example, a workout may include a 1a exercise paired with a 1b and a 1c exercise. In this scenario, the athlete performs the *a* exercise, followed by the *b* exercise, and finally the *c* exercise, then takes the prescribed rest before beginning his next set. He completes all indicated sets of this pairing before moving on to the next pairing or exercise.

Table 12.4   Novice Training Program: Monday, Weeks 1 to 4

MOVEMENT SKILLS SESSION		WEEK 1		WEEK 2		WEEK 3		WEEK 4	
	Exercise	Sets × reps (intensity)	Rest	Sets × reps (intensity)	Rest	Sets × reps (intensity)	Rest	Sets × reps (intensity)	Rest
Active dynamic warm-up (chapter 1)	General movement prep								
	Walking series								
	Ground series								
	Standing series								
Acceleration training (chapter 7)	Wall drill (1-count, 2-count, 3-count)	2×4 each side	60 sec	2×4 each side	60 sec	1×4 each side	60 sec	None	NA
	A-skip	1×2 (10 yd)	WB	1×2 (10 yd)	WB	1×2 (10 yd)	WB	1×2 (10 yd)	WB
	Resisted A-march	1×2 (10 yd)	WB	1×2 (10 yd)	WB	1×2 (10 yd)	WB	1×2 (10 yd)	WB
	Resisted A-run	1×3 (5 yd)	WB	1×3 (5 yd)	WB	1×3 (5 yd)	WB	1×3 (5 yd)	WB
	Two-point acceleration start*	1×2 (10 yd)	120 sec each rep/180 sec each set	2×2 (10 yd)	120 sec each rep/180 sec each set	3×2 (10 yd)	120 sec each rep/180 sec each set	2×2 (10 yd)	120 sec each rep/180 sec each set
	Three-point acceleration start*	3×3 (15 yd)	120 sec each rep/180 sec each set	3×3 (15 yd)	120 sec each rep/180 sec each set	3×3 (15 yd)	120 sec each rep/180 sec each set	None	NA

(continued)

Table 12.4 (continued)

WEIGHT ROOM SESSION		WEEK 1		WEEK 2		WEEK 3		WEEK 4	
	Exercise	Sets × reps (intensity)	Rest	Sets × reps (intensity)	Rest	Sets × reps (intensity)	Rest	Sets × reps (intensity)	Rest
CNS stimulation	1a. Box jump	3×2	120 sec	3×3	120 sec	4×3	120 sec	3×2	120 sec
	1b. Medicine ball drop	3×5		4×5		4×5		3×5	
Lower body 1	2a. Squat choice	Warm-up 1×5 (50% 1RM)	180 sec	Warm-up 1×5 (50% 1RM)	180 sec	Warm-up 1×5 (50% 1RM)	180 sec	Warm-up 1×5 (50% 1RM)	180 sec
		1×5 (60% 1RM)		1×3 (60% 1RM)		1×3 (60% 1RM)		1×5 (60% 1RM)	
		1×5 (70% 1RM)		1×3 (70% 1RM)		1×3 (70% 1RM)		1×5 (70% 1RM)	
		1×5 (75% 1RM)		1×3 (80% 1RM)		1×2 (75% 1RM)			
				1×3 (85% 1RM)		1×2 (80% 1RM)			
						1×2 (85% 1RM)			
	2b. Dumbbell squat jump	4×3		4×3		4×3		4×3	
Lower body 2	3a. Bulgarian split squat	3×5 each side	120 sec	4×5 each side	120 sec	5×5 each side	120 sec	3×5 each side	120 sec
	3b. Side plank	3×1 each side (20 sec)		3×1 each side (20 sec)		3×1 each side (20 sec)		3×1 each side (20 sec)	

WB = walk back

* Rest: 180 sec between sets plus an additional 60 sec for every 10 yards sprinted

Table 12.5 Novice Training Program: Tuesday, Weeks 1 to 4

MOVEMENT SKILLS SESSION		WEEK 1		WEEK 2		WEEK 3		WEEK 4	
	Exercise	Sets × reps (intensity)	Rest	Sets × reps (intensity)	Rest	Sets × reps (intensity)	Rest	Sets × reps (intensity)	Rest
Active dynamic warm-up (chapter 1)	General movement prep								
	Walking series								
	Ground series								
	Standing series								
Change of direction (chapter 8) and pro agility drill (chapter 3)	Crossover step (tall)	2×4 each side (5 yd)	60 sec	2×4 each side (5 yd)	60 sec	1×4 each side (5 yd)	60 sec	None	NA
	Pro agility drill to first touch	2×3 each side (5 yd)	60 sec	1×2 each side (5 yd)	60 sec	1×2 each side (5 yd)	60 sec	1×2 each side (5 yd)	60 sec
	Pro agility drill to second touch (tall)	2×3 each side (10 yd)	60 sec	1×3 each side (10 yd)	60 sec	1×3 each side (10 yd)	60 sec	1×3 each side (10 yd)	60 sec
	Pro agility drill (full drill)	1×2 each side (20 yd)	120 sec each rep/180 sec each set	2×2 each side (20 yd)	120 sec each rep/180 sec each set	3×2 each side (20 yd)	120 sec each rep/180 sec each set	2×2 each side (20 yd)	120 sec each rep/180 sec each set
	Agility ladder	3 drills × 4 reps each	1:6*	3 drills × 4 reps each	1:6	3 drills × 6 reps each	1:6	2 drills × 4 reps each	1:6
WEIGHT ROOM SESSION		WEEK 1		WEEK 2		WEEK 3		WEEK 4	
	Exercise	Sets x reps (intensity)	Rest	Sets x reps (intensity)	Rest	Sets x reps (intensity)	Rest	Sets x reps (intensity)	Rest
Upper body 1	1a. Barbell bench press	1×8 (55% 1RM)	120 sec	1×8 (55% 1RM)	120 sec	1×8 (55% 1RM)	120 sec	1×5 (50% 1RM)	120 sec
		1×5 (65% 1RM)		1×5 (65% 1RM)		1×5 (65% 1RM)		1×5 (55% 1RM)	
		1×5 (70% 1RM)		1×5 (70% 1RM)		1×5 (70% 1RM)		1×5 (60% 1RM)	
		1×5 (75% 1RM)		1×5 (75% 1RM)		1×5 (75% 1RM)			
				1×5 (80% 1RM)		1×5 (80% 1RM)			
	1b. Medicine ball drop	3×5		4×5		4×5		3×5	
	1c. Miniband lateral monster walk	3×10 yd each way		4×10 yd each way		4×10 yd each way		3×10 yd each way	

(continued)

Table 12.5 *(continued)*

WEIGHT ROOM SESSION		WEEK 1		WEEK 2		WEEK 3		WEEK 4	
	Exercise	Sets × reps (intensity)	Rest	Sets × reps (intensity)	Rest	Sets × reps (intensity)	Rest	Sets × reps (intensity)	Rest
Upper body 2	2a. Single-arm dumbbell row	4×5 each side	120 sec	2×5 each side	120 sec	1×5 each side	120 sec	3×5 each side	120 sec
				2×3 each side		1×3 each side			
						2×2 each side			
	2b. Side plank	3×1 each side (20 sec)		3×1 each side (20 sec)		3×1 each side (20 sec)		3×1 each side (20 sec)	
Upper body 3	3a. Dumbbell incline bench press	3×5	120 sec	4×5	120 sec	4×5	120 sec	3×5	120 sec
	3b. Post Ts	3×12		3×12		3×12		3×12	
Upper body 4	4a. Suspension trainer inverted row	3×8	90 sec	4×5	90 sec	5×5	90 sec	3×5	90 sec
	4b. Tempo push-up (2 sec going down/1 sec going up)	3×8		3×8		3×8		None	

* Work-to-rest ratio

Table 12.6 Novice Training Program: Thursday, Weeks 1 to 4

MOVEMENT SKILLS SESSION		WEEK 1		WEEK 2		WEEK 3		WEEK 4	
	Exercise	Sets × reps (intensity)	Rest	Sets × reps (intensity)	Rest	Sets × reps (intensity)	Rest	Sets × reps (intensity)	Rest
Active dynamic warm-up (chapter 1)	General movement prep								
	Walking series								
	Ground series								
	Standing series								
Top-end speed training (chapter 9)	Heel slide	2×3 (10 yd)	WB	2×3 (10 yd)	WB	3×3 (10 yd)	WB	3×3 (10 yd)	WB
	Stepover A-run	2×3 (10 yd)	WB	2×3 (10 yd)	WB	3×3 (10 yd)	WB	3×3 (10 yd)	WB
	Stepover A-skip	2×3 (15 yd)	WB	2×3 (15 yd)	WB	2×3 (15 yd)	WB	3×3 (15 yd)	WB
	Straight-leg shuffle	1×3 (5 yd)	WB	3×3 (5 yd)	WB	2×3 (5 yd)	WB	3×3 (5 yd)	WB
	40-yd buildup (to 75%)	1×3 (40 yd)	120 sec	1×3 (40 yd)	120 sec	2×2 (40 yd)	120 sec	1×2 (40 yd)	120 sec

WEIGHT ROOM SESSION		WEEK 1		WEEK 2		WEEK 3		WEEK 4	
	Exercise	Sets × reps (intensity)	Rest	Sets × reps (intensity)	Rest	Sets × reps (intensity)	Rest	Sets × reps (intensity)	Rest
CNS stimulation	1a. Medicine ball overhead throw	3×2	120 sec	3×2	120 sec	4×2	120 sec	None	NA
	1b. Medicine ball drop	3×5		4×5		4×5		None	
Lower body 1	2a. Dumbbell squat jump	3×3 (5% of body weight)	180 sec	4×3 (5% of body weight)	180 sec	5×3 (5% of body weight)	180 sec	3×3 (5% of body weight)	180 sec
	2b. Front plank	3×30 sec		3×30 sec		3×30 sec		3×30 sec	
Lower body 2	3a. Dumbbell step-up	3×5 each side	120 sec	4×5 each side	120 sec	4×5 each side	120 sec	3×5 each side	120 sec
	3b. Side plank	3×1 each side (20 sec)		3×1 each side (20 sec)		3×1 each side (20 sec)		None	

WB = walk back

Table 12.7 Novice Training Program: Friday, Weeks 1 to 4

MOVEMENT SKILLS SESSION		WEEK 1		WEEK 2		WEEK 3		WEEK 4	
	Exercise	Sets × reps (intensity)	Rest	Sets × reps (intensity)	Rest	Sets × reps (intensity)	Rest	Sets × reps (intensity)	Rest
Active dynamic warm-up (chapter 1)	General movement prep								
	Walking series								
	Ground series								
	Standing series								
Change of direction (chapter 8) and L-drill (chapter 3) training	L-drill to first touch	1×3 (5 yd)	60 sec	1×3 (5 yd)	60 sec	1×2 (5 yd)	60 sec	1×2 (5 yd)	60 sec
	L-drill to second touch	1×3 (10 yd)	60 sec	1×3 (10 yd)	60 sec	2×2 (10 yd)	60 sec	2×2 (10 yd)	60 sec
	L-drill figure eight (from second touch)	1×3 (20 yd)	90 sec	2×3 (20 yd)	90 sec	2×2 (20 yd)	90 sec	2×2 (20 yd)	90 sec
	L-drill full drill (80% speed)	2×2 (30 yd)	120 sec	2×2 (30 yd)	120 sec	3×2 (30 yd)	120 sec	2×2 (30 sec)	120 sec

(continued)

Table 12.7 (continued)

WEIGHT ROOM SESSION		WEEK 1		WEEK 2		WEEK 3		WEEK 4	
	Exercise	Sets × reps (intensity)	Rest	Sets × reps (intensity)	Rest	Sets × reps (intensity)	Rest	Sets × reps (intensity)	Rest
Upper body 1	1a. Alternating dumbbell incline press	1×8 each arm	120 sec	1×8 each arm	120 sec	4×2 each arm	120 sec	3×5 each arm	120 sec
		3×5 each arm		4×5 each arm					
	1b. Miniband lateral monster walk	3×10 each way		3×10 each way		3×10 each way		3×10 each way	
Upper body 2	2a. Bent-over barbell row	1×8	120 sec	5×5	180 sec	4×2	180 sec	3×5	180 sec
		3×5							
	2b. Dumbbell squat jump	4×3		4×3		4×3		4×3	
Upper body 3	3a. Tempo push-up (2 sec going down/1 sec going up)	3×10	120 sec	3×12	120 sec	3×15	120 sec	3×5	120 sec
	3b. Post Ts	3×12		3×12		3×12		3×12	
Upper body 4	4a. Suspension trainer inverted row	3×10	NA	3×12	NA	3×15	NA	3×5	NA
	4b. Supine breathing drill (rest)	3×60 sec		3×60 sec		3×60 sec		3×60 sec	

Table 12.8   Novice Training Program: Monday, Weeks 5 to 8

MOVEMENT SKILLS SESSION		WEEK 5		WEEK 6		WEEK 7		WEEK 8	
	Exercise	Sets × reps (intensity)	Rest	Sets × reps (intensity)	Rest	Sets × reps (intensity)	Rest	Sets × reps (intensity)	Rest
Active dynamic warm-up (chapter 1)	General movement prep								
	Walking series								
	Ground series								
	Standing series								
Acceleration training (chapter 7)	Wall drill (1-count, 2-count, 3-count)	None	NA	None	NA	1×4 each side	60 sec	None	NA
	A-skip	1×2 (10 yd)	WB	1×2 (10 yd)	WB	1×2 (10 yd)	WB	1×2 (10 yd)	WB
	Resisted A-march	1×2 (10 yd)	WB	3×2 (10 yd)	WB	3×2 (10 yd)	WB	2×3 (10 yd)	WB
	Resisted A-run	2×3 (5 yd)	WB	3×3 (5 yd)	WB	3×3 (5 yd)	WB	2×3 (5 yd)	WB

MOVEMENT SKILLS SESSION		WEEK 5		WEEK 6		WEEK 7		WEEK 8	
	Exercise	Sets × reps (intensity)	Rest	Sets × reps (intensity)	Rest	Sets × reps (intensity)	Rest	Sets × reps (intensity)	Rest
	Two-point acceleration start*	1×2 (10 yd)	120 sec each rep/180 sec each set	1×2 (10 yd)	120 sec each rep/180 sec each set	1×3 (10 yd)	120 sec each rep/180 sec each set	2×2 (10 yd)	120 sec each rep/180 sec each set
	Three-point acceleration start*	2×3 (15 yd)	120 sec each rep/180 sec each set	3×3 (15 yd)	120 sec each rep/180 sec each set	3×4 (15 yd)	120 sec each rep/180 sec each set	1×3 (10 yd)	NA

WEIGHT ROOM SESSION		WEEK 5		WEEK 6		WEEK 7		WEEK 8	
	Exercise	Sets × reps (intensity)	Rest	Sets × reps (intensity)	Rest	Sets × reps (intensity)	Rest	Sets × reps (intensity)	Rest
CNS stimulation	1a. Medicine ball overhead throw	3×2	120 sec	3×3	120 sec	4×2	120 sec	3×2	120 sec
Lower body 1	2a. Squat choice	1×5 (65% 1RM)	180 sec	1×5 (65% 1RM)	180 sec	1×5 (65% 1RM)	180 sec	1×2 (50% 1RM)	180 sec
		1×5 (70% 1RM)		1×5 (70% 1RM)		1×3 (70% 1RM)		1×2 (55% 1RM)	
		1×5 (75% 1RM)		1×3 (75% 1RM)		1×2 (75% 1RM)		1×2 (60% 1RM)	
		1×5 (80% 1RM)		1×3 (80% 1RM)		1×2 (80% 1RM)			
	2b. Standing broad jump	3×2		None		3×2		None	
	2b. Dumbbell squat jump	None		3×2		None		3×2	
Lower body 2	3a. Bulgarian split squat	3×5 each side	120 sec	3×3 each side	120 sec	3×2 each side	120 sec	None	60 sec
	3b. Side plank	3×1 each side (20 sec)		3×1 each side (20 sec)		3×1 each side (20 sec)		3×1 each side (20 sec)	

WB = walk back

* Rest: 180 sec between sets plus an additional 60 sec for every 10 yards sprinted

Table 12.9   Novice Training Program: Tuesday, Weeks 5 to 8

MOVEMENT SKILLS SESSION		WEEK 5		WEEK 6		WEEK 7		WEEK 8	
	Exercise	Sets × reps (intensity)	Rest	Sets × reps (intensity)	Rest	Sets × reps (intensity)	Rest	Sets × reps (intensity)	Rest
Active dynamic warm-up (chapter 1)	General movement prep								
	Walking series								
	Ground series								
	Standing series								
Change of direction (chapter 8) and pro agility drill (chapter 3)	Crossover step (tall)	2×4 each way (5 yd)	60 sec	2×4 each way (5 yd)	60 sec	1×4 each way (5 yd)	60 sec	None	NA
	Pro agility drill to first touch	2×3 (5 yd)	60 sec	1×2 (5 yd)	60 sec	1×2 (5 yd)	60 sec	1×2 (5 yd)	60 sec
	Pro agility drill to second touch (tall)	2×3 (10 yd)	60 sec	3×2 (10 yd)	60 sec	3×2 (10 yd)	60 sec	2×3 (10 yd)	60 sec
	Pro agility drill (full drill)	1×2 (20 yd)	120 sec each rep/180 sec each set	1×4 (20 yd)	120 sec each rep/180 sec each set	3×2 (20 yd)	120 sec each rep/180 sec each set	2×1 (20 yd)	120 sec each rep/180 sec each set
	Agility ladder	3 drills × 4 reps each	1:6*	3 drills × 6 reps each	1:6	3 drills × 4 reps each	1:6	2 drills × 4 reps each	1:6
WEIGHT ROOM SESSION		**WEEK 5**		**WEEK 6**		**WEEK 7**		**WEEK 8**	
	Exercise	Sets × reps (intensity)	Rest	Sets × reps (intensity)	Rest	Sets × reps (intensity)	Rest	Sets × reps (intensity)	Rest
Upper body 1	1a. Barbell bench press	1×5 (65% 1RM)	90 sec	1×5 (65% 1RM)	90 sec	1×5 (65% 1RM)	90 sec	3×5 (60% 1RM)	180 sec
		1×5 (70% 1RM)	120 sec	1×5 (70% 1RM)	120 sec	1×3 (70% 1RM)	120 sec		
		1×5 (75% 1RM)	120-180 sec	1×3 (75% 1RM)	120-180 sec	1×2 (75% 1RM)	120-180 sec		
		1×5 (80% 1RM)		1×3 (80% 1RM)		1×2 (80% 1RM)			
	1b. Medicine ball drop	3×5		4×5		4×5		3×5	
	1c. Miniband lateral monster walk	3×10 yd each side		4×10 yd each side		4×10 yd each side		4×10 yd each side	

WEIGHT ROOM SESSION		WEEK 5		WEEK 6		WEEK 7		WEEK 8	
	Exercise	Sets × reps (intensity)	Rest	Sets × reps (intensity)	Rest	Sets × reps (intensity)	Rest	Sets × reps (intensity)	Rest
Upper body 2	2a. Single-arm dumbbell row	Warm-up 1×8 each side (55% 1RM)	120 sec	Warm-up 1×8 each side (55% 1RM)	120 sec	4×2 each side (55% 1RM)	120 sec	1×5 (50% 1RM)	120 sec
		1×5 (65% 1RM)		1×3 (60% 1RM)		1×3 (60% 1RM)		1×5 (55% 1RM)	
		1×5 (70% 1RM)		1×3 (70% 1RM)		1×3 (70% 1RM)		1×5 (60% 1RM)	
		1×5 (75% 1RM)		1×3 (80% 1RM)		1×2 (75% 1RM)			
				1×3 (85% 1RM)		1×2 (80% 1RM)			
						1×2 (85% 1RM)			
	2b. Side plank	3×1 each side (20 sec)		3×1 each side (20 sec)		3×1 each side (20 sec)		3×1 each side (20 sec)	
Upper body 3	3a. Incline dumbbell bench press	3×5	120 sec	4×5	120 sec	4×5	120 sec	3×5	120 sec
	3b. Post Ts	3×12		3×12		3×12		3×12	
Upper body 4	4a. Suspension trainer inverted row	3×8	120 sec	4×8	120 sec	4×8	120 sec	3×5	120 sec
	4b. Serratus step-up	3×1 (25 sec continuous)		3×1 (25 sec continuous)		3×1 (25 sec continuous)		3×1 (25 sec continuous)	

* Work-to-rest ratio

Table 12.10 Novice Training Program: Thursday, Weeks 5 to 8

MOVEMENT SKILLS SESSION		WEEK 5		WEEK 6		WEEK 7		WEEK 8	
	Exercise	Sets × reps (intensity)	Rest	Sets × reps (intensity)	Rest	Sets × reps (intensity)	Rest	Sets × reps (intensity)	Rest
Active dynamic warm-up (chapter 1)	General movement prep								
	Walking series								
	Ground series								
	Standing series								

(continued)

Table 12.10 (continued)

MOVEMENT SKILLS SESSION		WEEK 5		WEEK 6		WEEK 7		WEEK 8	
	Exercise	**Sets × reps (intensity)**	**Rest**	**Sets × reps (intensity)**	**Rest**	**Sets × reps (intensity)**	**Rest**	**Sets × reps (intensity)**	**Rest**
Top-end speed training (chapter 9)	Heel slides	1×3 (10 yd)	WB	1×3 (10 yd)	WB	1×3 (10 yd)	WB	1×3 (10 yd)	WB
	Stepover run	2×3 (10 yd)	WB	2×3 (10 yd)	WB	3×3 (10 yd)	WB	1×3 (10 yd)	WB
	Flying 10s	1×2 (30 yd)	WB	1×2 (30 yd)	WB	1×3 (30 yd)	WB	None	NA
	Flying 20s	1×3 (40 yd)	WB	3×3 (40 yd)	WB	2×3 (40 yd)	WB	None	NA
	40-yd buildup (to 75%)	None	NA	None	NA	None	NA	1×2 (40 yd)	180 sec
WEIGHT ROOM SESSION		**WEEK 5**		**WEEK 6**		**WEEK 7**		**WEEK 8**	
	Exercise	**Sets × reps (intensity)**	**Rest**	**Sets × reps (intensity)**	**Rest**	**Sets × reps (intensity)**	**Rest**	**Sets × reps (intensity)**	**Rest**
CNS stimulation	1a. Medicine ball overhead throw	3×2	120 sec	3×3	120 sec	4×2	120 sec	None	NA
	1b. Medicine ball drop	3×5		4×5		4×5			
Lower body 1	2a. Dumbbell squat jump	3×3 (5% of body weight)	180 sec	4×3 (5% of body weight)	180 sec	5×3 (5% of body weight)	180 sec	3×3 (5% of body weight)	180 sec
	2b. Front plank	3×30 sec		3×30 sec		3×30 sec		3×30 sec	
Lower body 2	3a. Dumbbell step-up	3×5 each side	120 sec	4×5 each side	120 sec	4×5 each side	120 sec	3×5 each side	120 sec
	3b. Side plank	3×1 each side (20 sec)		3×1 each side (20 sec)		3×1 each side (20 sec)		3×1 each side (20 sec)	

WB = walk back

Table 12.11 Novice Training Program: Friday, Weeks 5 to 8

MOVEMENT SKILLS SESSION		WEEK 5		WEEK 6		WEEK 7		WEEK 8	
	Exercise	**Sets × reps (intensity)**	**Rest**	**Sets × reps (intensity)**	**Rest**	**Sets × reps (intensity)**	**Rest**	**Sets × reps (intensity)**	**Rest**
Active dynamic warm-up (chapter 1)	General movement prep								
	Walking series								
	Ground series								
	Standing series								

MOVEMENT SKILLS SESSION		WEEK 5		WEEK 6		WEEK 7		WEEK 8	
	Exercise	Sets × reps (intensity)	Rest	Sets × reps (intensity)	Rest	Sets × reps (intensity)	Rest	Sets × reps (intensity)	Rest
Change of direction (chapter 8) and L-drill (chapter 3) training	L-drill to first touch	2×3 (5 yd)	60 sec	2×2 (5 yd)	60 sec	1×2 (5 yd)	60 sec	1×2 (5 yd)	60 sec
	L-drill to second touch	2×3 (10 yd)	60 sec	2×2 (10 yd)	60 sec	2×2 (10 yd)	60 sec	2×2 (10 yd)	60 sec
	L-drill figure eight (from second touch)	2×2 (20 yd)	90 sec	2×2 (20 yd)	90 sec	2×2 (20 yd)	90 sec	2×2 (20 yd)	90 sec
	L-drill full drill (80% speed)	1×2 (30 yd)	120 sec	2×2 (30 yd)	120 sec	3×2 (30 yd)	120 sec	2×2 (30 sec)	120 sec

WEIGHT ROOM SESSION		WEEK 5		WEEK 6		WEEK 7		WEEK 8	
	Exercise	Sets × reps (intensity)	Rest	Sets × reps (intensity)	Rest	Sets × reps (intensity)	Rest	Sets × reps (intensity)	Rest
Upper body 1	1a. Alternating dumbbell incline bench press	3×5 each arm	120 sec	3×3 each arm	120 sec	3×3 each arm	120 sec	3×5 each arm	120 sec
	1b. Lateral miniband monster walk	3×10 each way		3×10 each way		3×10 each way		3×10 each side	
Upper body 2	2a. Bent-over barbell row	1×8 3×5	120 sec	5×5	180 sec	4×2	180 sec	3×5	180 sec
	2b. Side plank	3×1 each side (20 sec)		3×1 each side (20 sec)		3×1 each side (20 sec)		3×1 each side (20 sec)	
Upper body 3	3a. Tempo push-up (2 sec going down/1 sec going up)	3×10	120 sec	3×12	120 sec	3×15	120 sec	3×5	120 sec
	3b. Post Ts	3×12		3×12		3×12		3×12	
Upper body 4	4a. Suspension trainer inverted row	3×10	NA	3×12	NA	3×15	NA	3×5	NA
	4b. Supine breathing drill (rest)	3×60 sec		3×60 sec		3×60 sec		3×60 sec	

Table 12.12   Elite Training Program: Monday, Weeks 1 to 4

MOVEMENT SKILLS SESSION		WEEK 1		WEEK 2		WEEK 3		WEEK 4	
	Exercise	Sets × reps (intensity)	Rest	Sets × reps (intensity)	Rest	Sets × reps (intensity)	Rest	Sets × reps (intensity)	Rest
Active dynamic warm-up (chapter 1)	General movement prep								
	Walking series								
	Ground series								
	Standing series								

(continued)

Table 12.12 *(continued)*

MOVEMENT SKILLS SESSION		WEEK 1		WEEK 2		WEEK 3		WEEK 4	
	Exercise	**Sets × reps (intensity)**	**Rest**	**Sets × reps (intensity)**	**Rest**	**Sets × reps (intensity)**	**Rest**	**Sets × reps (intensity)**	**Rest**
Acceleration training (chapter 7)	A-skip	1×3 (10 yd)	WB	2×3 (10 yd)	WB	2×3 (10 yd)	WB	1×3 (10 yd)	WB
	Resisted A-march	3×2 (10 yd)	WB	1×2 (10 yd)	WB	1×2 (10 yd)	WB	1×2 (10 yd)	WB
	Resisted A-run	3×3 (5 yd)	WB	3×2 (5 yd)	WB	3×2 (5 yd)	WB	2×3 (5 yd)	WB
	Two-point acceleration start*	3×3 (10 yd)	120 sec each rep/180 sec each set	3×3 (10 yd)	120 sec each rep/180 sec each set	3×3 (10 yd)	120 sec each rep/180 sec each set	2×3 (10 yd)	120 sec each rep/180 sec each set
	Three-point acceleration start*	None	NA	2×3 (10 yd)	120 sec each rep/180 sec each set	3×3 (15 yd)	120 sec each rep/180 sec each set	2×2 (15 yd)	120 sec each rep/180 sec each set
	Overhead throw	2×3 (8-12 lb)	60-90 sec	3×3 (8-12 lb)	60-90 sec	3×3 (8-12 lb)	60-90 sec	3×1 (8-12 lb)	60-90 sec

WEIGHT ROOM SESSION		WEEK 1		WEEK 2		WEEK 3		WEEK 4	
	Exercise	**Sets × reps (intensity)**	**Rest**	**Sets × reps (intensity)**		**Sets × reps (intensity)**		**Sets × reps (intensity)**	**Rest**
CNS stimulation	1a. Box jump	3×3	120 sec	3×3	120 sec	3×1	120 sec	None	NA
	1b. Medicine ball drop	3×5		4×5		4×5		None	
Lower body 1	2a. Clean	1×3 (50% 1RM)	180 sec	1×3 (55% 1RM)	180 sec	1×5 (50% 1RM)	180 sec	1×1 (50% 1RM)	180 sec
		1×3 (60% 1RM)		1×3 (65% 1RM)		1×3 (60% 1RM)		1×1 (60% 1RM)	
		1×3 (65% 1RM)		1×3 (70% 1RM)		1×2 (70% 1RM)		1×1 (65% 1RM)	
		1×3 (70% 1RM)		1×3 (75% 1RM)		1×2 (75% 1RM)			
						1×2 (80% 1RM)			
	2b. Snap down	3×2		None**		None		None	
	2b. Reactive drop	None		4×3		None		None	
	2b. Box jump	None		None		4×2		4×2	

WEIGHT ROOM SESSION		WEEK 1		WEEK 2		WEEK 3		WEEK 4	
	Exercise	Sets × reps (intensity)	Rest	Sets × reps (intensity)	Rest	Sets × reps (intensity)	Rest	Sets × reps (intensity)	Rest
Lower body 2	3a. Squat choice Velocity-based training: strength priority (bar speed of 0.5-0.75 m/s)	Warm-up 1×8 (135 lb)	180 sec	Warm-up 1×8 (135 lb)	180 sec	Warm-up 1×8 (135 lb)	180 sec	Warm-up 1×8 (135 lb)	180 sec
		1×5 (50% 1RM)		1×5 (50% 1RM)		1×5 (50% 1RM)		1×3 (50% 1RM)	
		1×5 (60% 1RM)		1×3 (60% 1RM)		1×3 (60% 1RM)		1×2 (60% 1RM)	
		1×5 (70% 1RM)		1×3 (70% 1RM)		1×3 (70% 1RM)		1×2 (70% 1RM)	
		1×5 (75% 1RM)		2×3 (80% 1RM)		1×2 (75% 1RM)			
						1×2 (80% 1RM)			
						1×2 (85% 1RM)			
	3b. Dumbbell squat jump	4×3		4×3		None		3×2	
	3b. Standing vertical jump (Vertec)	None		None		5×2		None	
	3c. Low plank	3×1 (30 sec)		3×1 (30 sec)		3×1 (30 sec)		3×1 (30 sec)	
Lower body 3	4a. Bulgarian split squat	3×5 each side (1 sec pause at bottom)	120 sec	3×3 each side (2 sec pause at bottom)	120 sec	3×3 each side (3 sec pause at bottom)	120 sec	None	60 sec
	4b. Backward ankle hop	3×1 (5 yd)		3×1 (5 yd)		3×1 (5 yd)		3×1 (5 yd)	
Plank series	5a. Low plank	2×1 (30 sec)	60 sec	2×1 (30 sec)	60 sec	2×1 (30 sec)	60 sec	2×1 (30 sec)	60 sec
	5b. Side plank	2×1 each side (20 sec)		2×1 each side (20 sec)		2×1 each side (20 sec)		2×1 each side (20 sec)	

WB = walk back

* Rest: 180 sec between sets plus an additional 60 sec for every 10 yards sprinted

** Offensive and defensive linemen continue snap down for week 2; no reactive drop.

Table 12.13 Elite Training Program: Tuesday, Weeks 1 to 4

MOVEMENT SKILLS SESSION		WEEK 1		WEEK 2		WEEK 3		WEEK 4	
	Exercise	Sets × reps (intensity)	Rest	Sets × reps (intensity)	Rest	Sets × reps (intensity)	Rest	Sets × reps (intensity)	Rest
Active dynamic warm-up (chapter 1)	General movement prep								
	Walking series								
	Ground series								
	Standing series								
Change of direction (chapter 8) and pro agility drill (chapter 3)	Crossover step (tall)	2×4 (5 yd)	60 sec	2×4 (5 yd)	60 sec	1×4 (5 yd)	60 sec	1×2 (5 yd)	60 sec
	Pro agility drill to first touch	2×3 (5 yd)	60 sec	1×2 (5 yd)	60 sec	1×2 (5 yd)	60 sec	1×2 (5 yd)	60 sec
	Pro agility drill to second touch (tall)	2×3 (10 yd)	60 sec	3×2 (10 yd)	60 sec	3×2 (10 yd)	60 sec	2×3 (10 yd)	60 sec
	Pro agility drill (full drill)	1×2 (20 yd)	120 sec each rep/180 sec each set	1×4 (20 yd)	120 sec each rep/180 sec each set	3×2 (20 yd)	120 sec each rep/180 sec each set	2×1 (20 yd)	120 sec each rep/180 sec each set
	Position-specific drills	3 drills × 4 reps each	1:6*	4 drills × 4 reps each	1:6	5 drills × 3 reps each	1:6	None	NA
WEIGHT ROOM SESSION		**WEEK 1**		**WEEK 2**		**WEEK 3**		**WEEK 4**	
	Exercise	Sets × reps (intensity)	Rest	Sets × reps (intensity)	Rest	Sets × reps (intensity)	Rest	Sets × reps (intensity)	Rest
Upper body 1	1a. Dumbbell flat bench press (increase weight each set; no failure reps)	1×8	120 sec	1×8	120 sec	1×8	120 sec	3×5 each side (alternating)	120 sec
		4×5		5×5		5×5			
	1b. Miniband lateral monster walk	3×5 yd each way		4×5 yd each way		3×5 yd each way		2×5 yd each way	
Upper body 2	2a. Pull-up (weighted)	4×5	120 sec	5×5	120 sec	5×5	120 sec	3×5	120 sec
	2b. Physioball plank hold	3×1 (30 sec)		3×1 (30 sec)		3×1 (30 sec)		3×1 (30 sec)	
Upper body 3	3a. Incline dumbbell bench press (increase weight each set; no failure reps)	4×5	120 sec	5×5	120 sec	5×5	120 sec	3×5 each side (alternating)	120 sec
	3b. Post Ts	3×12		3×12		3×12		3×12	

WEIGHT ROOM SESSION		WEEK 1		WEEK 2		WEEK 3		WEEK 4	
	Exercise	Sets × reps (intensity)	Rest	Sets × reps (intensity)	Rest	Sets × reps (intensity)	Rest	Sets × reps (intensity)	Rest
Upper body 4	4a. Dumbbell single-arm row	4×5 each side	90 sec	5×5 each side	90 sec	5×5 each side	90 sec	3×5 each side	90 sec
	4b. Serratus step-up	3×1 (25 sec continuous)		3×1 (25 sec continuous)		3×1 (25 sec continuous)		3×1 (25 sec continuous)	

* Work-to-rest ratio

Table 12.14 Elite Training Program: Thursday, Weeks 1 to 4

MOVEMENT SKILLS SESSION		WEEK 1		WEEK 2		WEEK 3		WEEK 4	
	Exercise	Sets × reps (intensity)	Rest	Sets × reps (intensity)	Rest	Sets × reps (intensity)	Rest	Sets × reps (intensity)	Rest
Active dynamic warm-up (chapter 1)	General movement prep								
	Walking series								
	Ground series								
	Standing series								
Top-end speed training (chapter 9)	Tall kneeling arm action	1×1 (3-8 sec at 50% speed)	NA	1×1 (3-8 sec at 50% speed)	NA	1×1 (3-8 sec at 50% speed)	NA	1×1 (3-8 sec at 50% speed)	NA
		1×1 (3-8 sec at 75% speed)	NA	1×1 (3-8 sec at 75% speed)	NA	1×1 (3-8 sec at 75% speed)	NA	1×1 (3-8 sec at 75% speed)	NA
		1×1 (3-8 sec at 90% speed)	NA	1×1 (3-8 sec at 90% speed)	NA	1×1 (3-8 sec at 90% speed)	NA	1×1 (3-8 sec at 90% speed)	NA
	Heel slide	1×2 (10 yd)	WB	1×2 (10 yd)	WB	1×2 (10 yd)	WB	1×2 (10 yd)	WB
	Stepover run	1×3 (10 yd)	WB	1×3 (10 yd)	WB	3×3 (10 yd)	WB	2×3 (10 yd)	WB
	Stepover skip	2×3 (15 yd)	WB	2×3 (15 yd)	WB	2×3 (15 yd)	WB	2×3 (15 yd)	WB
	Straight-leg shuffle	1×3 (5 yd)	WB	3×3 (5 yd)	WB	3×3 (5 yd)	WB	2×3 (5 yd)	WB
	40-yd buildup	1×3 (75%)	120 sec	1×3 (85%)	120 sec	2×2 (90%)	120 sec	2×1 (100%)	120 sec

(continued)

Table 12.14 (continued)

WEIGHT ROOM SESSION		WEEK 1		WEEK 2		WEEK 3		WEEK 4	
	Exercise	Sets × reps (intensity)	Rest	Sets × reps (intensity)	Rest	Sets × reps (intensity)	Rest	Sets × reps (intensity)	Rest
CNS stimulation	1a. Dumbbell squat jump	3×3 (10% of body weight)	120 sec	3×2 (10% of body weight)	120 sec	3×1 (10% of body weight)	120 sec	None	NA
	1b. Medicine ball drop	3×5 (8-12 lb)		4×5 (8-12 lb)		4×5		None	
	1c. Plank	3×1 (30 sec)		3×1 (30 sec)		3×1 (30 sec)		3×1 (30 sec)	
Lower body 1	2a. Clean	1×3 (50% 1RM)	180 sec	1×3 (55% 1RM)	180 sec	1×3 (50% 1RM)	180 sec	1×2 (60% 1RM)	180 sec
		1×3 (60% 1RM)		1×3 (65% 1RM)		1×3 (60% 1RM)		2×3 (70% 1RM)	
		1×3 (65% 1RM)		1×3 (70% 1RM)		1×2 (65% 1RM)			
		1×3 (70% 1RM)		1×3 (75% 1RM)		1×2 (70% 1RM)			
						1×2 (75% 1RM)			
	2b. Snap down	3×2		None		None		None	
	2b. Dumbbell squat jump	None		None		3×2 (10% of body weight)		3×1 (10% of body weight)	
	2b. Reactive drop	None		4×3		None		None	
	2c. Post Ts	3×12		3×12		3×12		3×12	
Lower body 2	3a. Barbell speed squat Velocity-based training: strength-speed priority (bar speed of 0.75-1.0 m/s)	1×8 (135 lb)	120 sec	1×8 (135 lb)	120 sec	1×8 (135 lb)	120 sec	1×8 (135 lb)	120 sec
		1×5 (50% 1RM)		1×3 (55% 1RM)		1×2 (55% 1RM)		1×3 (55% 1RM)	
		1×5 (60% 1RM)		1×3 (65% 1RM)		1×2 (65% 1RM)		1×3 (60% 1RM)	
		1×5 (65% 1RM)		1×3 (70% 1RM)		1×2 (70% 1RM)		1×3 (65% 1RM)	
		1×5 (70% 1RM)		1×3 (75% 1RM)		3×2 (75% 1RM)			
	3b. Standing vertical jump (Vertec)	None		3×2		None		3×2	
	3b. Standing broad jump	3×2		None		3×2		None	

WEIGHT ROOM SESSION		WEEK 1		WEEK 2		WEEK 3		WEEK 4	
	Exercise	Sets × reps (intensity)	Rest	Sets × reps (intensity)	Rest	Sets × reps (intensity)	Rest	Sets × reps (intensity)	Rest
Lower body 3	4a. Bulgarian split squat	4×5 each side (1 sec pause at bottom)	120 sec	2×5 each side (2 sec pause at bottom)	120 sec	1×5 each side (3 sec pause at bottom)	120 sec	None	120 sec
				2×3 each side		1×3 each side			
						2×2 each side			
	4b. Backward ankle hop	3×1 (5 yd)		3×1 (5 yd)		3×1 (5 yd)		3×1 (5 yd)	
	4c. Side plank	3×1 each side (20 sec)		3×1 each side (20 sec)		3×1 each side (20 sec)		3×1 each side (20 sec)	

WB = walk back

Table 12.15   Elite Training Program: Friday, Weeks 1 to 4

MOVEMENT SKILLS SESSION		WEEK 1		WEEK 2		WEEK 3		WEEK 4	
	Exercise	Sets × reps (intensity)	Rest	Sets × reps (intensity)	Rest	Sets × reps (intensity)	Rest	Sets × reps (intensity)	Rest
Active dynamic warm-up (chapter 1)	General movement prep								
	Walking series								
	Ground series								
	Standing series								
Change of direction (chapter 8) and L-drill (chapter 3) training	L-drill to first touch	1×3 (5 yd)	60 sec	1×3 (5 yd)	60 sec	1×2 (5 yd)	60 sec	1×2 (5 yd)	60 sec
	L-drill to second touch (tall)	1×3 (5 yd)	60 sec	1×3 (5 yd)	60 sec	1×2 (5 yd)	60 sec	1×2 (5 yd)	60 sec
	L-drill figure eight (from second touch)	1×3 (20 yd)	90 sec	1×2 (20 yd)	90 sec	1×1 (20 yd)	90 sec	1×1 (20 yd)	90 sec
	L-drill (full drill at 80% speed)	1×3 (30 yd)	120 sec	1×4 (30 yd)	120 sec	2×3 (30 yd)	120 sec	2×2 (30 yd)	120 sec

(continued)

Table 12.15 *(continued)*

WEIGHT ROOM SESSION		WEEK 5		WEEK 6		WEEK 7		WEEK 8	
	Exercise	Sets × reps (intensity)	Rest	Sets × reps (intensity)	Rest	Sets × reps (intensity)	Rest	Sets × reps (intensity)	Rest
Upper body 1	1a. Single-arm dumbbell row	3×5 each side	120 sec	3×3 each side	120 sec	3×3 each side	120 sec	3×3 each side	120 sec
	1b. Kneeling ankle mobility	3×8 each side		3×8 each side		3×8 each side		3×8 each side	
Upper body 2	2. Barbell bench press (maximum repetitions test)	1×8 (135 lb)	60 sec	1×8 (135 lb)	60 sec	1×8 (135 lb)	60 sec	1×8 (135 lb)	60 sec
		1×5 (185 lb)	90 sec	1×5 (185 lb)	90 sec	1×5 (185 lb)	90 sec	1×5 (185 lb)	90 sec
		1×2-3 (225 lb)	120 sec	1×2-3 (225 lb)	120 sec	1×2-3 (225 lb)	120 sec	1×2-3 (225 lb)	120 sec
		1×1 (275 or 315 lb)*	180-300 sec	1×1 (275 or 315 lb)*	180-300 sec	1×1 (275 or 315 lb)*	180-300 sec	1×1 (275 or 315 lb)*	180-300 sec
		Repetitions to failure (225 lb)	NA	Repetitions to failure (205 lb)	NA	Repetitions to failure (225 lb)	NA	Repetitions to failure (205 lb)	NA
Upper body 3	3a. Chest supported dumbbell row	3×5	120 sec	4×5	120 sec	4×5	120 sec	3×5	120 sec
	3b. Miniband single-leg abduction	3×10 each side		3×10 each side		3×10 each side		3×10 each side	
Upper body 4	4a. Suspension trainer inverted row	3×1 round, repetitions to failure	120 sec	3×1 round, repetitions to failure	120 sec	3×1 round, repetitions to failure	120 sec	3×1 round, repetitions to failure	120 sec
	4b. Isometric push-up hold (top position)	3×60 sec		3×60 sec		3×60 sec		3×60 sec	

* If athlete can perform 15 or more reps at 225 lb, he uses 275 lb. If he can perform 20 or more reps at 225 lb, he uses 315 lb. If he performs fewer than 10 reps at 225 lb, he performs 1×2-3 at 225 lb.

Table 12.16 Elite Training Program: Monday, Weeks 5 to 8

MOVEMENT SKILLS SESSION		WEEK 5		WEEK 6		WEEK 7		WEEK 8	
	Exercise	Sets × reps (intensity)	Rest	Sets × reps (intensity)	Rest	Sets × reps (intensity)	Rest	Sets × reps (intensity)	Rest
Active dynamic warm-up (chapter 1)	General movement prep								
	Walking series								
	Ground series								
	Standing series								

MOVEMENT SKILLS SESSION		WEEK 5		WEEK 6		WEEK 7		WEEK 8	
	Exercise	**Sets × reps (intensity)**	**Rest**	**Sets × reps (intensity)**	**Rest**	**Sets × reps (intensity)**	**Rest**	**Sets × reps (intensity)**	**Rest**
Acceleration training (chapter 7)	A-skip	1×2 (10 yd)	WB	1×4 (10 yd)	WB	1×4 (10 yd)	WB	None	NA
	Resisted A-march	3×2 (10 yd)	WB	1×2 (10 yd)	WB	1×2 (10 yd)	WB	1×2 (10 yd)	WB
	Resisted A-run	3×3 (5 yd)	WB	3×2 (5 yd)	WB	3×2 (5 yd)	WB	2×3 (5 yd)	WB
	Two-point acceleration start*	3×3 (10 yd)	120 sec each rep/180 sec each set	3×3 (10 yd)	120 sec each rep/180 sec each set	3×3 (10 yd)	120 sec each rep/180 sec each set	2×3 (10 yd)	120 sec each rep/180 sec each set
	Three-point acceleration start*	2×3 (15 yd)	120 sec each rep/180 sec each set	3×3 (15 yd)	120 sec each rep/180 sec each set	2×3 (15 yd)	120 sec each rep/180 sec each set	2×2 (15 yd)	120 sec each rep/180 sec each set
	Medicine ball overhead throw	3×2 (8-12 lb)	90 sec	4×2 (8-12 lb)	90 sec	6×1 (8-12 lb)	90 sec	3×1 (8-12 lb)	90 sec
WEIGHT ROOM SESSION		**WEEK 5**		**WEEK 6**		**WEEK 7**		**WEEK 8**	
	Exercise	**Sets × reps (intensity)**	**Rest**	**Sets × reps (intensity)**	**Rest**	**Sets × reps (intensity)**	**Rest**	**Sets × reps (intensity)**	**Rest**
CNS stimulation	1a. Vertimax	3×3	120 sec	3×2	120 sec	3×1	120 sec	None	NA
	1b. Medicine ball drop	3×5 (8-12 lb)		3×5 (8-12 lb)		3×5 (8-12 lb)		None	
	1c. Plank	3×1 (30 sec)		3×1 (30 sec)		3×1 (30 sec)		None	
Lower body 1	2a. Clean	1×3 (50% 1RM)	180 sec	1×3 (50% 1RM)	180 sec	1×3 (55% 1RM)	180 sec	1×2 (55% 1RM)	180 sec
		1×3 (55% 1RM)		1×3 (60% 1RM)		1×2 (65% 1RM)		1×1 (60% 1RM)	
		1×3 (60% 1RM)		1×2 (70% 1RM)		2×1 (70% 1RM)		1×1 (65% 1RM)	
		2×3 (70% 1RM)		2×2 (75% 1RM)					
	2b. Standing vertical jump (Vertec)	3×2		3×2		3×2		3×2	

(continued)

Table 12.16 (continued)

WEIGHT ROOM SESSION		WEEK 5		WEEK 6		WEEK 7		WEEK 8	
	Exercise	Sets × reps (intensity)	Rest	Sets × reps (intensity)	Rest	Sets × reps (intensity)	Rest	Sets × reps (intensity)	Rest
Lower body 2	3a. Squat choice Velocity-based training: speed-strength priority (bar speed of 1.0 m/s or greater)	1×5 (135 lb)	120 sec	1×5 (135 lb)	120 sec	1×5 (135 lb)	120 sec	1×5 (135 lb)	120 sec
		1×5 (50% 1RM)		1×5 (50% 1RM)		1×2 (50% 1RM)		1×1 (50% 1RM)	
		1×3 (60% 1RM)		1×3 (60% 1RM)		1×2 (60% 1RM)		1×1 (55% 1RM)	
		1×3 (65% 1RM)		1×2 (65% 1RM)		3×2 (65% 1RM)		2×1 (60% 1RM)	
		1×3 (70% 1RM)		2×2 (70% 1RM)					
		2×3 (75% 1RM)							
	3b. Dumbbell squat jump	None		3×2 (last 3 sets of squat)		None		3×2 (last 3 sets of squat)	
	3b. Standing broad jump	3×2 (last 3 sets of squat)		None		3×2 (last 3 sets of squat)		None	
	3c. Low plank	3×1 (30 sec)		3×1 (30 sec)		3×1 (30 sec)		3×1 (30 sec)	
Lower body 3	4a. Bottom-up step-up	3×5 each side (moderate load)	120 sec	1×5 each side (moderate to heavy)	120 sec	3×3 each side (moderate to heavy)	120 sec	3×2 each side (heavy load)	120 sec
				2×3 each side (moderate to heavy)					
	4b. Backward ankle hop	3×1 (10 yd)		3×1 (10 yd)		3×1 (10 yd)		3×1 (5 yd)	
	4c. Side plank	2×1 each side (20 sec)		2×1 each side (20 sec)		2×1 each side (20 sec)		2×1 each side (20 sec)	

WB = walk back

* Rest: 180 sec between sets plus an additional 60 sec for every 10 yards sprinted

Table 12.17   Elite Training Program: Tuesday, Weeks 5 to 8

MOVEMENT SKILLS SESSION		WEEK 5		WEEK 6		WEEK 7		WEEK 8	
	Exercise	Sets × reps (intensity)	Rest	Sets × reps (intensity)	Rest	Sets × reps (intensity)	Rest	Sets × reps (intensity)	Rest
Active dynamic warm-up (chapter 1)	General movement prep								
	Walking series								
	Ground series								
	Standing series								
Change of direction (chapter 8) and pro agility drill (chapter 3)	Crossover step (tall)	2×4 (5 yd)	60 sec	2×4 (5 yd)	60 sec	1×4 (5 yd)	60 sec	2×2 (5 yd)	60 sec
	Pro agility drill to first touch	2×3 (5 yd)	60 sec	1×2 (5 yd)	60 sec	1×2 (5 yd)	60 sec	1×2 (5 yd)	60 sec
	Pro agility drill to second touch (tall)	2×3 (10 yd)	60 sec	3×2 (10 yd)	60 sec	3×2 (10 yd)	60 sec	2×3 (10 yd)	60 sec
	Pro agility drill (full drill)	1×2 (20 yd)	120 sec each rep/180 sec each set	1×4 (20 yd)	120 sec each rep/180 sec each set	3×2 (20 yd)	120 sec each rep/180 sec each set	2×1 (20 yd)	120 sec each rep/180 sec each set
	Position-specific drills	3 drills × 4 reps each	1:6*	4 drills × 4 reps each	1:6	5 drills × 3 reps each	1:6	2 drills × 3 reps each	1:6
WEIGHT ROOM SESSION		**WEEK 5**		**WEEK 6**		**WEEK 7**		**WEEK 8**	
	Exercise	Sets × reps (intensity)	Rest	Sets × reps (intensity)	Rest	Sets × reps (intensity)	Rest	Sets × reps (intensity)	Rest
Upper body 1	1a. Dumbbell flat bench press	1×8	120 sec	1×8	120 sec	1×8	120 sec	4×3	120 sec
		5×5		5×5		5×5			
Upper body 2	2a. Single-arm row	5×5 each side	120 sec	5×5 each side	120 sec	5×5 each side	120 sec	4×3 each side	120 sec
	2b. Physioball plank hold	3×1 (30 sec)		3×1 (30 sec)		3×1 (30 sec)		3×1 (30 sec)	
Upper body 3	3a. Dumbbell incline bench press	3×5	120 sec	4×5	120 sec	5×5	120 sec	4×3	120 sec
	3b. Post Ts	3×12		3×12		3×12		3×12	
Upper body 4	4a. Suspension trainer inverted row (3 sec pause at top)	3×8	90 sec	4×5	90 sec	4×5	90 sec	3×5	90 sec
	4b. Tempo push-up (3 sec going down/1 sec going up)	3×1 (30-45 sec continuous)		3×1 (30-60 sec continuous)		3×1 (30-60 sec continuous)		3×1 (30 sec continuous)	

* Work-to-rest ratio

Table 12.18 Elite Training Program: Thursday, Weeks 5 to 8

MOVEMENT SKILLS SESSION		WEEK 5		WEEK 6		WEEK 7		WEEK 8	
	Exercise	Sets × reps (intensity)	Rest	Sets × reps (intensity)	Rest	Sets × reps (intensity)	Rest	Sets × reps (intensity)	Rest
Active dynamic warm-up (chapter 1)	General movement prep								
	Walking series								
	Ground series								
	Standing series								
Top-end speed training (chapter 9)	Tall kneeling arm action	1×1 (3-8 sec at 50% speed)	NA	1×1 (3-8 sec at 50% speed)	NA	1×1 (3-8 sec at 50% speed)	NA	1×1 (3-8 sec at 50% speed)	NA
		1×1 (3-8 sec at 75% speed)	NA	1×1 (3-8 sec at 75% speed)	NA	1×1 (3-8 sec at 75% speed)	NA	1×1 (3-8 sec at 75% speed)	NA
		1×1 (3-8 sec at 90% speed)	NA	1×1 (3-8 sec at 90% speed)	NA	1×1 (3-8 sec at 90% speed)	NA	1×1 (3-8 sec at 90% speed)	NA
	Heel slide	1×3 (10 yd)	WB	1×3 (10 yd)	WB	1×3 (10 yd)	WB	1×1 (10 yd)	WB
	Stepover run	1×3 (10 yd)	WB	1×3 (10 yd)	WB	1×3 (10 yd)	WB	1×1 (10 yd)	WB
	40-yd buildup (to 75%)	1×2 (40 yd)	120 sec	1×2 (40 yd)	120 sec	1×2 (40 yd)	120 sec	1×1 (40 yd)	240 sec
	Flying 10s	1×2 (30 yd)	180 sec	1×2 (30 yd)	180 sec	1×2 (30 yd)	180 sec	1×1 (30 yd)	180 sec
	Flying 20s	1×2 (40 yd)	240 sec	1×2 (40 yd)	240 sec	1×2 (40 yd)	240 sec	1×1 (40 yd)	240 sec
	40-yd dash (%)	1×2 (85%)	180 sec	2×2 (90%)	240 sec	2×1 (90%-100%)	300 sec	1×1 (90%-100%)	NA
WEIGHT ROOM SESSION		**WEEK 5**		**WEEK 6**		**WEEK 7**		**WEEK 8**	
	Exercise	Sets × reps (intensity)	Rest	Sets × reps (intensity)	Rest	Sets × reps (intensity)	Rest	Sets × reps (intensity)	Rest
CNS stimulation	1a. Dumbbell squat jump	2×2 (10% of body weight)	NA	3×2 (10% of body weight)	120 sec	3×2 (10% of body weight)	120 sec	3×1 (10% of body weight)	120 sec
	1b. Medicine ball drop	2×5 (8-12 lb)		3×5		4×5		3×5	
	1c. Plank	2×1 (30 sec)		3×1 (30 sec)		3×1 (30 sec)		3×1 (30 sec)	

WEIGHT ROOM SESSION		WEEK 5		WEEK 6		WEEK 7		WEEK 8	
	Exercise	Sets × reps (intensity)	Rest	Sets × reps (intensity)	Rest	Sets × reps (intensity)	Rest	Sets × reps (intensity)	Rest
Lower body 1	2a. Clean	1×3 (50% 1RM)	180 sec	1×2 (50% 1RM)	180 sec	1×1 (55% 1RM)	180 sec	3×1 (60% 1RM)	180 sec
		1×3 (60% 1RM)		1×2 (60% 1RM)		2×1 (60% 1RM)			
		1×3 (65% 1RM)		1×2 (65% 1RM)		2×1 (65% 1RM)			
		3×3 (70% 1RM)		3×2 (70% 1RM)					
	2b. Standing vertical jump (Vertec)	None		4×2		None		None	
	2b. Vertimax	4×2		None		3×3		3×2	
Lower body 2	3a. Barbell speed squat Velocity-based training: speed-strength priority (bar speed of 0.75-1.0 m/s)	1×5 (50% 1RM)	120 sec	1×5 (50% 1RM)	120 sec	1×2 (50% 1RM)	120 sec	1×1 (50% 1RM)	120 sec
		4×3 (55% 1RM)		1×3 (55% 1RM)		1×2 (55% 1RM)		2×1 (55% 1RM)	
				3×2 (60% 1RM)		2×2 (60% 1RM)			
						2×2 (65% 1RM)			
	3b. Standing vertical jump (Vertec)	3×2		None		3×2		None	
	3b. Standing broad jump	None		3×2		None		3×2	
Lower body 3	4a. Bottom-up step-up	3×5 each side (moderate weight)	120 sec	3×3 each side (moderate-heavy weight)	120 sec	3×2 each side (moderate-heavy weight)	120 sec	3×1 each side (heavy weight)	120 sec
	4b. Side plank	3×1 each side (20 sec)		3×1 each side (20 sec)		3×1 each side (20 sec)		3×1 each side (20 sec)	

WB = walk back

Table 12.19   Elite Training Program: Friday, Weeks 5 to 8

MOVEMENT SKILLS SESSION		WEEK 5		WEEK 6		WEEK 7		WEEK 8	
	Exercise	Sets × reps (intensity)	Rest	Sets × reps (intensity)	Rest	Sets × reps (intensity)	Rest	Sets × reps (intensity)	Rest
Active dynamic warm-up (chapter 1)	General movement prep								
	Walking series								
	Ground series								
	Standing series								
Change of direction (chapter 8) and L-drill (chapter 3) training	L-drill to first touch	1×3 (5 yd)	60 sec	1×3 (5 yd)	60 sec	1×2 (5 yd)	60 sec	1×2 (5 yd)	60 sec
	L-drill to second touch (tall)	1×3 (5 yd)	60 sec	1×3 (5 yd)	60 sec	1×2 (5 yd)	60 sec	1×2 (5 yd)	60 sec
	L-drill figure eight (from second touch)	1×3 (20 yd)	90 sec	1×2 (20 yd)	90 sec	1×1 (20 yd)	90 sec	1×1 (20 yd)	90 sec
	L-drill (full drill)	1×3 (30 yd)	120 sec	1×4 (30 yd)	120 sec	2×3 (30 yd)	120 sec	2×2 (30 sec)	120 sec
	Position-specific drill work								
	Long shuttle	2×1 (60 yd)	120 sec	None	NA	2×1 (60 yd)	120 sec	None	NA
WEIGHT ROOM SESSION		WEEK 5		WEEK 6		WEEK 7		WEEK 8	
	Exercise	Sets × reps (intensity)	Rest	Sets × reps (intensity)	Rest	Sets × reps (intensity)	Rest	Sets × reps (intensity)	Rest
Upper body 1	1a. Single-arm dumbbell row	3×5 each side	120 sec	4×3 each side	120 sec	4×3 each side	120 sec	3×2 each side	120 sec
	1b. Kneeling ankle mobility	3×8 each side		3×8 each side		3×8 each side		3×8 each side	
Upper body 2	2a. Barbell bench press, maximum repetitions test	1×8 (135 lb)	60 sec	1×8 (135 lb)	60 sec	1×8 (135 lb)	60 sec	1×8 (135 lb)	60 sec
		1×5 (185 lb)	90 sec	1×5 (185 lb)	90 sec	1×5 (185 lb)	90 sec	1×5 (185 lb)	90 sec
		1×2-3 (225 lb)	120 sec	1×2-3 (225 lb)	120 sec	1×2-3 (225 lb)	120 sec	1×2-3 (225 lb)	120 sec
		1×1 (275 or 315 lb)*	180-300 sec	1×1 (275 or 315 lb)*	180-300 sec	1×1 (275 or 315 lb)*	180-300 sec	1×1 (275 or 315 lb)*	180-300 sec
		Repetitions to failure (225 lb)	NA	Repetitions to failure (205 lb)	NA	Repetitions to failure (225 lb)	NA	Repetitions to failure (205 lb)	NA
Upper body 3	3a. Chest supported dumbbell row	3×5	120 sec	4×5	120 sec	4×5	120 sec	3×5	120 sec
	3b. Miniband single-leg abduction	3×6 each side		3×6 each side		3×6 each side		None	

WEIGHT ROOM SESSION		WEEK 5		WEEK 6		WEEK 7		WEEK 8	
	Exercise	**Sets × reps (intensity)**	**Rest**	**Sets × reps (intensity)**	**Rest**	**Sets × reps (intensity)**	**Rest**	**Sets × reps (intensity)**	**Rest**
Upper body 4	4a. Suspension trainer inverted row	3×1 round, repetitions to failure	120 sec	3×1 round, repetitions to failure	120 sec	3×1 round, repetitions to failure	120 sec	3×1 round, repetitions to failure	120 sec
	4b. Isometric push-up hold (top position)	3×60 sec		3×60 sec		3×60 sec		3×60 sec	

* If athlete can perform 15 or more reps at 225 lb, he uses 275 lb. If he can perform 20 or more reps at 225 lb, he uses 315 lb. If he performs fewer than 10 reps at 225 lb, he performs 1×2-3 at 225 lb.

Conclusion

This chapter focuses specifically on the architecture of training, displaying examples of how coaches at Landow Performance prepare athletes for football combines at the sport's different levels. Chapters 13 and 14 focus on other factors that strongly influence the athlete's combine training process: nutrition, sleep, recovery, and psychological preparation. These are fundamental variables that may seem automatic, but they can derail training when neglected. An athlete cannot successfully follow a demanding training plan such as the ones in this book if he is training on an empty stomach or on a lack of sleep, for example. Also detailed are strategies athletes can use to stay calm and physically primed throughout their testing events. The combination of all these factors is what drives a successful training outcome.

CHAPTER 13

Nutrition and Recovery

Much of this book covers what athletes spend only a small fraction of their combine preparation time doing: training. The choices athletes make during the rest of the time—how they eat, sleep, study, and relax—are just as critical as the quality of their movement and lifting sessions. For maximum results, their entire day must be structured around training to ensure optimal recovery. With proper recovery, their bodies will create physical and neural adaptations to the training.

Science of Adaptation in Athletics

Many of today's strength and conditioning principles are rooted in the work of pioneering endocrinologist Hans Selye, who is largely credited with having first postulated the concept of biological stress. Selye's general adaptation syndrome (GAS) model describes how organisms respond to a stressor via the stages of alarm, reaction, and exhaustion (Selye 1946). This model applies to many different types of organisms and in many ways, so we will focus on GAS solely as it relates to the athletic context of training adaptations. An initial stress response causes alarm within the nervous system, triggering a reaction from the body to resist the stressor with its available resources. As these resources become depleted through further stress, the body's physical capabilities begin to diminish to the point where the dose of training stress can either drive it to exhaustion or help it to become stronger based on the stressor's intensity and duration.

Practitioners must factor the GAS model into the training program's structure in order to help athletes to fully adapt and supercompensate in response to training stressors rather than enter an overtrained state (Bompa and Buzzichelli 2018). This means that training programs need built-in periods of reduced workout stress to allow athletes' bodies to regenerate and supercompensate. In the strength and conditioning world, these are referred to as deloading or downloading periods. The intensity of the exercises remains high, but their volume drops significantly; this way, the athlete gets an adequate neural stimulus to avoid detraining, but the volume is low enough for his body to ease out of the alarm and reaction phases. With this figurative breathing room from stress, the athlete's body can make physical and neurological adaptations in response to demands accumulated over the course of the training block.

An athlete could attack each workout with the utmost dedication, but if his body is never allowed to recover properly, he will never gain the full benefit of his training. Lifestyle, habits, sleep, and nutrition are the true building blocks of performance. A multitude of helpful strategies can be used to maximize recovery and performance gains, ranging from the most fundamental aspects of eating and sleeping to highly advanced recovery methods such as cryotherapy and dry needling.

Sleep and Nutrition

Combine training is a brief, intense stressor, designed to create quick and effective adaptations that will prime athletes for their testing days. Working hard on the field and in the weight room cannot make up for an unhealthy lifestyle outside of training. A player who stays out late drinking every night will severely limit his body's ability to adapt and make the desired performance gains. The regimented training approach laid out in this book demands that athletes live an equally disciplined lifestyle, structured to provide the nutrients and sleep they need to recover and adapt from intense training.

Sleeping for Success at the Combine

Sleep is one of the easiest factors for coaches to dismiss during the planning and execution of a football combine training cycle. Athletes understand that sleep is important, but their knowledge about it often begins and ends with the common recommendation that everyone get eight hours per night. Practitioners may design a training program assuming that an athlete gets consistent and adequate sleep, when in fact this is not a given. Once we better understand the factors governing an athlete's sleep patterns, we can help him optimize sleep's contribution to his performance gains.

Managing Circadian Rhythms

Sleep time and duration are determined in part by our own individual 24-hour sleep and wake cycles, otherwise known as circadian rhythms. The other major factor is "sleep pressure," or the sleepy feeling triggered by a gradual buildup of the chemical adenosine in the brain during waking hours (Walker 2017).

One of the major sleep-related training hindrances occurs when an athlete's circadian rhythms conflict with his training schedule. A player's lifestyle can drastically affect the amount and quality of his sleep. A "night owl" might prefer going to bed late and sleeping in; doing so, however, could cause him to lose out on two to four hours of sleep, missing crucial periods spent in rapid eye movement (REM) sleep (Samuels 2008).

Athletes must have sleep strategies to contend with these problems. Table 13.1 highlights some of the most commonly agreed upon sleep guidelines offered by scientists.

Table 13.1 Essential Sleeping Tips for Athletes

Avoid caffeine entirely, if possible.
Abstain from alcohol and other beverages and large meals near bedtime.
Do not take any naps after 3:00 p.m.
Develop a consistent nighttime routine that includes a relaxing activity to help you unwind before bed.
Sleep in a dark, cool, and comfortable environment.
Get at least 30 minutes of exposure to sunlight every day.

Adapted from M. Walker, *Why We Sleep: Unlocking the Power of Sleep and Dreams* (New York: Simon & Schuster, 2017).

Extending Sleep, Improving Performance

Sleep and performance are strongly linked, but researchers have found most collegiate athletes tend not to exhibit good sleep habits or quality. To combat this, athletes need to increase the total amount of time they sleep, improve their sleep environments, and identify any potential sleep disorders (Simpson, Gibbs, and Matheson 2017).

Athletes may get only a brief time window for combine or pro day training, but for many players this time period offers a rare chance to extend their sleeping hours and maximize their limited preparation time. Research indicates that adding time to one's nightly sleeping period results in performance benefits. College basketball players who extended their nightly sleep up to a minimum of 10 hours per night for a sustained period of five to seven weeks were found to have better sprint and reaction times, as well as improved self-reported mood and energy levels (Mah et al. 2011). Strength training workouts have also been found to improve both sleep quality and duration (Carandente et al. 2011), so training will help athletes extend their sleep and improve recovery.

Even for athletes with a well-tuned circadian rhythm, occasional nights with sleep loss are still likely. At such times, research has found that a post-lunch nap can help restore this sleep deficit and improve sprinting speed and reaction times (Waterhouse et al. 2007).

Nervousness the night before a combine event can also affect sleep quality for many players, most of whom have not been taught any relaxation strategies or routines to fall asleep in such a situation (Mah et al. 2011). Athletes traveling to combine events in a different time zone can use melatonin supplements to help restore their circadian rhythms and ensure that jet lag is not a factor in their testing performance (Atkinson et al. 2003).

Nutrition for Combine Prep and Testing

Nutrition is a highly personal area of human performance, and an approach that may work wonders for one athlete could be less effective for another. However, certain guidelines can be helpful in establishing and tweaking an athlete's diet. Table 13.2 lays out the recommended approach before and after workouts, as well as for the day of the athlete's combine event.

Table 13.2   Nutritional Strategies for Before and After Workouts and Combine Day

Nutritional window	General notes	Recommended carbohydrate	Recommended protein	Meal timing	Hydration	Foods to avoid
Pre-workout	Eat a smaller meal that is easily digested. Stick with a low glycemic index carbohydrate and a small amount of protein (for long workouts).	Sprouted whole grains Sprouted grain cereals/breads Fruits such as apples, pears, peaches, mangos Root vegetables (small amounts) such as beets, carrots, yucca Activated barley	Lean meat such as fish, chicken breast Sprouted brown rice protein Raw, organic grass-fed whey protein concentrate	Eat 90 minutes to 2 hours before workout.	Drink 2 or 3 cups of water, 15-30 minutes before workout.	Beef and other red meats Pork High-fiber foods Legumes such as beans, peas, peanuts Cruciferous vegetables such as Brussels sprouts, cauliflower, broccoli
Post-workout	Immediate post-workout nutrition contributes to neuromuscular repair. Consume a high glycemic index carbohydrate that can be digested quickly.	Raw whole fruit Fruit juices Raw honey	Raw, organic, grass-fed whey protein	First hour post training is most crucial, especially first 15 minutes.	For each 30 minutes of workout duration, drink 10 ounces (0.3 liters) of water. Continue to hydrate over the next few hours.	Fats of any kind (interferes with post-workout nutrient absorption)
Day of combine	Eat familiar foods that are easy to digest and slow-burning. Liquid nutrition, such as a shake or smoothie, is recommended. Optional: Eat small quantities of easily digested fat. During the event, consume instantly absorbable items.	Low-fiber and low-glycemic index Fruit juices without pulp	Sprouted brown rice protein Raw, organic grass-fed whey protein concentrate	Same as the athlete's preferred pre-workout meal timing (90-120 minutes prior). If needed, instantly absorbable items may be consumed during the event.	Maintain consistent, low-level hydration throughout the combine. Drink plenty of water with any food intake during the event.	New or unfamiliar foods High-fiber foods

Recovery Modalities

Coaches face several key considerations when constructing a holistic recovery circuit. Recovery methods may differ depending on the athlete's level and available resources. Lower-cost methods such as water immersion therapy, myofascial foam rolling, active isolated stretching (AIS), and specific joint mobilization and stabilization exercises are all popular and effective ways to aid in recovery and performance. In an elite-level training environment, access to more advanced methods may include forms of soft tissue treatments, infrared sauna, intermittent pneumatic compression, whole-body cryotherapy, and dry needling.

Contrast Showers

Water immersion therapy has become widely accepted as an effective and easily accessible method to aid in both neural and musculoskeletal recovery. The classic variation alternates between immersing the body in cold water (50 to 59 degrees Fahrenheit) and then in hot water (93 to 97 degrees Fahrenheit). Protocols may vary, but they generally consist of 30 to 300 seconds in one temperature range immediately followed by 30 to 300 seconds in the other. This routine can be repeated many times, lasting from 4 to 30 minutes in duration (Versey, Halson, and Dawson 2013). This protocol does not require a hot or cold tub, however; it can be performed in the shower by alternating hot and cold water. This is what is known as a contrast shower.

Hydrostatic pressure and temperature are two mechanisms that stimulate physiological changes in the body that may help accelerate and enhance recovery (Cochrane 2004). The alternating extreme temperatures help create a "vascular pumping" in the body: The cold water immersion stimulates vasoconstriction, helping to clear some of the exercise-induced metabolic waste products from the working muscle, then hot water immersion stimulates vasodilation, increasing blood flow and allowing greater transport of oxygen, nutrients, and hormones to muscle tissue (Wilcock, Cronin, and Hing 2006).

Foam Rolling Series

Exercise and physical stress can cause microtrauma and inflammation to the muscular system. As the inflammatory response occurs, fascial scar tissue may develop over time, which may lead to muscular dysfunction, decreased performance, and increased pain.

Self-myofascial release using a foam roller can be a noninvasive way to supplement traditional methods of massage that may help with restoring muscle length–tension relationship, increase blood flow, and act as a mood enhancer to mimic an ergogenic aid (Healey et al. 2014). The athlete lies on a foam roller and targets large muscle groups by rolling the length of the muscle. The best muscles to target with the roller are the quadriceps, hamstrings, lateral thigh, gluteus maximus, erector spinae group, pectoralis major, and latissimus dorsi.

Usually, 20 to 30 seconds per muscle group will suffice. However, it is best to use the foam roller after a workout or on recovery days. Rolling out prior to a workout is not advised; the foam roller may produce a pain response that can stimulate a relaxation signal to the muscles and decrease stiffness. This inhibitory response works well in a recovery scenario, but it is not ideal before a workout that involves high power output and joint stability demands.

Active Isolated Stretching (AIS)

Created by Aaron Mattes, AIS is a series of dynamic stretches to improve range of motion (Mattes 1996). Sherrington's law of reciprocal inhibition dictates that when an agonistic muscle contracts, the opposing antagonistic muscle will relax. The myotatic stretch reflex is inhibited by actively performing slow, controlled, rhythmic stretches that each last less than two seconds before returning to the starting position. This stretch can be repeated 5 to 15 times, depending on the muscle and its current state.

The muscle is slightly stretched beyond end range, to the point of light irritation, using an implement such as a band or rope to apply force during the stretch. Our goal in stretching should not be for the athlete to go as deep as he possibly can into a specific range of motion; rather, the coach should emphasize how well the athlete can control movement speed and tempo within a given range. Trying to stretch a muscle as far as possible without regard to other joint ranges of motion can risk negative consequences due to the immense strain placed on connective tissues.

Barefoot Stability Work

The foot's ability to maintain stability while moving as needed at different gait speeds is important because of its relation to noncontact soft tissue injuries. Teaching the foot to properly move in reaction to its environment can help improve proper recruitment of intrinsic foot musculature. Poor functioning at the foot can cause problems further up the kinetic chain, resulting in adverse effects in the knee, hip, or spine.

To build foot stability, the athlete performs the walking series from the warm-up (chapter 1) with his shoes off. This serves as an effective post-workout cooling-down method, which arguably carries more relevant performance benefits than using a stationary bike, treadmill, or elliptical machine to cool down. Barefoot stability work on solid flat surfaces can be extremely beneficial for balance, recovery, and postural restoration, and it is also a great tool to help flush postexercise toxins. The athlete holds each position for three to five seconds to ensure that his balance is secure and stable.

Soft Tissue Therapy

A wide array of soft tissue therapies can be employed during the combine preparation process. Muscle activation techniques (MAT), active release therapy (ART), and massage are specialized therapies that must be performed by a licensed or certified therapist. MAT is a nonmedical process that assesses, maintains, and improves muscle contractile efficiency.

PREP LIKE A PRO: ELITE LEVEL RECOVERY MODALITIES

At the highest levels of training, elite athletes need to recover as efficiently and effectively as possible. In addition to the other modalities covered in this chapter, Landow Performance athletes preparing for the NFL combine use several advanced recovery techniques to maximize their elite-level preparation.

Infrared Sauna

Infrared saunas have been used in clinical settings to help reduce pain and inflammation in patients with rheumatoid arthritis and ankylosing spondylitis. The addition of infrared radiation allows heat to penetrate deeper into the tissue in comparison to traditional heat treatment methods from Scandinavian saunas and water immersion (Oosterveld et al. 2009).

Intermittent Pneumatic Compression

Intermittent pneumatic compression units (from brands like NormaTec) have become popular in most collegiate and professional settings. The compression provides a mechanical squeezing around the affected limb to circulate blood and clear waste by-product from exercise. This circulation allows blood to be quickly reoxygenated by the heart and lungs, promoting faster oxygen reabsorption and healing to injured tissue (Hanson et al. 2013).

Cryotherapy

Whole-body cryotherapy consists of brief exposure to extremely cold air (–110 to –140 degrees Celsius) in a climate-controlled cryochamber. Research on the effects of cryotherapy is still inconclusive at this point, so its benefits are anecdotal, but cryotherapy has a devoted following, and it is widely used for trauma recovery and to prevent overtraining symptoms. The benefits may include cardiovascular improvements, muscular activation, and reduced inflammation.

Typical cryotherapy procedures require two minutes of exposure, but they can sometimes last up to three minutes depending on tolerance and protocol. Prior to entry to the cryochamber, there is a temperature acclimation phase in a vestibule at a temperature of –60 degrees Celsius for 30 seconds. During exposure, participants wear minimal clothing, and to avoid frostbite they may wear a bathing suit, socks, clogs or shoes, surgical mask, gloves, and a hat (Banfi et al. 2010).

Dry Needling

Dry needling is a minimally invasive procedure used to alleviate myofascial pain associated with "trigger points," also called MTrP (Travell and Simons 1983). An MTrP is a highly localized palpable spot found in taut bands of skeletal muscle fibers. They are hyperirritable and can elicit pain and a local twitch response. Dry needling is an intramuscular stimulation method in which an acupuncture needle penetrates directly into an MTrP to create mechanical stimulation in hopes of decreasing myofascial pain and dysfunction (Kalichman and Vulfsons 2010).

This form of soft tissue treatment aims to activate and improve the muscle's ability to contract, resulting in a more stable joint. This stability boost paves the way for mobility to begin improving as well. ART and massage are techniques for increasing muscular efficiency and decreasing muscular tightness through touch or specific trigger points that elicit a contract-relax response. They help promote a parasympathetic nervous system response so that athletes can calm themselves out of the fight-or-flight response of the sympathetic nervous system to allow for better recovery.

Conclusion

Though it may seem like a piece of cake compared to the intense physical challenges of training, properly caring for one's body during combine preparation requires a disciplined and detail-oriented approach. Human performance adaptation naturally requires proper food, hydration, and sleep, but these variables are much more nuanced than athletes and practitioners often realize. Athletes are best served when they employ consistent, well-timed nutrition habits and practice proper sleep hygiene. A wide array of modalities can be used at various budget levels to accelerate the body's recovery process between workouts. With the body now primed, the next chapter outlines some of the psychological factors one should consider during combine preparation, including how to be mentally ready for testing day.

CHAPTER 14

Day of Event and Psychological Preparation

Over the course of his combine preparation, a player may work with many different people, including performance coaches, position specialists, soft tissue therapists, and doctors, but on his testing day, he will stand at the starting line of the 40-yard dash alone. The outcome is now entirely up to him.

Such a high-pressure situation can be an immense mental stressor for athletes. As team sport athletes, many football players are unaccustomed to performing entirely on their own. Add in the pressure of performing in front of scouts and coaches, and the nervous butterflies in a player's stomach grow to the size of pterodactyls.

Performance coaches can play a pivotal role in alleviating the anxiety their athletes often experience at these high-stakes events. It would be a grave mistake to wait until late in the training process to begin mental preparation for the combine. This chapter details some of the ways athletes can improve their mental game, with insider tips about how to approach the combine day itself.

Psychological Preparation

A player's mental training for the combine begins on day one. Different types of mental training occur at the same time, however. For example, the athlete will need to put in significant time studying the Xs and Os of football strategy so that he can impress teams in private interviews. He also needs a strong psychological foundation to perform well on the field and in other tests.

Performance Coach's Role

A coach's relationship goal with athletes during this process should be to establish trust and rapport while also strategically managing their egos and vulnerabilities. This can be a delicate balance, and it starts on the first day of athlete intake and evaluations (covered in chapter 2). Players running the 40-yard dash during initial testing will almost always clock a slower time than they expect, and part of the performance coach's job is to help soften that blow to the athlete's ego. The coach's message could be that while the athlete may not be as fast as he'd thought, the good news is the right training can make him as fast as he thought he was. This conversation may not be a pleasant one, but it can be invaluable to the coach–athlete relationship.

Athletes must be able to trust their training and their coaches, even during times in the training cycle when it may seem like they are getting slower instead of faster. It can be alarming for athletes to see any fluctuation in their numbers and times, especially while they are preparing for such an important event.

At these times, coaches can help by giving their athletes context about the natural fluctuation of sprint times over the course of training, to reassure them that it is perfectly normal if their sprint times do not always match what they have recorded on previous days. Coaches should avoid giving their players intentionally low drill times during training to boost their self-confidence; in the long run this can undermine the coach–athlete relationship. An athlete needs to trust that his coach will tell him the truth even if the truth is unpleasant.

Mock Combine

Landow Performance puts on a mock combine for their athletes after three to four weeks of training. There is a training volume reduction during the fourth week of the training programs; this is done to accommodate the mock combine without placing too much physical stress on athletes.

The mock combine is the first time coaches can see how athletes put all the teaching pieces together in a rough draft of sorts. By this point, athletes should have a working familiarity with every combine drill, but this dress rehearsal is the first time since intake testing that the athletes have performed these drills all on the same day.

Local media are invited to the event; cameras, distractions, and unfamiliar faces help to create a necessary element of chaos and simulate the combine's uncertainty. These athletes need to become used to having cameras around them while they are working out. They might be used to playing football on TV, but they are not used to running around by themselves in shorts and a T-shirt. The mock combine also presents a good opportunity for players to work on their interview skills in front of the camera. Athletes do not need to be over-coached in this area; more than anything, they need to be authentic and not try to be someone different.

Cognitive Strategies for Combine Success

One of a coach's biggest challenges throughout the training cycle is managing athletes' performance-related anxieties. Athletes, especially those who compete at elite levels, tend to have perfectionist attitudes about their own performance. This is where mental preparation walks a fine line. Striving for perfection has actually been associated with lower anxiety and higher self-confidence in athletes, and researchers contend that how an athlete reacts to negative outcomes is much more influential on anxiety than whether the athlete is a perfectionist (Stoeber et al. 2007). This means that if we can help athletes to change their reactions to negative outcomes in their sport, we can change the level of anxiety they experience before and during the combine.

Performance anxiety may be addressed with an array of different coping techniques. These include (but are not limited to) meditation, visualization and breathing exercises, and positive self-talk. Research suggests that elite-level athletes use these coping techniques more effectively than their lower-tier peers (Parnabas, Parnabas, and Parnabas 2015).

Landow Performance combine preparation athletes are taught to imagine every drill that they have been working on and how they execute it, down to the most minute detail. Coaches walk athletes through visualizations to help with this process. For example, a visualization for the 40-yard dash start might be the following:

> *I want you to visualize what it feels like to have lead leg pressure. Visualize putting your arm up to the loaded position, holding still for that three-second count, and then pushing out explosively with great horizontal trajectory. Picture each step you take as you're climbing out of acceleration and finishing into top speed.*

These meditative techniques are powerful, and they can go a long way in calming athletes before the event and alleviating sleep issues.

Sleep, discussed in more detail in chapter 13, is also a vital component of mental preparedness. However, even athletes who have their circadian rhythms in tune will often struggle sleeping in the nights leading up to their combine. Research indicates that most athletes grapple with poor sleep the night before an important event, primarily due to nervous thoughts about the competition (Juliff, Halson, and Peiffer 2015). Developing a consistent and effective routine before sleep each night (often called "sleep hygiene" by researchers) has been shown to improve sleep quality and duration (Caia et al. 2018).

Mental Taper

The training taper (described fully in chapter 12) is much more than strictly a period for physical training adaptations. This 12-day period offers coaches a chance to lay the psychological foundation of combine day. In the final weeks leading up to the event, athletes should be reminded of the amazing opportunity in front of them. They have made major sacrifices to put their best foot forward and create playing opportunities at the next level. Now the event is almost here.

For the entire duration of the taper, the coach's job is to prep athletes mentally for what's to come, so that nothing is surprising to them on combine day. This preparation can take place in sidebar conversations that occur during the rest intervals because the rest and recovery is so much greater than the workload during a taper. This is also when coaches have the athletes' full attention. As the combine draws closer, athletes start to get anxious or worried. They benefit from a calming presence and a regular routine, which is why known routines such as the warm-up are critical to performance.

Day of Event

Combine preparation staff should help athletes get ready for the look and feel of combine day. The coaches' goal is to ensure that nothing catches their athletes off guard on testing day. This means studying the event's logistics and then giving athletes information so they can arrive at the event with a good idea of what to expect.

Travel and Event Logistics

Coaches should help their athletes prepare by going through a laundry list of every small logistical point, down to bringing protein and empty water bottles on the flight to the event. Athletes can benefit from a coach's guidance with these seemingly insignificant details.

For the NFL combine, coaches typically fly to Indianapolis a couple of days before the combine. Having someone guide them through travel and pre-event logistics can be a major stress reducer for athletes. Some pro days or high school combines may be located in-state for the athlete and coach. If the coach can travel with the athlete to his combine or pro day, this type of support can be immensely helpful.

When a player has arrived at his hotel but is still a day or two out from his combine, he should not rest the entire time. He should still complete soft tissue work, go through a warm-up, and practice his execution of drills. At this point he is still in his training taper, even though he has already arrived for the combine. Athletes can find space in their hotel or nearby for drill and sprint practice. Getting a few acceleration starts is key to keeping primed for testing day. Speed is an extremely neural-intensive quality, so it must be touched up constantly or it will begin to diminish within a few days.

Pro days and high school combines are often run differently than the NFL combine. Most of the tests are the same, but the ordering and pacing may be different. Coaches and players should try to learn the agenda early on so that they can be proactive in warming up for the order of events. If the bench press test is up first, then the coach takes the athlete through a simple warm-up for bench press. If the organizers announce that the day will begin with vertical jump and broad jump, the coach can warm the athlete up for those events. The warm-up should not create central nervous system fatigue that will negatively affect the athlete's jumps. It should be a familiar warm-up for the athlete, to help establish a level of comfort and normalcy in a new environment.

Routines for Combine Day

Coaches should teach athletes some of the helpful routines to follow during testing and then have the athletes rehearse them throughout the training cycle so they feel comfortable on combine day. For the 40-yard dash, for example, Landow Performance athletes are taught a specific routine: Walk to the starting line, hit a tuck jump, shake out the legs, and then set up in a three-point start. (For more information about the setup for a three-point start, refer to chapter 3.)

Once an athlete runs his first 40-yard dash, he is better off not asking the testing officials about his time. At this moment his time is irrelevant, and he should be focused on his second attempt. He should not immediately go and distract himself with his phone. Instead, he should walk back to the nearest wall and sit with his back on the floor and his legs up on the wall, not for stretching, but to restore normal blood flow and to calm his breathing. The player should visualize himself attacking the next repetition with flawless form. Relaxation techniques like this between sprints have been shown to positively affect athletes' maximum speed in subsequent sprint attempts (Pelka et al. 2017). After a minute with his legs on the wall, he sits up on the ground for two to three minutes, then starts walking, then begins getting into some skips, and finally takes some acceleration starts.

The player should hit his last acceleration start with about two to three minutes remaining to recover before his next turn. To get an idea of what his time allotment will be like between rounds, the player should pay attention to his alphabetical order within his testing group, relative to the group's size. The time in between repetitions goes by faster than one might think, so it helps to be aware and not lose track of time. In some cases, the athlete might not get enough time to go through this entire pre-40 routine. It is still a good idea to perform an abbreviated version of this routine with one's allotted time between attempts.

Embracing the Moment

Football combine events go by in a blur for players, whether the event takes one day or four days. Athletes often talk about these events as a burden, and they look forward to their completion like relieved high schoolers finishing the SAT. But players should relish the moment and the opportunity they have earned, rather than wishing for it to be over sooner. The best message that coaches can try to impart to athletes is, "When the opportunity of a lifetime presents itself, you have to act within the lifetime of that opportunity." At this point, the preparation is complete, and it is time for the athlete to put all his hard work on display.

Conclusion

Preparation for a football combine or pro day goes far beyond the purely physical. Working on tactical Xs and Os with position-specific coaches can be one example of nonphysical training; the psychological component of combine prep includes much more. Topics such as performance anxiety and reactions to undesired outcomes are critical to the athlete's performance. In addition to performing a mock combine, athletes should be practicing coping techniques and other activities such as helpful daily routines to prep themselves mentally in the weeks leading up to the event. Ultimately, if performance coaches follow this process diligently and coach with authenticity, their athletes will be feeling confident on combine day—and beyond.

References

Introduction

Associated Press. 2017. Christian McCaffrey makes up for poor bench press. *USA Today*, March 3, 2017. www.usatoday.com/story/sports/nfl/2017/03/03/christian-mccaffrey-makes-up-for-poor-bench-press/98715874

Crouse, K. 2007. Players are seen and unseen at NFL Scouting Combine. *The New York Times*, February 23, 2007. www.nytimes.com/2007/02/23/sports/football/23combine.html

ESPN. 2016. Pac-12 conference player rushing stats 2016. ESPN.com. www.espn.com/college-football/stats/player/_/stat/rushing/season/2016/group/9

Ghigiarelli, J.J. 2011. Combine performance descriptors and predictors of recruit ranking for the top high school football recruits from 2001 to 2009: Differences between position groups. *Journal of Strength and Conditioning Research*, 25(5): 1193-1203. doi:10.1519/jsc.0b013e318215f546.

Knaak, J. 2018. Early days of the combine. Raiders.com, February 28, 2018. https://raiders.exposure.co/early-days-of-the-combine

Lombardi, D. 2015. Christian McCaffrey racks up 461 total yards, breaks Barry Sanders' mark. ESPN.com, December 5, 2015. www.espn.com/college-football/story/_/id/14298775/christian-mccaffrey-stanford-cardinal-breaks-barry-sanders-ncaa-single-season-record-all-purpose-yardage

Modrak, T. 1980. The REAL offensive line: Scouting department reason for Steelers success. *Beaver County Times*, August 7, 1980.

Sports TV Ratings. 2015. Saturday's NFL Network Scouting Combine viewership up 91% to 529,000. *Sports TV Ratings*, February 23, 2015. https://sportstvratings.com/saturdays-nfl-network-scouting-combine-viewership-up-91-to/1520

Chapter 1

Ajemian, R., A. D'Ausilio, H. Moorman, and E. Bizzi. 2010. Why professional athletes need a prolonged period of warm-up and other peculiarities of human motor learning. *Journal of Motor Behavior*, 42(6): 381-388.

Katzowitz, J. 2014. NFL combine: Chris Johnson's 4.24 40 moves him into 1st round in 2008. CBSSports.com, February 19, 2014. www.cbssports.com/nfl/news/nfl-combine-chris-johnsons-424-40-moves-him-into-1st-round-in-2008

Pagaduan, J.C., H. Pojskić, E. Užičanin, and F. Babajić. 2012. Effect of various warm-up protocols on jump performance in college football players. *Journal of Human Kinetics*, 35(1): 127-132.

Chapter 2

Balyi, I., and A. Hamilton. 2004. Long-term athlete development: Trainability in childhood and adolescence. *Olympic Coach*, 16(1): 4-9.

Balyi, I., and R. Way. 2005. The role of monitoring growth in long-term athlete development. *Canadian Sport for Life*, 8-10.

Cook, G., L. Burton, B.J. Hoogenboom, and M. Voight. 2014a. Functional movement screening: The use of fundamental movements as an assessment of function, part 1. *International Journal of Sports Physical Therapy*, 9(3): 396.

Cook, G., L. Burton, B.J. Hoogenboom, and M. Voight. 2014b. Functional movement screening: The use of fundamental movements as an assessment of function, part 2. *International Journal of Sports Physical Therapy*, 9(4): 549.

Lloyd, R.S., J.B. Cronin, A.D. Faigenbaum, G.G. Haff, R. Howard, W.J. Kraemer, L.J. Micheli, G.D. Myer, and J.L. Oliver. 2016. National Strength and Conditioning Association position statement on long-term athletic development. *Journal of Strength and Conditioning Research*, 30(6): 1491-1509.

Matveyev, L.P. 1977. *Osnovy sportivnoy trenirovki [Fundamentals of sports training]*. Moscow: FiS. p. 66.

Chapter 6

Bompa, T.O. 1996. *Power Training for Sport: Plyometrics for Maximum Power Development.* Oakville, ON: Mosaic Press.

Cormie, P., M.R. McGuigan, and R.U. Newton. 2010. Changes in the eccentric phase contribute to improved stretch-shorten cycle performance after training. *Medicine & Science in Sports & Exercise,* 42(9): 1731-1744.

DeWeese, B.H., G. Hornsby, M. Stone, and M.H. Stone. 2015. The training process: Planning for strength–power training in track and field. Part 1: Theoretical aspects. *Journal of Sport and Health Science,* 4(4): 308-317.

Fouré, A., A. Nordez, P. McNair, and C. Cornu. 2011. Effects of plyometric training on both active and passive parts of the plantarflexors series elastic component stiffness of muscle–tendon complex. *European Journal of Applied Physiology,* 111(3): 539-548.

Haynes, T., C. Bishop, M. Antrobus, and J. Brazier. 2019. The validity and reliability of the My Jump 2 app for measuring the reactive strength index and drop jump performance. *Journal of Sports Medicine and Physical Fitness,* 59(2): 253-258.

Hill, A.V. 1938. The heat of shortening and the dynamic constants of muscle. *Proceedings of the Royal Society of London. Series B-Biological Sciences,* 126(843): 136-195.

Hunter, G.R., J.P. McCarthy, S.J. Carter, M.M. Bamman, E.S. Gaddy, G. Fisher, K. Katsoulis, E.P. Plaisance, and B.R. Newcomer. 2015. Muscle fiber type, Achilles tendon length, potentiation, and running economy. *Journal of Strength and Conditioning Research,* 29(5): 1302-1309.

Komi, P.V. 1984. Physiological and biomechanical correlates of muscle function: Effects of muscle structure and stretch-shortening cycle on force and speed. *Exercise and Sport Sciences Reviews,* 12(1): 81-122.

Nuzzo, J.L., J.M. McBride, P. Cormie, and G.O. McCaulley. 2008. Relationship between counter-movement jump performance and multijoint isometric and dynamic tests of strength. *Journal of Strength and Conditioning Research,* 22(3): 699-707.

Ross, S.E., and K.M. Guskiewicz. 2003. Time to stabilization: A method for analyzing dynamic postural stability. *Athletic Therapy Today,* 8(3): 37-39.

Young, W. 1995. Laboratory strength assessment of athletes. *New Studies in Athletics,* 10: 89-89.

Chapter 7

Aagaard, P., E.B. Simonsen, J.L. Andersen, P. Magnusson, and P. Dyhre-Poulsen. 2002. Increased rate of force development and neural drive of human skeletal muscle following resistance training. *Journal of Applied Physiology,* 93(4): 1318-1326.

Haff, G.G., and S. Nimphius. 2012. Training principles for power. *Strength and Conditioning Journal,* 34(6): 2-12.

Hunter, J.P., R.N. Marshall, and P.J. McNair. 2005. Relationships between ground reaction force impulse and kinematics of sprint-running acceleration. *Journal of Applied Biomechanics,* 21(1): 31-43.

Kugler, F., and L. Janshen. 2010. Body position determines propulsive forces in accelerated running. *Journal of Biomechanics,* 43(2): 343-348.

Lockie, R.G., A.J. Murphy, A.B. Schultz, T.J. Knight, and X.A.J. de Jonge. 2012. The effects of different speed training protocols on sprint acceleration kinematics and muscle strength and power in field sport athletes. *Journal of Strength and Conditioning Research,* 26(6): 1539-1550.

McBride, J.M., D. Blow, T.J. Kirby, T.L Haines, A.M. Dayne, and N.T. Triplett. 2009. Relationship between maximal squat strength and five, ten, and forty yard sprint times. *Journal of Strength and Conditioning Research,* 23(6): 1633-1636.

Murphy, A.J., R.G. Lockie, and A.J. Coutts. 2003. Kinematic determinants of early acceleration in field sport athletes. *Journal of Sports Science and Medicine,* 2(4): 144.

Nagahara, R., T. Matsubayashi, A. Matsuo, and K. Zushi. 2014. Kinematics of transition during human accelerated sprinting. *Biology Open,* 3(8): 689-699.

Newton, I., A. Motte, and N.W. Chittenden. 1850. *Newton's Principia: The Mathematical Principles of Natural Philosophy.* New York: Geo. P. Putnam.

Pfaff, D. 2019. Head coach, Altis, in discussion with the author, February 2019.

Young, W., B. McLean, and J. Ardagna. 1995. Relationship between strength qualities and sprinting performance. *Journal of Sports Medicine and Physical Fitness,* 35(1): 13-19.

Chapter 8

DeWeese, B., and S. Nimphius. 2016. Speed and agility program design and technique. In *Essentials of Strength and Conditioning,* edited by N.T. Triplett and G.G. Haff. Champaign, IL: Human Kinetics, pp. 521-557.

Holmberg, P.M. 2009. Agility training for experienced athletes: A dynamical systems approach. *Strength and Conditioning Journal,* 31(5): 73-78.

Loturco, I., S. Nimphius, R. Kobal, A. Bottino, V. Zanetti, L.A. Pereira, and I. Jeffreys. 2018. Change-of direction deficit in elite young soccer players. *German Journal of Exercise and Sport Research,* 48(2): 228-234.

Nimphius, S. 2014. Agility development. In *High-Performance Training for Sports,* edited by D. Joyce and D. Lewindon. Champaign, IL: Human Kinetics, pp. 185-197.

Nimphius, S., G. Geib, T. Spiteri, and D. Carlisle. 2013. Change of direction deficit measurement in Division I American football players. *Journal of Australian Strength and Conditioning,* 21(S2): 115-117.

Prabhu, N.S. 1987. *Second Language Pedagogy.* Vol. 20. Oxford: Oxford University Press.

Sheppard, J.M., and W.B. Young. 2006. Agility literature review: Classifications, training, and testing. *Journal of Sports Sciences,* 24: 919-932.

Skehan, P. 1998. *A Cognitive Approach to Language Learning.* Oxford: Oxford University Press.

Sorichter, S., B. Puschendorf, and J. Mair. 1999. Skeletal muscle injury induced by eccentric muscle action: Muscle proteins as markers of muscle fiber injury. *Exercise Immunology Review,* 5: 5-21.

Spiteri, T., J.L. Cochrane, N.H. Hart, G.G. Haff, and S. Nimphius. 2013. Effect of strength on plant foot kinetics and kinematics during a change of direction task. *European Journal of Sport Science,* 13(6): 646-652.

Spiteri, T., R.U. Newton, M. Binetti, N.H. Hart, J.M. Sheppard, and S. Nimphius. 2015. Mechanical determinants of faster change of direction and agility performance in female basketball athletes. *Journal of Strength and Conditioning Research,* 29(8): 2205-2214.

Spiteri, T., and S. Nimphius. 2013. Relationship between timing variables and plant foot kinetics during change of direction movements. *Journal of Australian Strength and Conditioning,* 21(Supplement 1): 73-77.

Chapter 10

Comfort, P., A. Haigh, and M.J. Matthews. 2012. Are changes in maximal squat strength during preseason training reflected in changes in sprint performance in rugby league players? *Journal of Strength and Conditioning Research,* 26(3): 772-776.

McGuigan, M.R., G.A. Wright, and S.J. Fleck. 2012. Strength training for athletes: Does it really help sports performance? *International Journal of Sports Physiology and Performance,* 7(1): 2-5.

Schoenfeld, B.J. 2010. Squatting kinematics and kinetics and their application to exercise performance. *Journal of Strength and Conditioning Research,* 24(12): 3497-3506.

Chapter 11

Baker, D. 2001. Acute and long-term power responses to power training: Observations on the training of an elite power athlete. *Strength and Conditioning Journal,* 23(1): 47-56.

Chu, D.A., and L. Plummer. 1984. The language of plyometrics. *Strength and Conditioning Journal,* 6(5): 30-31.

Cronin, J.B., and K.T. Hansen. 2005. Strength and power predictors of sports speed. *Journal of Strength and Conditioning Research,* 19(2): 349-357.

Mann, B. 2016. *Developing Explosive Athletes: Use of Velocity Based Training in Athletes.* Muskegon, MI: Ultimate Athlete Concepts.

Rhea, M.R., J.G. Kenn, and B.M. Dermody. 2009. Alterations in speed of squat movement and the use of accommodated resistance among college athletes training for power. *Journal of Strength and Conditioning Research,* 23(9): 2645-2650.

Rhea, M.R., M.D. Peterson, J.R. Oliverson, F.N. Ayllón, and B.J. Potenziano. 2008. An examination of training on the VertiMax resisted jumping device for improvements in lower body power in highly trained college athletes. *Journal of Strength and Conditioning Research,* 22(3): 735-740.

Seitz, L.B., and G.G. Haff. 2015. Application of methods of inducing postactivation potentiation during the preparation of rugby players. *Strength and Conditioning Journal,* 37(1): 40-49.

Seitz, L.B., E.S. de Villarreal, and G.G. Haff. 2014. The temporal profile of postactivation potentiation is related to strength level. *Journal of Strength and Conditioning Research,* 28(3): 706-715.

Chapter 13

Atkinson, G., B. Drust, T. Reilly, and J. Waterhouse. 2003. The relevance of melatonin to sports medicine and science. *Sports Medicine,* 33(11): 809-831.

Banfi, G., G. Lombardi, A. Colombini, and G. Melegati. 2010. Whole-body cryotherapy in athletes. *Sports Medicine,* 40(6): 509-517.

Bompa, T.O., and C. Buzzichelli. 2018. *Periodization: Theory and Methodology of Training.* Champaign, IL: Human Kinetics.

Carandente, F., A. Montaruli, A. Angeli, C. Sciolla, E. Roveda, and G. Calogiuri. 2011. Effects of endurance and strength acute exercise on night sleep quality. *International SportMed Journal,* 12(3): 113-124.

Cochrane, D.J. 2004. Alternating hot and cold water immersion for athlete recovery: A review. *Physical Therapy in Sport,* 5(1): 26-32.

Hanson, E., K. Stetter, R. Li, and A. Thomas. 2013. An intermittent pneumatic compression device reduces blood lactate concentrations more effectively than passive recovery after Wingate testing. *Journal of Athletic Enhancement,* 2(3).

Healey, K.C., D.L. Hatfield, P. Blanpied, L.R. Dorfman, and D. Riebe. 2014. The effects of myofascial release with foam rolling on performance. *Journal of Strength and Conditioning Research,* 28(1): 61-68.

Kalichman, L., and S. Vulfsons. 2010. Dry needling in the management of musculoskeletal pain. *Journal of the American Board of Family Medicine,* 23(5): 640-646.

Mah, C.D., K.E. Mah, E.J. Kezirian, and W.C. Dement. 2011. The effects of sleep extension on the athletic performance of collegiate basketball players. *Sleep,* 34(7): 943-950.

Mattes, A.L. 1996. Active isolated stretching. *Journal of Bodywork and Movement Therapies,* 1(1): 28-33.

Oosterveld, F.G.J., J.J. Rasker, M. Floors, R. Landkroon, B. van Rennes, J. Zwijnenberg, M.A.F.J. van de Laar, and G.J. Koel. 2009. Infrared sauna in patients with rheumatoid arthritis and ankylosing spondylitis. A pilot study showing good tolerance, short-term improvement of pain and stiffness, and a trend towards long-term beneficial effects. *Clinical Rheumatology,* 28(1): 29-34.

Samuels, C. 2008. Sleep, recovery, and performance: The new frontier in high-performance athletics. *Neurologic Clinics,* 26(1): 169-180.

Selye, H. 1946. The general adaptation syndrome and the diseases of adaptation. *Journal of Clinical Endocrinology,* 6(2): 117-230.

Simpson, N.S., E.L. Gibbs, and G.O. Matheson. 2017. Optimizing sleep to maximize performance: Implications and recommendations for elite athletes. *Scandinavian Journal of Medicine & Science in Sports,* 27(3): 266-274.

Travell, J.G., and D.G. Simons. 1983. *Myofascial Pain and Dysfunction: The Trigger Point Manual* (Vol. 2). Philadelphia: Lippincott Williams & Wilkins.

Versey, N.G., S.L. Halson, and B.T. Dawson. 2013. Water immersion recovery for athletes: Effect on exercise performance and practical recommendations. *Sports Medicine,* 43(11): 1101-1130.

Walker, M. 2017. *Why We Sleep: Unlocking the Power of Sleep and Dreams.* New York: Simon and Schuster.

Waterhouse, J., G. Atkinson, B. Edwards, and T. Reilly. 2007. The role of a short post-lunch nap in improving cognitive, motor, and sprint performance in participants with partial sleep deprivation. *Journal of Sports Sciences,* 25(14): 1557-1566.

Wilcock, I.M., J.B. Cronin, and W.A. Hing. 2006. Physiological response to water immersion. *Sports Medicine,* 36(9): 747-765.

Chapter 14

Caia, J., T.J. Scott, S.L. Halson, and V.G. Kelly. 2018. The influence of sleep hygiene education on sleep in professional rugby league athletes. *Sleep Health,* 4(4): 364-368.

Juliff, L.E., S.L. Halson, and J.J. Peiffer. 2015. Understanding sleep disturbance in athletes prior to important competitions. *Journal of Science and Medicine in Sport,* 18,(1): 13-18.

Parnabas, V.A., J. Parnabas, and A.M. Parnabas. 2015. The effect of coping strategies techniques on football players. *International Journal of Physical and Social Sciences,* 5(4): 381-391.

Pelka, M., S. Kölling, A. Ferrauti, T. Meyer, M. Pfeiffer, and M. Kellmann. 2017. Acute effects of psychological relaxation techniques between two physical tasks. *Journal of Sports Sciences,* 35(3): 216-223.

Stoeber, J., K. Otto, E. Pescheck, C. Becker, and O. Stoll. 2007. Perfectionism and competitive anxiety in athletes: Differentiating striving for perfection and negative reactions to imperfection. *Personality and Individual Differences,* 42(6): 959-969.

Drill Finder

WARM-UP AND MOVEMENT PREP

Ankle Rocker	22
Back Rocker	13
Bodyweight Squat	23
Carioca	6
Elbow to Instep	22
Fire Hydrant	8
Hip Circle	9
Inchworm	20
Lateral Leg Reach	10
Leg Cradle	19
Prone Straight-Leg Abduction	13
Scorpion	9
Side-Lying Straight-Leg Abduction	11
Side-Lying Straight-Leg Adduction	12
Skips (Cross-Body Arm Swing, Windmill Arm Swing)	5
Straight-Leg March	20
Straight-Leg Skip	21
Supine Straight-Leg Lift	11
Toe Grab	24
Walking Knee Hug	18
Walking Quad Stretch	18
Walking Toe Touch	19
Windshield Wipers	15

PHYSIOLOGICAL ASSESSMENTS AND ATHLETE BACKGROUND

Active Straight-Leg Raise   31

Deep Squat   27

Hurdle Step   28

In-Line Lunge   29

Rotary Stability   33

Shoulder Mobility   30

Trunk Stability Push-Up   32

GENERAL ATHLETICISM DRILLS

40-Yard Dash   46

L-Drill   50

Pro Agility (5-10-5)   49

60-Yard Shuttle   51

Standing Broad Jump   44

225-Pound Bench Press   52

Vertical Jump   42

DEFENSIVE POSITION-SPECIFIC DRILLS

Backpedal and React   56

Body Control Drill   63

Close and Speed Turn   58

Four-Bag Agility Drill   62

Four-Bag Shuffle Drill   61

Pass Drop and Hip Rotation   59

Pass Rush Drill   60

Three-Man Bag Drill   63

W Drill   57

OFFENSIVE POSITION-SPECIFIC DRILLS

Blast Read   69

Block Explosion   73

Find the Ball   70

Gauntlet 71

Hip Rotation Drop 75

Long Pull 74

Nine (Go) Route 67

Off-Tackle Reaction 69

Out Route 66

Over-the-Shoulder Adjust 72

Pass Protection Mirror Drill 74

Post-Corner Route 68

Sideline Toe-Tap 71

ACCELERATION

A-Skip 100

Partner-Resisted A-March/A-Run 103

PVC Acceleration Sprint 109

PVC A-March/A-Skip 97

Tall Kneeling Arm Action Drill 108

Three-Point Acceleration Start 107

Two-Point Acceleration Start 106

Wall Drill: March and 1, 2, 3 Count 101

AGILITY AND DECELERATION

Carioca Knee Punch Without Rotation 130

Carioca Knee Punch With Rotation (Bridging Movement) 131

Carioca Small Step Without Rotation 129

Carioca Small Step With Rotation 129

Crossover Step 127

Cyclical Acceleration to Deceleration 134

Cyclical Acceleration to Pivot 135

Five-Yard Shuffle Down and Back to Deceleration 126

Five-Yard Shuffle to Deceleration 125

Lateral Shuffle Drop Step Back to Acceleration 139

Lateral Shuffle to Acceleration 138

Lateral Shuffle to 45-Degree Acceleration 138

Lateral Shuffle to Return Acceleration 139

Lateral Squat Push   124

Shuffle to Reactive Deceleration   126

Shuffle With Reactive Change of Direction   126

Submaximal Acceleration to Bilateral Deceleration   132

Submaximal Acceleration to Split-Stance Deceleration   134

TOP-END SPEED

40-Yard Buildup   152

Fast Claw   147

Flying 10s and 20s   151

Heel Slide   148

Stepover A-Run   149

Stepover A-Skip   151

TRAINING FOR STRENGTH

Banded Post T   176

Barbell Back Squat   158

Barbell Bench Press   162

Bent-Over Barbell Row   166

Bottom-Up Step-Up   160

Bulgarian Split Squat   161

Chest Supported Row   167

Dead Bug   172

Dumbbell Incline Bench Press
   or Alternating Dumbbell Incline Bench Press   168

Front Plank or Isometric Push-Up Hold in the Top Position   170

Kneeling Ankle Mobility   178

Monster Walk   174

No-Back Dumbbell Shoulder Press   165

Physioball Plank Hold   174

Pull-Up   164

Serratus Step-Up   177

Side Plank   171

Single-Arm Dumbbell Row   164

Single-Leg Abduction   175

Step-Back Lunge   159

Supine Breathing   178

Suspension Trainer Inverted Row   167

Tempo Push-Up   169

TRAINING FOR POWER

Backward Ankle Hop   195

Barbell Speed Squat   193

Box Blast   188

Box Jump   186

Dumbbell Squat Jump   194

Medicine Ball Closed Rotation   192

Medicine Ball Drop   188

Medicine Ball Open Rotation   191

Medicine Ball Overhead Throw   192

Plyo Push-Up   190

Power Clean   184

Snap Down   194

Standing Broad Jump   186

About the Authors

© Adam Bratten

Loren Landow, CSCS,*D, has been a sports performance coach for over two decades. He joined the Denver Broncos staff as head strength and conditioning coach in 2018 after spending 10 years as the owner and director of Landow Performance, a training facility in Centennial, Colorado. During his 20 years coaching in the private sector, he designed and led a training program to prepare prospective pro football players for their combines and pro days, including more than 20 NFL Draft first-round picks.

Landow has coached thousands of athletes over the course of his career, including more than 700 professional athletes associated with the NFL, NHL, MLB, UFC, WNBA, and Olympics. In addition to his expertise on biomechanics and maximizing athletic performance, he is renowned for his emphasis on injury prevention and rehabilitation. He developed the ACL prevention program and the ACL return-to-sport protocols for the world-renowned Steadman Hawkins Clinic.

Landow has been a keynote speaker at the conferences of NSCA in the United States, ASCA in Australia, SPRINZ in New Zealand, and UKSCA in the United Kingdom. He is the author of two other books, *My Off-Season With the Denver Broncos: Building a Championship Team (While Nobody's Watching)* and *Ultimate Conditioning for Martial Arts.*

© Adam Bratten

Chris Jarmon, CSCS, is a sports performance coach at Landow Performance in Centennial, Colorado. He previously worked as an intern and volunteer assistant coach for the University of Denver sports performance staff.

Prior to his career in the sports performance field, Jarmon worked at ESPN for four years as a content associate, traveling with ESPN production crews to work behind the scenes on live sporting event TV broadcasts, including *Monday Night Football,* the NFL Draft, the X Games, MLS matches, and the FIFA World Cup.

You read the book—now complete the companion CE exam to earn continuing education credit!

Find and purchase the companion CE exam here:
US.HumanKinetics.com/collections/CE-Exam
Canada.HumanKinetics.com/collections/CE-Exam

50% off the companion CE exam with this code

APPT2021

HUMAN KINETICS